ENDORSEMENTS

Finally, someone has had the courage to deepen our understanding on ethnicity, culture, and Christianity. In this groundbreaking book, Pastor Matthew Ashimolowo brings together a robust view of the black person. This challenging new work reveals the unique ability of the author to communicate the achievement of blacks in the past, their contribution in laying the foundation of civilization, the richness of their continent, and the tragedy of their fall from grace.

Pastor Ashimolowo brings you face to face with the challenges that have held our communities down for so long and comforts us with the truth that there will be transformation for people of color. I encourage all people to read this thought-provoking work. Remember, you cannot help others if you don't understand their struggles. I believe that none of us can rest until all of us have come into God's purposes and promises.

We must move beyond what is politically correct and deal with what is spiritually relevant. No longer ignored, blacks, whites, and browns are breaking the silence and seeking common threads, deeper respect, and ultimately a greater sense of unity through a long overdue dialog about who we are and what we have to offer each other from our unique perspectives!

T.D. Jakes

Pastor and best-selling author

Pastor Ashimolowo writes from the unique perspective influenced by an African heritage and a Westernized sensitivity. He addresses ancient stereotypes, traditional misconceptions, and old questions with timeless principles of a renewed mind. His scholarship is transcended only by his experiential sensitivity and theological insight. The content is ethnic. The truths are universal. Travel with Pastor Matthew on a historical, cultural, and biblical journey from myths and mysteries to revelation and renewal.

Bishop Kenneth C. Ulmer, Presiding Bishop

Macedonia International Bible Fellowship

This is one of the most gripping works I have ever read. It is well researched, honest, realistic, engaging, and impacting. This book is destined to be a defining reference for understanding the history, the journey, plight, and present state of the people of African decent. Pastor Matthew unearths questions and provides answers to correct and heal the wounds of history.

Dr. Myles Munroe, Founder and Senior Pastor

Bahamas Faith Ministries International

Nassau, Bahamas

What Is Wrong With Being Black? transcends all other books that I have read on the subject. The most engaging aspect of this book is Pastor Matthew's marriage of all elements of the challenges that Black people have faced. He discusses not only the role that politics, society, and economics play in the equation, but also the most vital role of religion or spirituality.

Let me caution you. If you are looking for a "woe is me" book that caters to a fault-finding mission, this is not the book for you. Pastor Matthew very directly outlines the role that Black people have played in their own bondage. Although it acknowledges outside forces and the detrimental influences they have played, *What Is Wrong With Being Black?* encourages Black people to take responsibility for their part in history.

What is wrong with being Black? Absolutely nothing.

Bishop Eddie L. Long, Senior Pastor

New Birth Missionary Baptist Church

WHAT IS WRONG WITH
BEING BLACK?

Celebrating Our Heritage,

Confronting Our Challenges

MATTHEW ASHIMOLOWO

DESTINY IMAGE® PUBLISHERS, INC.
P.O. Box 310, Shippensburg, PA 17257-0310

"Speaking to the Purposes of God for this Generation and for the Generations to Come."

This book and all other Destiny Image, Revival Press, Mercy Place, Fresh Bread, Destiny Image Fiction, and Treasure House books are available at Christian bookstores and distributors worldwide.

For a U.S. bookstore nearest you, call 1-800-722-6774.

For more information on foreign distributors, call 717-532-3040.

Reach us on the Internet: www.destinyimage.com.

ISBN 10: 0-7684-2638-3
ISBN 13: 978-0-7684-2638-0

For Worldwide Distribution, Printed in the U.S.A.

1 2 3 4 5 6 7 8 9 10 11 / 09 08

Table of Contents

Introduction

In the past years the state of the Black person globally has become paramount on my mind. I have observed that wherever Black people are, whether it is Australia—among the Aborigines, Africa, Europe, Latin America, the Caribbean, or North America, we seem to belong at the bottom of the pile, or the bottom of the pyramid, economically, socially, physically, mentally, etc. It makes one ask several questions:

1. What is responsible for these 2,000 years of "Black backwardness"?

   Recorded history as we have it, dating back 2,000 years, portrays Blacks as being backward and not making any impact on civilization, neither were they contributing by way of inventions, discoveries, etc.

2. Why do we seem to fail even where we are in the majority?

   Black nations have not given us any respite. A good chunk of aid is sent to Africa. Caribbean nations are economically challenged as well.

3. Is the Black man victimized; and is he a victim of his own circumstances, pathologies, or of other people's opinions and decisions?

4. Have Blacks always been this way?

In the subsequent chapters we will see that the Black man has known great and glorious days, and that there have been conscious efforts to suppress his achievements, dignity, royalty, and impact on past world civilizations.

5. Are we descended from "Kunta Kinteh" or from kings?

This question requires an urgent, detailed, honest, as well as a historical answer, because the dignity of a people cannot be divorced from their history and contribution to the advancement of humankind.

6. If Blacks are not cursed, what did they do to deserve almost 2,000 years of oppression, lack, etc.?

Again, it will be established from Scripture that although people of color may not have been cursed, yet by their actions they might have brought certain curses upon themselves.

The debate has often been whether Blacks were cursed when Ham was cursed. It could not have been, because Blacks prospered even after the curse was placed on Canaan, a son of Ham. It was not placed on Cush or Mizraim, from whom Blacks descended.

7. What is responsible for Africa being the richest continent and yet inhabited by the poorest people?

This is an interesting question, and in our exegesis it will be obvious that a purely sociological, economical, and educational approach cannot be given to the question of poverty in Africa, without reference to the spiritual reasons.

8. If Black means only one sixteenth of skin, why are Blacks unable to overcome the "victimitis" or pressure that comes with it?

Certainly the man of color cannot just disappear into various cultures, since his color distinguishes him. Albeit, there are people also of a dark color, of Asiatic origin who have been able to make a certain degree of progress, in spite of such stereotypes that may have been associated with their color. In effect it is deeper than a skin problem.

The use of skin color to classify people is itself no more than 300 years old, as we will see later. Therefore the challenges confronting Blacks dates back further than the prejudice that follows the color of their skin.

9. Is there a conspiracy to keep Blacks at the bottom?

The conspiracy theory has been a well-flogged argument, particularly by Blacks. Marginalizations in Europe, which is one of the pathologies of Blacks and a certain degree of experience when Blacks have gone for interviews, have shown that the possibilities of a conspiracy are there.

However, even as I write, the fact that you are more likely to die from a fellow Black man's bullet on the streets of New York, Cape Town, or Lagos, makes the conspiracy theory a hard pill to swallow.

10. Why do Black nations constitute the biggest borrower nations?

In the following pages, you will read about pathologies such as misgovernance and Post Colonial heritages, which have exposed African nations to the theory of "easy pickings," that is going rather for the borrowing and later the "sorrowing," instead of delaying their gratification as a nation to produce the best for the people.

11. If Blacks are not cursed, is their land cursed?

The African continent has probably the richest mineral deposits in the world. It would be hard in a lot of ways to disassociate the wealth that built previous civilizations, and particularly Western Europe in its days of Industrial Revolution, without making reference to the plundering of Africa. However, while the content of the land may be there, consider this passage in Ezekiel.

And the land of Egypt shall become desolate and waste; then they will know that I am the Lord, because He said, "The River is mine, and I have made it. Indeed, therefore I am against you and against, your rivers, and I will make the land of Egypt utterly waste and utterly waste and desolate, from Migdol to Syene, as far as the border of Ethiopia (Ezekiel 29:9-10).

12. Africans are religious by nature, and where they have become Christians they have been committed. Why are they still not making progress?

Being religious could be deceptive, we will see as we consider how Blacks can break this 2,000-year jinx. One of the things we need in the end is a transformation of the mind.

13. Why is there such a gap between White dominated and Black dominated nations?

As we consider this question, we have to be honest with ourselves. South Africa and Zimbabwe were run essentially by Whites. South Africa and particularly certain parts of it look like European cities uprooted and planted in Africa. However, there is also such a striking resemblance for all of the slums in Black communities—the slums of the Caribbean, Watts in Los Angeles, the slums of Australia where the Aborigines live, and much of Haiti, are as if you were in the slums of Lagos or Uganda. Why?

14. What are the pathologies responsible for the state of Blacks in different settings?

We intend to consider 21 pathologies. What shaped the life of Black people in the United States of America in the majority is different from Black pathology in Australia. South Africa has gone through 300 years of apartheid; it would be foolhardy for the Blacks there to think that their attainment of independence also means political and economic sophistication, when they have been deliberately denied maximum exposure although they live in a 21st century system.

15. Can there be healing for the atrocities committed against Blacks in the past?

In the words of Glen Laurie, "No people can be genuinely free, so long as they look to others for their deliverance." The ability to help oneself may be the first action that leads to freedom. This book is not merely about Black sociology; it is about finding true transformation. This is what I intend to establish as the answer to breaking the gripvarious pathologies mentioned in this book have on Blacks.

If Blacks were cursed, then 2,000 years of punishment seems to outmatch the offense. It is not life imprisonment here; it seems like an eternal damnation. Truly it seems as if the punishment has gone on in perpetuity; however, the obvious truth is that history keeps repeating itself. For example, it will be established that, though in his glorious state, the Black man had the opportunity to pioneer civilization, advancement, and economic wealth before other civilizations, his pursuit and commitment to idolatry triggered the challenges he faces; and even as this pen is put to paper, this is still essentially a Black man's burden.

16. Some African nations have the highest number of educated citizens, yet Africa in modern times has not contributed significantly to discoveries or inventions.

For most colonized Africans, there has been a continuous exposure to Western education for at least 90 years, yet Africa remains perpetually tied to the apron strings of the first world. Because almost everything is being imported from tablecloths and toilet rolls to super conductors, computers, and cars, this makes Africa and its citizens perpetual slaves—economic slaves at least.

17. What is the future of the Black person?

For much of our study of why things went wrong for the man of color, we shall be looking at Isaiah 19 and Jeremiah 29. Going forward, how do Blacks deal with the negative identities attached to them?

18. If there is a future, what is the key to that future?

Certainly a different approach has been recommended in different places. In the majority of the cases, what people think Black people need is information. Black people have some of the finest minds on earth. What they need is not information, but rather transformation.

19. When will the Black man's day of manifestation come?

These questions point to the fact that something has gone awry, and there is the need for a detailed examination which identifies and confronts the issues facing the people of color globally. An attempt to do this is not an expression of self-hate, self-criticism, or knocking oneself down, but rather constructive self-examination.

Any culture, group of people, or civilization that forbids intellectual, as well as a psychological study of its challenges, has in itself forbidden the ability to find help, healing, and progress for the future. It is the inability to study what has gone wrong with the Blacks that confirms what the African American scholar Milton Morris said, "When Black people slaughter other Black people on the street, they all come back to 'look what the white people made us do'."[1]

A school of thought within the Black community feels that to analyze and confront the challenges, the conformations within the Black community is to align with the oppressors and to take on the conduct of the oppressor. Some are seeing it as playing into the hands of people with a negative perception of the Black community. However, each culture on earth has its own integrity. The points from which the conformities of the Black communities will be viewed in this book will be as it stands parallel to the Bible.

It is my opinion that there is no culture that transcends any other culture, or stands superior to other cultures. The Bible is raised as the standard here because it is in it that we find what I consider the key root to Black pathologies and the final solution that will cause Blacks to come into the fullness of who they will be. It is the Bible that will cause them to come to a place of the true identification of their gift in God, transformation and a manifestation of the gifts and abilities that have been deposited in them from time immemorial.

As a Black person who is 53 years old and has lived the first 31 years in Africa and the last 22 years in Europe, I think I might bring to the table a balanced evaluation. Who can truly evaluate a group of people other than a member of the same group.

Melville Herskovits puts it this way in *Cultural Relativism: Perspectives in Cultural Pluralism*: "Evaluations are relative to the cultural background out of which they arrive. The very definition of what is normal or abnormal is relative to the cultural prim of reference. In studying a culture one does not study the moods of behavior one is describing, rather one seeks to understand the sanctions of behavior in terms of the established relationships within the culture itself."[2]

As a Black man I therefore do not see the years in the forests of Africa, or the days of the rulership of the Black person as being savage, primitive, advanced, inferior, or superior. We are what we are.

The questions raised earlier seem to predict the content of this book; however, we must maintain that millions of Blacks around the world are hard-working people who maintain great families, raise good children, and contribute to the economy wherever they are. There are African nations with challenges that are making efforts to see that the general populace in such nations enjoy the benefits of their citizenship. The church or the religious community in many of these Black nations are making efforts and are becoming rallying points for the general populace.

In conclusion, around the world Blacks are still confronted with challenges. A civil rights movement in the United States of America fought strongly against segregation. They fought for the achievement of the right to vote. They were followed closely by the reformist movement in the United States, who have called for justice and equality and an attempt to seek integration. Whether that is possible for a people whose color is distinctly different is only a matter for the future.

Of the poorest countries in the world, 22 out of 25 are in Africa. Fifty-four percent of Africans live below the United Nations' poverty line. Africa is the only part of the world where poverty is expected to increase significantly over the next couple of years. The total debt of African nations, as of 1999, stood at $313 billion—more than twice the total income that comes through its export. The United Nations has earmarked along with the World Bank, the International Monetary Fund, and some international agencies, $25 billion for debt relief. But considering the fact that this could only pay the interest for one year on the debt of the African nations, where do we go from here?

In 1995, $231 billion was invested in third world countries. Only $2 billion of the total went to Africa. Where did the rest go? Businessmen have chosen to go elsewhere. Is the Black man hopeless? Is there no future?

It is only when we look into his past that we can understand his present predicament; and understanding his present predicament, we can then turn to the Christian Bible to find hope, direction, and purpose. It is not time for Blacks, whether in the Caribbean, Australasia, America, or Africa to give up. It took Europe centuries to build itself up. Some of the Black majority nations have had only 100 years of self-rule.

Many of these nations have had fragile economies, politics, and systems that brought together ethnic groups that are different or were previously enemies. Post colonial Black-led nations therefore need time to develop strong economies and governments, but to effectively use time there must be a diagnosis before there can be a prescription for the pathologies of the Black person.

ENDNOTES

1. "Endangered Family," *Newsweek*, August 30, 1993, 29.

2. Melville J. Herskovits, *Cultural Relativism: Perspectives in Cultural Pluralism* (New York: Random House, 1972).

PART I

His Glorious Past

CHAPTER I

Man—A Masterpiece of Creation

The Bible's account of the creation of man is the most comfortable one in which the dispersal of nations sits properly, particularly as it relates to the Black race. In Genesis 1:28 we are told that this man who was created was blessed to be fruitful, to multiply, replenish the earth, subdue it, and have dominion. This was intended for all humankind and not a particular color. That empty shell who was molded by God became a living being as the life of God was birthed into him. Again what distinguishes man is not his color, but the fact that he was specifically created and that the life of God was breathed into him. In what pigmentation he later shows is secondary. Man was fully loaded for what he was called to be; he was fully loaded for what he was created to manifest.

At the time of creation the life of God was imparted into man; this in effect means that everything a man is supposed to be was already imparted into him. It was not going to be a matter of striving or trying hard to be. All humankind appeared fully loaded. As the creation of God we were created to manifest His grace. Our revelation on earth was not our beginning. We were already a finished handiwork of God before the foundation of the world. We were revealed on this planet, packaged with everything we need in order to become whom God wants us to be. It is left to individuals to find what grace and ability has been deposited in them, follow that grace, and function in the ability.

Wherefore I put thee in remembrance that thou stir up the gift of God, which is in thee by the putting on of my hands (2 Timothy 1:6).

It is not only talent and ability that was deposited in us at creation. We were packaged with everything we would ever need in life. Everything we would need was put in us from the beginning of time.

I know that, whatsoever God doeth, it shall be for ever: nothing can be put to it, nor any thing taken from it: and God doeth it, that men should fear before him. That which hath been is now; and that which is to be hath already been; and God requireth that which is past (Ecclesiastes 3:14-15).

The onus rests on the individual to bring out and manifest that ability. At creation we were loaded to be all that we could be. The failure to achieve in any community is not by reason of discrimination from the Creator. We cannot add or remove from what God has already deposited in us. We cannot reduce things that were packaged into us.

For the earnest expectation of the creature waiteth for the manifestation of the sons of God (Romans 8:19).

With this in mind we do ourselves no good when we only talk of how useless we are or sing songs that denigrate us, either in the name of humility or because we have allowed ourselves to determine the composition of our songs. We sing songs such as, "Oh well, I am tired, I am so weary." Or, "I'm just a pilgrim passing through this world." Some others sing, "It's not an easy road we are travelling to Heaven." One of the greatest failures comes when we do not link up with the God who made the deposit in us. He can stir up what He had already stored up.

We then, as workers together with Him, beseech you also that ye receive not the grace of God in vain (2 Corinthians 6:1).

In effect Genesis chapter 1 is the beginning of God's purpose for our lives. The manifestation of that purpose or the lack of it is what makes peoples' lives fulfilled or frustrated.

According to the eternal purpose which He purposed in Christ Jesus our Lord: (Ephesians 3:11).

The purpose God gave man, the dominion we have, is to dominate the earth and to continue the process God Himself began. He rested so we can continue. When we fail to recognize that purpose and stay in the remit of that purpose, we pursue our own intentions. We pursue other gods and therefore miss our connection with the One who initiated our purpose and whose counsel we must follow.

When purpose is not followed, things do not work; when purpose is not followed, things get out of sync. A very basic illustration would be the result if you pour gasoline in the water tank of your car. They are both liquids, water and gasoline, but they serve different purposes and go into different departments. When people fail to stay in the purpose of God, it is impossible to fulfill the original intention of God. We are all here to carry out specific assignments—to be the person God wants us to be. It is only abiding within that purpose that causes us to fulfill our calling.

The intention of God for creating man is to reveal His glory, His righteousness, and to reflect His beauty on earth. That is why at creation God looked at the work of His hands, that was man, and said, *"very good."*

And God saw every thing that he had made, and, behold, it was very good. And the evening and the morning were the sixth day (Genesis 1:31).

Please note the word *made* in this passage, *asah* in the Hebrew, means "to procure, furnish, or thoroughly equip." The implication therefore is that at creation, black or white, brown or yellow, when you were made, God procured everything you needed, furnished you with all that you would require. You were thoroughly equipped to be all that you should be. So you are not just an old banger, an old hag that is just passing through this world.

Genesis 2:3 goes on to say,

And God blessed the seventh day, and sanctified it: because that in it he had rested from all His work which God created and made.

The word is *create* in this verse, while Genesis 1:31 says, *made*. One is the procuring, the furnishing, and the equipping. The latter *create* is the dispatching of what has been made. In other words after God had fully loaded, furnished, and thoroughly equipped you, He dispatched all humankind to become all they should be here on earth. He dispatched them with their blessings; He dispatched them with the favors they will ever experience; He dispatched them with all the blessings, the goodness, and the good things they would ever come into.

Remember when God completed His work of creation, He said all that He created was good. So at your dispatch, you were sent out with the best that you could be. Once you were dispatched, all that you would have and be had been fixed. All generations had been fixed, there would never be anything in the past that you would need. Everything you need is in the future; that is why a cry for the "good old days" is a waste of time because the future is better than the past.

You live in now, you were fixed for now, you were dispatched for now, but you were not dispatched empty handed. What does this mean? All races were dispatched in Adam, and they were sent to fulfill and become the best they could ever be. To summarize, when we were made, it was with the intention that we operate on earth as God Himself would have done.

Herein is our love made perfect, that we may have boldness in the day of judgment: because as He is, so are we in this world (1 John 4:17).

We were called to reflect the nature and authority of God on earth. We were meant to be an extension of Him and His Kingdom.

I have said, Ye are gods; and all of you are children of the most High (Psalm 82:6).

THE FALL OF MAN

The fall of man, the scattering of all generations, and the subsequent confusion of their language, introduced various cultures, traditions, and conformations. A form is a shape, pattern, mold, or template. The various forms in the world have shaped people. Most of these forms have taken people away from the purpose of God for their lives.

Some of the forms of the world that have shaped us are ideas, value systems, and concepts. It is therefore important for us to recognize the fact that there cannot be a change until we know those conformations that are determining our value systems, thoughts, and the way we view ourselves. Prior to this, we need to look further at the evolution and dominion that the Black man exercised.

CHAPTER 2

The Black Man's Dominion

After the fall of Adam and subsequent races, the account of the re-population of the earth can be found in Genesis chapter 9. Noah had three sons: Shem, Ham, and Japheth, but of particular interest to us is Ham.

And the sons of Ham; Cush, and Mizraim, and Phut, and Canaan. And the sons of Cush; Seba, and Havilah, and Sabtah, and Raamah, and Sabtechah: and the sons of Raamah; Sheba, and Dedan. And Cush begat Nimrod: he began to be a mighty one in the earth. He was a mighty hunter before the Lord: wherefore it is said, Even as Nimrod the mighty hunter before the Lord. And the beginning of his kingdom was Babel, and Erech, and Accad, and Calneh, in the land of Shinar. Out of that land went forth Asshur, and builded Nineveh, and the city Rehoboth, and Calah, And Resen between Nineveh and Calah: the same is a great city. And Mizraim begat Ludim, and Anamim, and Lehabim, and Naph-tuhim, And Pathrusim, and Casluhim, (out of whom came Philis-tim,) and Caphtorim. And Canaan begat Sidon his first born, and Heth, And the Jebusite, and the Amorite, and the Girgasite, And the Hivite, and the Arkite, and the Sinite, And the Arvadite, and the Zemarite, and the Hamathite: and afterward were the families of the Canaanites spread abroad. And the border of the Canaanites was from Sidon, as thou comest to Gerar, unto Gaza; as thou goest, unto Sodom, and Gomorrah, and Admah, and Zeboim, even unto Lasha. These are the sons of Ham, after their families, after their tongues, in their countries, and in their nations (Genesis 10:6-20).

The Bible's account of the dispersal of nations places all humankind immediately in the Mesopotamian valley, particularly the four sons of Ham—Cush, Mizraim, Phut, and Canaan. These sons will be the subject of our study in this section.

Cush is another word for Ethiopia. Ethiopia in much of the Bible is not a nation but a people. *Mizraim* was the ancient name for Egypt. Ethiopia and Egypt were known to be brothers. *Phut* was Libya, and *Canaan* was their brother. By implication, this in effect means that we would need to read our Bibles with an understanding that every time we read of a Canaanite, he was just as dark as a Cushite. This in itself also would change our perspective on several personalities in the Scripture. The immediate example, which jumps out of the passage we just read, is Nimrod.

Nimrod was a Cushite, an Ethiopian, and a Black person who built the Tower of Babel and much of Babylon, which was in the Mesopotamian Valley. This puts the extent of Black rule to as far as Asia.

INVENTIONS

The first greatest inventions were by the Hamites, even though modern history has not given justification to the work they did. In the words of Arthur Custance in his book *Noah's Three Sons* he writes, "The people whose inventiveness is to be explored and illustrated quite extensively are all assumed to be neither Shemites or Japethites and therefore descendants of Ham. This in a word includes all who are Negroid or Mongoloid, which comprehends as a matter of fact the founders of virtually all Asian civilization in the Middle East, Africa, the Far East and the New World, as well as presently existing or recently extinct primitive people."[1]

He continues in his argument about the inventions of the Hamites by saying, "Hamites, it can be shown have been in unexpected ways the world's greatest inventors though very few people, except perhaps Archaeologists, Ethnologists and Cultural Anthropologists have been aware of it. The acknowledgement of our own debt to them is long overdue."[2]

In his book *Slavery in History*, Gurowski writes, "Architects, artists, merchants, mechanics, operatives, sailors, agriculturists, and shepherds of ancient Egypt were undoubtedly of Negro stock."[3]

John W. Weatherwax in his writing, *The African Contribution* said, "Modern canons, flying missiles, ship propellers, automatic hammers, gas motors, meat cleavers and even the upholstery tack hammers were developed in Africa's early use of power."[4]

Volume 18 of *The History of Nations* says of Africa, "The African Continent is no recent discovery; it is not a new world like America or Australia. While yet Europe was the home of wandering Barbarians, one of the most wonderful civilizations on record had began to work out its destiny on the banks of the Nile."[5]

Thomas Sowell notes that ancient Europe was more underdeveloped than Africa. Concerning Britain he writes, "before ancient Britain was invaded and conquered by the Roman legions, not a single Briton had ever done anything to leave his name in the pages of history.... An estimated one thousand years passed before the material standard of living in Europe rose again to the level achieved under the Romans. As late as the early nineteenth century, no city in Europe had as dependable a water supply system as many European cities had in the days of the Roman Empire."[6]

Upon return from his voyage to Syria and Egypt, C.F. Volney said, "And this race of Blacks who nowadays are slaves and the objects of our scorn is the very one to which we owe our arts, our sciences and even the use of spoken word, and finally recollect that it is in the midst of the people claiming to be the greatest influence of liberty and humanity that the most barbarous of enslavement has been sanctioned, and the question raised whether Black men have brains of the same quality as those of white men."[7]

In 1893 Reclus commented on Egypt in his book *The Earth and Its Inhabitants* saying, "A great civilised power during the period in which Europe was being overrun by savage tribes. Arithmetic, architecture, geometry, astrology, all the arts and nearly all of today's industries and sciences were known while the Greeks lived in caves. The pattern of our thinking originated in Africa."[8]

Through their study of astronomy, the Egyptians for example were able to employ their knowledge of signs and seasons to determine certain days and the length of a year and especially to apply it to their seedtime and harvest time. The practice they initiated then still exists among many modern-day farmers who seldom will begin to set out seed for planting without consulting their farmer's almanac—their planting guide book that illustrates the phases and positions of the moon.

ARCHITECTURE

The Bible's account of the first high-rise building was the Tower of Babel which was initiated by a Black man, Nimrod, a Cushite, another word for Ethiopia. As stated earlier Ethiopia was not a nation but a people who occupied a span of land from as far as Asia to the continent of Africa. It is believed that Nimrod was the same man venerated in Greek mythology known as Hercules. As quoted earlier, Gurowski confirmed that artists, architects, merchants, mechanics, operatives, sailors, agriculturalists, and shepherds of ancient Egypt were of Negro stock.

We must therefore move our mind from viewing Blacks as just a group of people who occupied the gun-shaped continent called Africa. In the words of George Rawlinson in *Seven Great Monarchies*, "The Babylonians were Ethiopians by blood and the Chaldeans should be viewed as Negroes not Semites or Arameans."[9]

Another writer, Morris Jastro in his book *Hebrew and Babylonian Traditions*, stated that the Babylonians chose to call themselves the "Black head" people.[10] We must bear in mind that at these times color was not really used to categorize people; therefore, it did not matter if people were black, brown, or white.

The Encyclopedia Britannica mentions the fact that the earliest Sumerians of Babylonia were non-Semitic but negritic people. The earliest sculptural remains found in Elam, an Asian town in the Mesopotamian Valley that bordered Babylonia, presented indisputable evidence of early Negro regional dominance.[11] The reader must bear in mind that much of the world's method of writing, counting, and building was given to us by people of the Mesopotamian Valley.

ENDNOTES

1. Arthur C. Custance, *Noah's Three Sons: Human History in Three Dimensions* (Grand Rapids, MI: Zondervan, 1975).

2. Ibid.

3. Adam Gurowski, *Slavery in History* (Univ. of Michigan Library: Scholarly Publishing Office, 2005).

4. John W. Weatherwax, *Ancient Africa: The African Contribution* (Los Angeles: J. Henry and M.L.D. Bryant Foundation, 1962).

5. *The History of Nations, Vol. 18*, (1906), 1.

6. Thomas Sowell, *Race and Culture: A World View* (New York: Basic Books, 1994), 193-95.

7. C.F. Volney, *Report of 1787, Vol. 1*.

8. Elisee Reclus, *The Earth and Its Inhabitants, Vol. 1* (New York: D. Appleton and Co., 1893), 207.

9. George Rawlinson, *Seven Great Monarchies of the Ancient Eastern World, Volume 1* (John B. Alden, 1885), 29.

10. Morris Jastrow, *Hebrew and Babylonian Traditions* (New York: C. Scribner's Sons, 1914).

11. *Encyclopedia Britannica*, Volume A, (1959), 1018.

CHAPTER 3

The Great Empire Builders

EGYPT

Mizraim, which is another name for Egypt, was the second son of Ham. This makes him an African by blood. Mizraim, Cush, and Phut traveled and began to settle in the upper parts of Africa. Egypt occupied what was known as the Lower Egypt and the Upper Egypt. Following this dispersal, Egypt became a very strong empire with a vast army that protected its borders and a high culture that marked it to be superior to its neighboring nations. It had its own system of rulership made up mainly of the pharaohs. Great pharaohs rose; pharaohs like Amose, Mennis, Kofo Amenomorphis, Amenhotep, and Rameses II.

When Herodotus, the Greek historian, visited Egypt in 450 B.C. he described the nation southwest of Egypt to be Ethiopian and said, "Here gold is found in great abundance." We must establish again that when the Scripture refers to Ethiopia it is more than a nation; it is a people and in this case in the light of the fact that Egypt, or Mizraim was a Black person, so was Cush, an Ethiopian. These two names refer to a people who occupied a region of the world later known as Africa, not just two nations. While the word *Egypt* is not certain in its origin, *Ethiopia* is the Greek word or term for "burnt-faced people" or Black people.

Egypt was a land of advanced architecture; the world's oldest stone structures are found in ancient Egypt. The great pyramids, which constitute one of the Seven Wonders of the World, were built by the Egyptians. They were built with such perfect symmetry, emanating from the engineering skills of the early Egyptians. One of these pyramids, known as the Great Pyramid, is said to be large enough to adequately contain St. Paul's Cathedral, Westminster Abbey, the Basilica of Rome, the cathedrals of Florence, and Milan all together.

They built the Great Sphinx, and at that time it was the marvel of the world. The Egyptians also built the temple of Amon that stands 338 feet wide and 1,200 feet long; the largest of its kind built by human hands. The Egyptians not only mastered architecture, they also gave the world what has become modern calculus.

Early Africa was blessed with all kinds of minerals. In his book *The Civilization of Ancient Egypt* Paul Johnson writes, "They did manufacture and wear large quantities of fine jewellery, rings, diadems, earrings, anklets, bangles and girdles. Featuring gold, silver and electron and felspar, cornelium amethyst, jasper, lapis-lazuli, garnets and haemorites."[1]

The Egyptians excelled in making jewels; this establishes the fact that Africa has always been the land of abundance of minerals. The Egyptians were the first ones to tame wild horses, breeding them and bringing forth the finest horses on earth. We read in Second Chronicles 1:16-17 that Solomon bought horses from the Egyptians.

> *And Solomon had horses brought out of Egypt, and linen yarn: the king's merchants received the linen yarn at a price. And they fetched up, and brought forth out of Egypt a chariot for six hundred shekels of silver, and an horse for an hundred and fifty: and so brought they out horses for all the kings of the Hittites, and for the kings of Syria, by their means* (2 Chronicles 1:16-17).

Egypt's dominance and power started 3,300 years before Christianity with an initial amalgamation of the Lower and the Upper Egypt. They were both separate kingdoms until brought together; that is why great Pharaohs would wear a crown that had both the sign of a serpent and a hawk.

The snake stood for Lower Egypt, while the hawk for the Upper. It became a powerful government and built empires that extended in all directions having dominion over its brother, the Canaanites and Palestine for a longer period. Remember again that these were the Africans, the Black Egyptians; they were proficient in mathematics, medicine, engineering, and agriculture. They surveyed the land upon which they lived. It is believed that Pythagoras learned mathematics from them. It was Black Arabs who started algebra from the Arabic *algibr*. It was the same Moors or Black Arabs who conquered Spain and Portugal and carried algebra into Europe.

The spread of the Black race and its influence on world civilization is further captured in Herbert Wendt's book, *It Began in Babel*, where he states that, "Crete was the dominant power during and up to the second century B.C. and European civilization went forth from Crete."[2] Crete was founded by Blacks. Egypt as it relates to the whole of Africa is very important to the argument in this book as to why Blacks have found themselves in several economic, spiritual, and physical predicaments, hence the dedication of much material to it.

In its heyday Egypt was the fashion capital. The Bible talks of the fine flax or linen of Egypt.

> *Moreover they that work in fine flax, and they that weave networks, shall be confounded* (Isaiah 19:9).

> *I have decked my bed with coverings of tapestry, with carved works, with fine linen of Egypt* (Proverbs 7:16).

Egypt was also the first country in history to develop what might be called great artistry and culture. This counters the impression of many in the West who think that they brought civilization and culture to Black people. Egyptians, i.e., the Blacks, were the first civilization to emerge as a nation as opposed to a city culture. In ancient times you could have a city culture, but Egypt was the first to emerge as a nation as opposed to a city culture. Its arts and crafts dominated the Nile and eventually the world. The Greeks came to learn culture from the

Egyptians who were advanced in it from 2900 B.C. to 600 B.C. when Egypt began to fall apart.

Egypt's advancement in education was known around the world. We are told in Scripture that Moses was taught in all of the wisdom of the Egyptians.

And Moses was learned in all the wisdom of the Egyptians, and was mighty in words and in deeds (Acts 7:22).

The wisdom of Solomon was compared to the wisdom of Egypt.

And Solomon's wisdom excelled the wisdom of all the children of the east country, and all the wisdom of Egypt (1 Kings 4:30).

By 2900 B.C. mathematics was a formal subject to be studied in Egyptian universities. This wisdom and knowledge was to become one of the things that destroyed Egypt, as it became its source of arrogance and its draw into idolatry.

And the spirit of Egypt shall fail in the midst thereof; and I will destroy the counsel thereof: and they shall seek to the idols, and to the charmers, and to them that have familiar spirits, and to the wizards (Isaiah 19:3).

Its capital, Noph, was a formidable city of incredible beauty; but unfortunately great sculptures and idols lined the streets like streetlights from end to end. It was the seat of government, the center of worship of Ptah the Egyptian god of creation, known today as Memphis. It was a city God sent a word to, which we shall see later, because of the idolatry of Egypt.

The word that the Lord spake to Jeremiah the prophet, how Nebuchadrezzar king of Babylon should come and smite the land of Egypt. Declare ye in Egypt, and publish in Migdol, and publish in Noph and in Tahpanhes: say ye, Stand fast, and prepare thee; for the sword shall devour round about thee. Why are thy valiant men swept away? they stood not, because the Lord did drive them. He made many to fall, yea, one fell upon another: and they said, Arise, and let us go again to our own people, and to the land of our nativity, from the oppressing sword.

They did cry there, Pharaoh king of Egypt is but a noise; he hath passed the time appointed. As I live, saith the King, whose name is the Lord of hosts, surely as Tabor is among the mountains, and as Carmel by the sea, so shall he come (Jeremiah 46:13-18).

God predicted that Memphis would fall and there would be a lot of wailing and crying. Several pharaohs ruled there until the city was conquered in 569 B.C. by Ahmose II—a man we will see later as the Black Pharaoh who enslaved the Israelites and was succeeded by his son Psamtik III in 525 B.C.; who was later conquered by Cambeses, the king of Persia.

Egypt the great became a mere province of Persia. The final blow was struck against Egypt and particularly Memphis by Alexander the Great in 332 B.C. The fall of Memphis and its desolation was complete with the advent of Christianity, when Christian zealots attacked the city about the fifth century A.D. and dismantled it.

With the rise of Islam also, there was an invasion of Egypt in A.D. 640, this began the "Arabization" of Egypt with a gradual reduction of Black presence. Prior to this, historians like Herodotus alluded to Egyptians being "black and curly-haired." This is coming from a person more used to seeing Mediterranean brunettes. In another passage concerning the fable of the Dodonian Oracle, Herodotus said the Egyptians were swarthy in color.

One of the early Greek playwrights, Aeschylus, mentioned a boat seen from the shores, and declares that the crew was Egyptian because of their black complexion.

Today Memphis, the former capital, is a desolate place called Mennufr with no one living there but only statues and idols standing, thus fulfilling the Scripture in Jeremiah.

O thou daughter dwelling in Egypt, furnish thyself to go into captivity: for Noph shall be waste and desolate without an inhabitant (Jeremiah 46:19).

ETHIOPIA

And Cush begat Nimrod: he began to be a mighty one in the earth. He was a mighty hunter before the Lord: wherefore it is said, Even as Nimrod the mighty hunter before the Lord. And the beginning of his kingdom was Babel, and Erech, and Accad, and Calneh, in the land of Shinar. Out of that land went forth Asshur, and builded Nineveh, and the city Rehoboth, and Calah, And Resen between Nineveh and Calah: the same is a great city (Genesis 10:8-12).

Though we have looked at Mizraim (Egypt), Cush (Ethiopia) was the first-born of Ham. Ethiopia, again as we have said earlier, is not a nation but a people, a people of Black color. Cush had six sons: Seba, Havilah, Sabtah, Raamah, Sabtecha, and Nimrod. Their original place of settlement was in the Mesopotamian Valley, as you would observe from the names of the towns they built. Nimrod in particular was said to have built Babel. *Babel* is a short form of Babylon, in modern-day Iraq. His reign and establishment extended as far as China, India, and Afghanistan.[3]

Josephus, Jewish historian and contemporary of the Lord Jesus Christ, gives an account of the nation of Cush, who is the grandson of Noah. He said, "For of the sons of Ham, time has not at all hurt the name of Cush, for the Ethiopians, over whom he reigned, are even at this day, both by themselves and by all men in Asia, called Chusites."[4]

The locality of the domain of the Cushites has been questioned, some believe it referred to countries south of the Israelites while others think it refers to parts of Africa such as Ethiopia.

Scholars like Johann Michaelis and Johann Christian Rosenmuller have proposed that the name Cush was applied to tracts of country on both sides of the Red Sea. The fifth century A.D. Himyarites in the south of Arabia were called Cushaens and Ethiopians by Syrian writers.[5]

Babylonian inscriptions mention the Kashishi or Kassites, and it was once held that it signified a possible explanation of Cush, the ancestor of Nimrod in Genesis chapter 8.

Ethiopia controlled China, India, and Afghanistan for ages. In the words of J. Johnson, "To this very day dwellers of those lands retain the old Ethiopian symbols, fine art and concepts of science, medicine and then engineering. The original architectural structures and municipalities were modified and sometimes mutilated but never destroyed."[6]

Ethiopia was known to be the brother of Egypt, and often did things together, albeit, they also fought wars against each other. Ethiopians were known to have engaged Persians, Hebrews, Assyrians, Arabians, and Greeks in wars. Alexander the Great conquered Egypt easily, but when he decided to devastate and destroy Ethiopia, he suffered grief and aggravation because Ethiopia forced him to retreat to Egypt in 332 B.C. Augustus Caesar also fought Ethiopia but was defeated by Ethiopia in 25 B.C. Ethiopia was known to be ferocious in its warfare.

Come up, ye horses; and rage, ye chariots; and let the mighty men come forth; the Ethiopians and the Libyans, that handle the shield; and the Lydians, that handle and bend the bow (Jeremiah 46:9).

As a result of this defeat of Augustus Caesar, the Roman Empire was contained at the borders of Ethiopia. The present nation that bears the name Ethiopia goes on record as the one nation in Africa that was never colonized. It is also on record as the only nation that has had 3,000 years of monarchy up to the reign of Haille Selassie. Ethiopia's combined effort with Egypt, his brother, made them formidable allies who made an impact on other nations in the field of mathematics, engineering, medicine, and agriculture.

Ethiopia in particular kept a winning edge in matters of the powers of government, war, and conquest. It was the habit of the great Greek historian Herodotus to describe beauty as it relates to the Ethiopian.

ENDNOTES

1. Paul Johnson, *The Civilization of Ancient Egypt* (New York: Harper Collins, 1978).

2. Herbert Wendt, *It Began in Babel* (New York: Dell Publishing Company, 1964), 89.

3. Harry H. Johnston, *Colonization of Africa*: Negro Princes in India (Cooper Square Publishers, 1905), 92. M. Ilin, *Men and Mountains* (J.B. Lippincott Co., 1935), 135. Tells of seeing Afghans who were as Black as Negroes.

4. Ladipo Solank's *United West Africa at the Family of Nations* (1906, Part 1, page 18) says, "Imperial Ethiopia was the central seat of civilization before Rome was seen on the map."

5. Gertrude Emerson, *The Pageant of India's History*, (David McKay, New York:1948), 152. The author states, "The Cushan Empire included Northern India as well as Afghanistan and Bactria."

6. John L. Johnson, *The Black Biblical Heritage* (Chicago: Lushena Books, 1999), 23.

CHAPTER 4

The Great Black Personalities

It is important to continue to reiterate that this book is not about Afrocentricism; it is about studying the burdens and pathologies that have shaped Black people over the generations and the Bible's answer for their transformation for the future. Unless we have a good grasp of the past, we will not be able to understand the future.

Dr. John Johnson in his book, *The Black Biblical Heritage* quotes Edmund Burke who said, "A people will never look forward to posterity, who never look back to their ancestors."[1] The interesting thing about the Bible is that it gives account of events, people, and places without attaching much to their color, except on some rare occasions.

Before we go through the names of some of these Black people, please remember that the four sons of Ham were Cush (Ethiopia), Mizraim also known as Egypt, Phut, and Canaan. It would not be possible for Ethiopia alone to have been Black, while others of the same parent did not share the complexion of their brothers.

The implication here is that everyone who the Scriptures describe as an Amorite, Canaanite, Cushite, Hittite, Hivite, Jebusite, Mizraim,

Phut, Sidon, or Heth would have to come from one of these four brothers.

Nimrod

Nimrod was a descendant of Cush, the Ethiopian. He was notoriously recorded in Scripture as the one who led the revolt against God at the building of the city called Babel, which is really an abbreviation for Babylon. As late as in the days of Micah the prophet, Babylon and its region was still known as the land of Nimrod.

> *And this man shall be the peace, when the Assyrian shall come into our land: and when he shall tread in our palaces, then shall we raise against him seven shepherds, and eight principal men. And they shall waste the land of Assyria with the sword, and the land of Nimrod in the entrances thereof: thus shall he deliver us from the Assyrian, when he cometh into our land, and when he treadeth within our borders* (Micah 5:5-6).

Nimrod must have been a fine architect and builder to have initiated the building of this tower.

Negro Babylonians dominated the area where he lived, the Ur of the Chaldeans, located south of Mesopotamia and east of Babylon. As we established earlier, ancient records connect this area to Ethiopia from the religion and science practiced there.

Alexander Hislop, in the book *The Two Babylons*, argues that Nimrod and his mother had sexual copulation and this possibly resulted in him being killed by the Lord.[2] The book further argues that upon his death, his mother initiated the worship of Nimrod—this was later to be known as the worship of a mother and her son.

The subsequent dispersal of nations was responsible for the spread of this form of religious worship.

Lady Keturah

In Genesis chapter 25, the Scripture's account says, "Then Abraham took a wife and her name was Keturah." In order to establish who she was in reference to our study, verse 3 establishes the names of her descendants: "And the names of Keturah's grandchildren, Sheba and Dedan." These names being Cushite names, it begins to show us that Keturah must have been a Cushite who lived in Canaan.

Sarah had her "son of promise," Isaac. Hagar had Ishmael. But it was Keturah who had more children for Abraham. Keturah brought comfort to Abraham after the death of his wife. Her first child, Zimran, has a name which means "musical." That should not be surprising at all. Her second son, Jokshan, gave birth to Sheba and Dedan. *Jokshan* means "insidious." Her last son, Shua, has a name which means "humility or to be humble."

Ahmose[3]

The pharaoh who knew not Joseph.

Now there arose up a new king over Egypt, which knew not Joseph (Exodus 1:8).

Four hundred years after the invasion and subsequent rulership of Egypt by the Hyksos, a Semitic tribe who had affinities with the Israelites, Black Egyptians became discontented with minority rule. This led to a revolt and rulership by the Black Egyptians. Of particular interest is Ahmose. His name means "moon child."

He was the first Pharaoh of the 18th Egyptian dynasty, according to J.A. Rogers in his book *The World's Great Men of Color*.[4] Scholars believe that the Hyksos were in power in Egypt when the Hebrews came down. This close affinity as being fellow Semites may have influenced their accommodation of Israel and his sons. The Hyksos were still aliens in Egypt.

In the providence of God, the Hyksos pharaoh was on the throne when Joseph came. God had possibly sent him ahead to put on the throne and make the prime minister out of Joseph. With time the Israelites grew and the discontented native Egyptians wanted a change in government.

In his book *From Babylon to Timbuktu*, Rudolph Windsor puts it this way, "Much points to the fact that the new Pharaoh who ascended the throne was Ahmose I or Ahmese, the first king of the brilliant eighteenth dynasty 1480-1557 B.C.. He re-established the government at Thebes, expelled the Hyksos, and instituted something of a Fascist form of government. The government was an autocratic nationalist regime exercising regimentation of industry, rigid censorship, and forcible suppression of opposition."[5]

In his opinion this influenced a turning point and a change in fortune for the Hebrews, who once were highly favored, but were now in trouble with the Black Pharaoh who had taken over.

Ahmose was the husband of the Ethiopian queen Nefertari who was the grandmother of queen Hatshepsut who ruled Egypt stringently, and reminded the Egyptians that they may go back to being ruled by the minority if they did not rule with an iron hand. And so came his word:

Come on, let us deal wisely with them; lest they multiply, and it come to pass, that, when there falleth out any war, they join also unto our enemies, and fight against us, and so get them up out of the land (Exodus 1:10).

Ahmose, of course, inherited a sophisticated system from Hyksos, which included their superiority in the use of horse-drawn chariots for fighting. Everyone who lived in Egypt who was not originally Egyptian was forced into slavery. This included the brother of Egypt, which is Ethiopia. Ethiopians, Nubians, Canaanites, Syrians, and people from as far as the Aegean Islands were forced into slavery.

Therefore they did set over them taskmasters to afflict them with their burdens. And they built for Pharaoh treasure cities, Pithom and Raamses. But the more they afflicted them, the more they multiplied and grew. And they were grieved because of the children of Israel. And the Egyptians made the children of Israel to serve with rigour: And they made their lives bitter with hard bondage, in morter, and in brick, and in all manner of service in the field: all their service, wherein they made them serve, was with rigour. And the king of Egypt spake to the Hebrew midwives, of which the name of the one was Shiphrah, and the name of the other Puah: And he said, When ye do the office of a midwife to the Hebrew women, and see them upon the stools; if it be a son, then ye shall kill him: but if it be a daughter, then she shall live (Exodus 1:11-16).

From the days of Ahmose, this oppression of the slaves continued until the reign of the Rameses, the pharaoh Rameses. In the words of Rudolph Windsor quoted earlier, "During the period that the Hebrews were slaves for pharaoh they built many of the megalithic structures: the Hebrews erected some pyramids, they dug a great many channels for the river, they built walls for the cities and ramparts, they constructed the halls at Karnak for Thutmose I, they built temple pylons, hypostyle halls and an obelisk for Amenhotep III; by the edict of Rameses II they constructed at Thebes the temple of the Ramesessian with its colossal statues of himself and they built the treasure cities of Pithon and Rameses."[6]

The 18th Egyptian dynasty is as follows:

1. Ahmose I
2. Amenophis I
3. Thotmes I
4. Thotmes II
5. Hatshepsut
6. Thotmes III
7. Amenophis II
8. Thotmes IV
9. Amenophis III
10. Amenophis IV
11. Akhenaton
12. Smenkhare
13. Tutukhamen
14. Ay
15. Horemhab

Pharaoh's Daughter

The princess who declared, "this is one of the Hebrew children" was said to bear the name Thermuthis by Josephus, a contemporary of the Lord Jesus Christ. She was daughter of Setti I. Josephus called her a black princess. She named the child Moses and raised him in the palace of Pharaoh along with the other princes. The blackness of Egypt at such times, we have already established in various findings. In his book *The Black Biblical Heritage*, Dr. Johnson quotes H.M. Stanley who said, "The ancient sculpture of Egypt's monuments, most mummies, the sphinx, wooded and stone statutes bear a strong resemblance to the Afro-Asians (keep in mind that the early Asians were Negroes through Cush and Canaan)." He goes on to say that the Egyptians were dark-haired people.[7]

Rameses II[8]

Over 400 years after Ahmose had introduced Black rulership in Egypt, the pharaoh on the throne who was the most obstinate, difficult taskmaster who refused to let go of Israel, was Rameses II. He was Black, a descendant of Cush and Mizraim, the first and second son of Ham.[9]

The *Interpreter's Commentary* on the Bible confirms that Rameses was Pharaoh of the oppression in the Book of Exodus.[10]

The king of the 19th dynasty who ruled from 1292-1225 was the son of Seti I. The Egyptian historian Manetho, who was a priest under Ptolemy, wrote that the son of Amenophis was Rameses, and that Rameses was a Black king and father of Seti who was now the father of Raameses II. He was a war-like pharaoh; he was industrious, energetic, and ruled Egypt for 67 years. He engaged several Canaanite kings, his own cousins, the Hittites, and others in battle.

Rameses II was also known as the pharaoh of the oppression. He had an ambition to build sphinxes and pyramids, and this brought an incredible burden upon the three million Hebrew slaves. He used the slaves to build treasure cities like Pithom and Rameses around the Nile Delta. The slaves were used to build the Colonnades at Luxor and the gigantic pylons in front of which he placed six massive statues of himself. Each of these statues, which were built with solid stone, was 60 feet high. With free labor he brought natural prosperity to his people but indirectly a curse for oppressing the people of God.

The prophecies of Moses, predicting the pestilences that humiliated the various gods of Egypt, examined later in our study, brought freedom to the Hebrews at about 1230 B.C. The Bible's account shows that Rameses II drowned in the Red Sea, and after his son Mermepth took over, Egypt began to decline rapidly; by the 20th dynasty there was a revolt across the whole empire.

Zipporah

Her name means "beauty." She was an Ethiopian who married Moses the prophet, and the daughter of the Midian priest, Jethro. Her story is carried in Exodus 2:16-22; Exodus 4:25-26; Exodus 18:24; and Numbers 12:1.

> *Now the priest of Midian had seven daughters: and they came and drew water, and filled the troughs to water their father's flock. And the shepherds came and drove them away: but Moses stood up and helped them, and watered their flock. And when they came to Reuel their father, he said, How is it that ye are come so soon to day? And they said, An Egyptian delivered us out of the hand of the shepherds, and also drew water enough for us, and watered the flock. And he said unto his daughters, And where is he? why is it that ye have left the man? call him, that he may eat bread. And Moses was content to dwell with the man: and he gave Moses Zipporah his daughter. And she bare him a son, and he called his name Gershom: for he said, I have been a stranger in a strange land (Exodus 2:16-22).*

> *Then Zipporah took a sharp stone, and cut off the foreskin of her son, and cast it at his feet, and said, Surely a bloody husband art thou to me. So He let him go: then she said, A bloody husband thou art, because of the circumcision (Exodus 4:25-26).*

> *So Moses hearkened to the voice of his father in law, and did all that he had said (Exodus 18:24).*

And Miriam and Aaron spake against Moses because of the Ethiopian woman whom he had married: for he had married an Ethiopian woman (Numbers 12:1).

Zipporah was given to Moses for his defense of the daughters of Jethro as a gesture of appreciation and as the manner of people who were in the Middle East in Bible times. This Black woman bore two sons for Moses, Gershom and Eliezer, though their marriage had challenges, particularly when it came to the circumcision of her sons. Bible scholars are still divided on why the circumcision of her sons caused such aggravation since the Negro Ethiopians were the only ones who frowned on circumcision. All other African Negroes were known to tolerate circumcision. Dr. John Johnson, again in *The Black Biblical Heritage*, quotes Josephus that "circumcision was learned by the Greeks from the Africans."[11] He also makes reference to Herodotus, the great Greek historian, as having supported Josephus.[12]

Time will not permit us to comment on every Canaanite of note in the Bible. They include Gershom and Eliezer, the sons of Moses to Hobab, Og the giant, Rahab, Purim, Cusham Rishathaim (whose first name means "blackness"), Ziba and Zalmuner, Abimilech of Shechem, Delilah, Boaz, Goliath, Ahimelech, Arunah of Ornan, and many others.

Simon of Cyrene

Simon, a Black man from Libya, or Cyrene, helped to bear the cross of the Lord Jesus Christ to Mount Calvary. The account of his work is found in Matthew 27:32; Mark 15:21; and Luke 23:26.

At that time, the population of the world was fluid and people moved around frequently. Simon was standing in the crowd when Jesus bore the cross. He was compelled to share in the burden of Christ to the Place of the Skull. This man became an ardent follower of the Lord Jesus Christ; his two sons followed after him and became leaders in the church. One of his sons, Rufus, was committed in ministry and many times put his life on the line, just like his father had for the work of Paul in ministry.

Simon the Canaanite

One of the greatest omissions of artists who have painted the Last Supper is to make the twelve men around Jesus look like they all were blond-haired Europeans, when one of them was clearly called a Canaanite. Remember again that Canaan was the fourth son of Ham, a brother of Cush, Ethiopia, and Mizraim. This Canaanite must have been a Jew by naturalization or nationality and culture, but not through genealogy since he was specifically referred to as a Canaanite.

Of the twelve apostles, he was the only one whose nationality was specified so that we would recognize and appreciate that in the providence of God, men of color were around the table with the Lord Jesus Christ as His apostles, breaking down the wall of partition.

Simeon the Niger and Lucius of Cyrene

Now there were in the church that was at Antioch certain prophets and teachers; as Barnabas, and Simeon that was called Niger, and Lucius of Cyrene, and Manaen, which had been brought up with Herod the tetrarch, and Saul. As they ministered to the Lord, and fasted, the Holy Ghost said, Separate me Barnabas and Saul for the work whereunto I have called them (Acts 13:1-2).

At the ordination of Paul the apostle and the sending forth for missionary work, four men laid hands on Paul and committed him and Barnabas to ministry. Of these men, two of them had their nationality specifically mentioned again for us to be able to see that God, who knew that one day the man of color may find himself discriminated against, needed us to appreciate that the gift and calling of God are without repentance.

Simon who was called Niger, the word *Niger* here is derived from an old European word for black. It is from the root words "negri, negrillo, negrito, negros, negro, nigger." This in effect shows that Simon was a Black man from Africa, but specifically from a different part of Africa that must have been recognized as Niger.

The second Black man on that occasion was Lucius of Cyrene. Niger being the people of the south of Africa, Cyrene was Libya. These two men were part of the ordination as demanded by the Holy Spirit. Incidentally much of what is known today as Bible theology was developed in North Africa under the auspices of great African Bible scholars like St. Augustine, Irenaeus, etc.

Cyrene and Alexandria were the guardians of what we today have as acceptable doctrines of the Bible at a time when all kinds of false doctrines were flying around. We will not spend time on the Ethiopian eunuch whom Philip baptized or Queen Candace on whose errand he was engaged when he came to Israel.

Rufus and Alexander

These were two sons of Simon the Cyrene, the man who was ordered to bear the cross for the Lord Jesus Christ.

Salute Rufus chosen in the Lord, and his mother and mine (Romans 16:13).

Rufus, whose name means black or jet black or dark brown, can comfortably be said to be another person of color in the Bible. Many believe that he and Alexander were sons of Simon the Cyrene. The apostle Paul specifically took time to appreciate the work of Rufus as he served with him in ministry.

CELEBRATION OF BLACKS IN ANTIQUITY

Until 300 years ago, as mentioned earlier, color was not often used to classify people, even though people in certain parts of the world tend to be ethnocentric. Among Greeks, a high view was held of Black people.

Frank M. Snowden Jr., Professor Emeritus of Classics at Howard University, has written two books on racism entitled *Blacks in Antiquity* and *Before Color Prejudice*. He analyzed the literature, numismatic artistry, and archaeology of ancient civilization to establish evidence of encounters between the Europeans and Blacks in the ancient Mediterranean.

Snowden's argument is that Europeans and Blacks were not unaware of their color difference. In fact this was discussed in pungent and frank terms, yet nothing of their discussions suggested that either the Europeans or the Blacks felt superior to each other.[13]

This attitude obviously must have been influenced by the fact that at this time certain parts of Africa, particularly what was later to be known as Ethiopia and Europe had been influenced by Christianity and therefore racial superiority had no room. After all, the Bible says, "...in Christ, there is neither Jew nor Greek...male nor female" (Gal. 3:28).

In subsequent literature Snowden argues that Homer actually placed Blacks at a level as being as blameless as the gods.[14] Dioderus, another Greek writer, spoke of their widespread reputation of being religious.[15] The Greek Seneca found them to be notable for their courage and their love of freedom.[16] Lucien respected their astrological knowledge, and acknowledged them as being the wisest of men. Herodotus the historian whom we have quoted earlier was the first European to comment on the physical appearance of Blacks described them as "the most handsome of men."[17]

At the time of these writings of most of these Greeks, certain Blacks were slaves in Greece but this did not hinder their appreciation for the Black person. Martial noted that while he was pursued by a woman whiter than a swan, he sought and desired the affection of a Black woman who was "blacker than pitch."[18] We must observe that these are the Greeks who had a certain disdain for people who did not sound like them, particularly people whose language has a lot of "bah bah" in it, whom they therefore called Barbarians. We know for a fact that the Greeks did not associate Blacks with being unintelligent.

In his book *Black Athena*, Martin Bernal, professor of Government at Cornell University and formerly a fellow of King's College Cambridge, asserts that Greeks, although haughty about their own accomplishments, were curious about and respectful of Black people. If anything, he said, they considered Northern Europeans to be the ones lacking in the rudiments and cultures of civilization.[19]

ENDNOTES

1. Dr. John L. Johnson, *The Black Biblical Heritage*, (Chicago: Lushena Books, 1999).

2. Alexander Hislop, *The Two Babylons*, (Neptune, NJ: Loizeaux Brothers, 1959).

3. Additional references to Ahmose can be found in:

   ❖ S. Birch, *Egypt From the Earliest Times*, (London, 1875), 83.

   ❖ Specimens of ancient culture society of Delettanti.

   ❖ *Bulletins et Memorie Dossier De Paris, Number 1*, (1901, pages 393 and 403); written by Lucien, Galan, and Block who journeyed to Egypt at different periods, all agreed that the Egyptians large, flat nose and puffy lips were proof of their Negro origin.

   ❖ Montet, *Eternal Egypt* (New York: New American Lib.) 21.

   ❖ J.A. Rogers, *World's Great Men of Color* (New York: Futuro Press, Inc., 1947).

   ❖ H.R. Hall, *Ancient History of the Near East*; page 271, in which he affirmed that the 18th dynasty was controlled by Negroes.

4. Rogers, *World's Great Men of Color.*

5. Rudolph Windsor, *From Babylon to Timbuktu: A history of the ancient Black races including the Black Hebrews*, (Atlanta: Windsor's Golden Series, 1988).

6. Ibid.

7. Johnson, *The Black Biblical Heritage*; quotes H.M. Stanley, *North American Review Vol. 170*, (1900), 656.

8. Further reading on Raameses II can be found in:

   ❖ Windsor, *From Babylon*, 69, 143.

   ❖ *The Story of Ancient Egypt* (New York: 1887), 252.

   ❖ Browns, Filzmyre and Murphy, *The Interpreters Commentary on the Bible, Vol. 1* (London: 1875), 35-36.

❖ J.D. Douglas, *The New Bible International Dictionary*, Vol. 4 (Grand Rapids, MI: Zondervan, 1999), 980.

❖ Montet, *Eternal Egypt*, 104, 114.

❖ Rogers, *Men of Color*; 11, 28, 64.

❖ Cheikh Anta Diop, *The African Origin of Civilization: Myth or Reality (New York: L. Hill, 1974)*, 230.

❖ D. Cappart, *Reflect Dummond;* (1956).

❖ Giuseppe Sergi, *The Mediterranean Race* (London: W. Scott, 1901); page 243 in which he said, "The features of Ramesses II showed marked resemblance to the notorious Negro king of Uganda, Mtesa."

9. H.M. Stanley, *The North American Review Vol. 170* (1900), 656.

10. *The Interpreter's Commentary on the Bible, Vol. One.*

11. Johnson, *The Black Biblical Heritage.*

12. *Herodotus, Vol. 5*; 175.

13. Frank Snowden, *Blacks in Antiquity* (Cambridge: Harvard University Press, 1970).

14. Frank Snowden, *Before Color Prejudice* (Cambridge: Harvard University Press, 1983).

15. Snowden, *Blacks in Antiquity.*

16. Ibid.

17. Ibid.

18. Ibid.

19. Martin Bernal, *Black Athena* (New Brunswick: Rutgers University Press, 1987), 28.

CHAPTER 5

The Wealthy Continent

Because of the wealth of Africa, it has been referred to as the "Golden Continent." There are records of the wealth of Egypt, Ethiopia, Timbuktu, and South Africa from as far back as 2000 B.C. to about A.D. 1500. Egypt was known for its abundance of gold—in fact it was the chief export. Egypt had greater fame for its gold than its military success.

In her book *Bible Legacy of the Black Race*, Joyce Andrews quotes King Tushratta of Mitanni, a Syrian king, in his letter to Pharaoh Amenophis III in which he said, "My brother, pray send gold in very great quantities such as cannot be counted. My brother, please send me that and my brother, please send me more gold than my father got from you, for in the land of my brother is not gold as plentiful as the dust upon the ground."[1]

The wealth of Africa was the chief attraction for many people from ancient times. Greek historian Herodotus referred to the wealth of Ethiopia when he said, "The furthest inhabited country towards the South West is Ethiopia, and here gold is found in great abundance." From ancient times until now, the continent of Africa still stands as possibly the wealthiest on earth, but the irony of it is that the wealthiest continent has the poorest occupants. The wealthiest continent has the inhabitants who seek for gifts and aid from around the world.

The measure of wealth in the whole Egyptian empire is revealed by the kind of gold and precious things found in the chambers around the tombs of the various pharaohs such as the tomb of King Tutenkamen discovered in 1922. His burial chambers were full of chariots, fine furniture, artistically painted chests, boxes full of fine linen and silk, innumerable clothing, fifty thousand beads. Even the sentinels to guide his chambers of burial wore sandals that were decorated with pure gold. Because of the negative influence of 19th and 20th century opinion about Egypt, it was concluded by some that the artistically crafted chests surpassed the kind that Egypt produced.

There was found fine bronze work, plaques of pearl and gold was everywhere. There were other treasure rooms that were studded with gold. Chest upon chest contained various kinds of artistically made products and as they were opened they contained more chests within chests. The final tomb itself was gorgeous and there were four shrines. The working on the tomb was with skilled artistry and intense workmanship. What was found was incomprehensible by those who felt that the culture of agrarian Egypt was not sophisticated enough for the craftsmanship they found.

The tomb in which Tutenkamen was laid weighed 2,500 pounds, and when it was removed there was revealed a magnificent golden effigy of the great young king. His final casket was said to weigh 1,800 pounds, and in monetary value over $1 million.

Egypt became the playing field of archaeologists who returned to Europe with a few artifacts and became very wealthy. Certainly the burial of Tutenkamen with his face covered with gold, and his mummified body with 143 objects that were also gold, must have been a most expensive and outstanding burial. This was Africa at its best; this was Africa before its fall and decline.

The decline of Africa only preserved the precious minerals in it until the plundering by European countries. Although the stealing of African wealth started in the 15th century A.D., with the visiting of places like Benin in Nigeria by the Portuguese, at the Berlin conference of 1884-85,

European countries staked claims over African nations, in view of the fact that they considered the natives a bunch of ignorant people who were led by chiefs. With the chiefs bought over, they were able to have uncontrolled access.

With the exception of Abyssinia (Ethiopia) and Liberia, the whole of Africa was shared among five European nations in the majority: United Kingdom, Germany, France, Belgium, and the Netherlands. France took political responsibility for one-third of Africa. Belgium had only seven and a half million people at the time in its population, yet it became responsible for African territories that were in some cases 95 times larger than it.

The Portuguese were five and a half million at the time, and they became responsible for Angola and Mozambique, nations that were 21 times larger.

Please take note here that racism and slavery were justified by making these African natives look inferior to their colonial masters and that by the art of slavery, the Europeans justified their actions as helping the slaves gain a better life. They were made to look like there was nothing to their continent and they were merely surviving. This began the use of Africa as a warehouse for raw materials to be used for the benefit of Europe. In the meantime, the Africans, the natives, reaped no benefit other than being given jobs on their own land as they exported their own raw materials.

Take South Africa, for example, where there has been White rule for 300 years. The digging of diamonds in mines began immediately upon European occupation. A great majority of the workers at the mines were the Black Africans themselves who were paid almost nothing and treated as if to dull their minds.

In his book *Mine Boy*, Peter Abrahams writes of how drinking parlors were built around the mines, so that immediately upon receiving their salary, these natives used the money to drown their sorrow in alcohol.[2] The natives also provided domestic service in the various homes.

Natural Resources Wealth

Africa is not only rich in gold and diamonds; it is a continent where no nation is bereft of national resources. One third of the world's bauxite reserve is found in Africa. This particular ore is used in the making of aluminium.

Other mineral-rich African nations include:

❖ The Democratic Republic of Congo has over a million metric tons of cobalt metal.

❖ Morocco has a similar cobalt metal.

❖ Beryllium is found in Madagascar, Mozambique, the Democratic Republic of Congo, and Zimbabwe.

❖ Chromium is found in the whole of South Africa and parts of West Africa.

❖ Manganese is found in most of West Africa as well as in the Kalahari Desert.

❖ Gabon has oil fields and vanadium, a rare element used to make steel tougher and shock resistant.

❖ Nigeria has not just oil fields or oil wells. Nigeria has 32 trillion tons of natural gas. It has been burning away for the past 30 years, and the deposit still remains at 32 trillion. Nigeria also has titanium, and a metallic element tanatlom, a metallic element resembling titanium.

❖ Lithium is found in large deposits in the Democratic Republic of Congo and Rwanda. This is used in some cases to make mobile phones.

❖ Platinum deposits are found in South Africa.

❖ The Democratic Republic of Congo is the world's chief source of radium.

❖ Uranium is found in the Democratic Republic of Congo, but the largest deposit of uranium is found in Niger just above Nigeria.

❖ Most of Africa's copper is found in Central Africa, particularly Zambia, Malawi, Central Africa Republic. Zambia has 36 million tons. The Democratic Republic of Congo has 26 million tons of copper. Botswana, a very small country, has 530,000 tons of copper metal reserves. Mauritania has the largest reserve of copper in West Africa, 740,000 tons. Uganda has 200,000 tons of copper.

❖ The whole of Africa has a billion tons of lead reserve. North Africa, though, is the largest producing region. Zinc deposits in Africa is 16.5 million tons. Morocco and Algeria have large deposits of zinc.

❖ Phosphate is found in large deposits in North Africa, the Democratic Republic of Congo, and some parts of Nigeria. Morocco and Western Sahara have large deposits of phosphate to the tune of 20,000 billion tons. The regions of Western Sahara, Algeria, and Tunisia together have 12,000 billion tons of phosphate. Egypt has 660 million tons of phosphate. Togo has 60 million tons of phosphate.

❖ Senegal has 140 million tons of phosphate. The world's only source of aluminium phosphate is found in Senegal. It is estimated to be 100 million tons.

❖ Other phosphate deposits are found in Tanzania, 10 million tons; Uganda, 180 million tons; Malawi, 18 million tons.

❖ Granite is found in Morocco and Nigeria. Nigeria's granite being of particular interest, the only unique, sandy-looking granite in the world. Vast reserves of granite are found in Burkina Faso.

❖ Quartzite is found in Uganda and the Democratic Republic of Congo.

❖ Dolerite is produced in South Africa.

❖ Marble is found in Nigeria, Mali, Togo, and South Africa.

❖ Limestone is a key element in the production of cement worldwide and it is found in large deposits in West Africa. It goes from West Africa across to Central Africa, down to the Atlantic coasts, with major deposits in Togo, Ghana, as well as East African countries like Kenya, Tanzanian, Uganda, Zambia, and South Africa.

❖ North Africa has a major reserve of jepson on the Mediterranean coast. This also is used in building. Somalia has a reserve of 30 million tons of jepson.

❖ Nigeria has an unquantified deposit of bitumen. It is so much it
   is taking over farmlands, and yet the country *imports* bitumen.

❖ Major metallic deposits are also found all across Africa.

❖ In Algeria, iron ore is said to be 1.5 billion metric tons. This is
   also found in Western Mauritania.

❖ In Mauritania there are 27 million tons of copper ore. Manganese is also found in Algeria.

❖ In Algeria in particular, various metallic deposits that are necessary for different works are found. This list includes tin, nickel,
   chromium, zinc, lead, cobalt, silver, gold, platinum, and molyb-
   denum, a metallic element used in strengthening steel. Wolfram
   is used as a source of tungsten in electricity; thorium, a radioactive metallic element; and uranium.

WEALTHIEST CONTINENT, POOREST PEOPLE

Was Africa poor? Was Africa the most destitute, dark continent? No,
it was and still is the wealthiest continent, occupied by the poorest of people. This makes the words of Ali Mazrui, professor of Sociology at Keny-
ata University, true, "Africa is producing what they do not use and using
what they do not produce."[3]

Africa produces two-thirds of the world's gold and two-thirds of the
world's cobalt. Much of the uranium used for nuclear energy or weapons
comes from African mines. If all these deposits are found in Africa, then
the interesting thing is that the technology needed for the development
and the processing of all these resources seems to be beyond the Africans.

As of the writing of this book, it is sad and interesting to understand that
Sierra Leone is still struggling with the consequences of a protracted civil
war that has thrown most of the nation into darkness and electric power almost non-existent. Yet Sierra Leone's rich fields are worked for diamonds—one of its most valuable exports. It is believed that smugglers have
taken out an estimated $30 billion worth of diamonds from Sierra Leone.

Guinea, a neighboring country to Sierra Leone, has the richest reserve of bauxite in the world. But interestingly enough, the company that mines aluminium in Guinea is owned jointly by U.S., French, British, and West German firms—and, by the way, gold and diamonds are also mined in Guinea.

The town of Lubumbashi in the Democratic Republic of Congo is rich in copper. In the 1970s it possessed 56 percent of the world's reserve. For many years Congo was the source of the mining of radium, a radioactive element useful in medicine for the cure of tumors. Thorium and Uranium also come out of the Congo; some of these minerals give you an insight as to why there is a continuous divide and rule in most of these parts of the world.

According to the *New Encyclopedia Britannica*, "Industrial diamonds are more closely associated with Africa. The continent contains ninety-five percent of the total world reserves. The stones are found in a number of major belts south of the Sahara." The principle reserves of diamonds in their primary form in the rough are in South Africa's Val belts. Is it not interesting also that South Africa has a high rate of crime because of the presence of poverty and wealth at the same time?

One of the sources of diamonds in Africa is Namibia, a nation that has a large deposit. Namibia has gem diamonds that have no comparison anywhere else in the world.

The largest deposit of coal on the continent of Africa is found in South Africa, 65 billion tons.

Tanzania has a wide variety of biological resources including tropical hardwoods, mahogany, teak, and soft woods; large deposits of coal, 304 million tons; and adequate waterways.

Gabon has gold, manganese, uranium, and petroleum.

Cameroon has aluminium, gold, limestone, and petroleum.

Free State (formerly Orange Free State) produces gold up to 8 million carats according to 1989 World Almanac.

The wealth of Africa was so great that even the Whites fought among themselves. This is what led to the Boer War, when the British fought the Dutch settlers from 1899 to 1902 over who owned what in Africa.

South Africa's gross national product for the year 2006 was $587.5 billion.[4]

ENDNOTES

1. Joyce Andrews, *Bible Legacy of the Black Race: The Prophecy Fulfilled* (Chicago, IL: Lushena Books, Inc., 2000).

2. Peter Abrahams, *Mine Boy* (Portsmouth, NH: Heinemann, 1989).

3. Ali Mazurui, *The Africans: A Triple Heritage* (Chicago: PMI Films).

4. http://www.cia.gov/library/publications/the-world-fact book/geos/sf.html.

PART II

Conformations
and Pathologies

Introduction

What Is Conformation?

To conform, according to the New International Webster's Comprehensive Dictionary of the English Language Encyclopedia Edition, is:

- ❖ To make like or similar in form or character;

- ❖ To act in accord;

- ❖ To correspond;

- ❖ To comply;

- ❖ To be or become a 'conformist'; a conformist is one who conforms or complies.

A better definition is seen when looking at the meaning of the word *form.* A *form* is a "mold, or a frame for shaping."

As it applies to this book, Webster's dictionary defines *form* as "behavior or conduct according to custom, ceremony, decorum, formality or manners."

Form is to give shape to, fashion or construct, devise, combine into, develop, acquire and make to be like. If we combine the definition of conformation and that of form, it in effect means:

- ❖ To give shape to a thing until it corresponds, conforms, or complies.
- ❖ To make a thing similar in its character or form to the others.

One of the simplest illustrations of conformation is water, whether it is used to make tea, coffee, or mixed with fruit juice, it adjusts to the form of the container in which we pour it.

WHAT IS THE BLACK MAN'S BURDEN?

It is a fact that when we look around, we see that certain things shaped his world, and because he has found himself in this for hundreds of years, it is becoming difficult to break out of the mold.

In an attempt to do justice as to why Blacks are the way they are or have found themselves where they are, I have also asked myself many of the questions others have asked. Is the Black man cursed? Is his fate fixed? What could be responsible for these 2,000-3,000 years of burden? It is my conviction that the number one reason for the challenges facing Blacks is *idolatry*!

CHAPTER 6

Idolatry

There is no reference in Genesis to idolatry until Nimrod led a revolt against God. May I even be bolder in saying that Black people started every religion that has pointed man away from the only true God? In Genesis chapter 8 following the flood, Noah built an altar to the Lord making his sons see the true way to approach God.

> *And Noah builded an altar unto the Lord; and took of every clean beast, and of every clean fowl, and offered burnt offerings on the altar. And the Lord smelled a sweet savour; and the Lord said in his heart, I will not again curse the ground any more for man's sake; for the imagination of man's heart is evil from his youth; neither will I again smite any more every thing living, as I have done* (Genesis 8:20-21).

His three sons Shem, Japheth, and Ham began to spread across the world. Our interest in this book is Cush, the firstborn of Ham.

Nimrod

Genesis 10:8-10 tells us that Cush gave birth to Nimrod who began to be a mighty hunter before the Lord.

And Cush begat Nimrod: he began to be a mighty one in the earth. He was a mighty hunter before the Lord: wherefore it is said, Even as Nimrod the mighty hunter before the Lord. And the beginning of his kingdom was Babel, and Erech, and Accad, and Calneh, in the land of Shinar (Genesis 10:8-10).

The Scriptures clearly establish the fact that Nimrod, a Cushite, the firstborn of Cush, a Black person, built Babel, which is an abbreviation of Babylon. Babel actually means the "gate of the god." Some historians have tried to belittle the impact of the Black person by arguing that at this time no Cushites out of Africa could have come as far as where Babylon was situated, (in today's Iraq), and they argue that an Asiatic Cush existed only in the imagination of Biblical interpreters. Yet earliest Babylonian monuments show that the primitive Babylonians, whose structures by Nebuchadnezzar's time were in ruin, had a vocabulary that was undoubtedly Cushite or Ethiopian in its style and structure.

The British historian H.G. Rawlinson was able to decipher the inscriptions in Babylonia chiefly by the help of the Galla and Mahra dialects that are found in today's Abyssinia or Ethiopia. Fausset's Bible Dictionary puts it this way, "The system of writing resembled the Egyptian being pictorial and symbolic, often both using the same symbols. Several words of the Babylonians and their kinsman the Susianians are identical with ancient Egyptian or Ethiopian roots. Thus Hyk or Hak found in the Egyptian name Hyksos or Shepherd king appears in the Babylonians and Susianian names as Khak."[1]

The Jewish Talmud says that the sight of the tower of Babel in Borsippa, which is called in Arabic Biris Nimrud, is seven and a half miles from Hillah, and from the northern ruins of Babylon.

According to Fausset's *Bible Dictionary*, "The French expedition found at Borsippa, a clay cake dated the thirtieth day of the sixth month of the sixteenth year of Nabonid, which established Borsippa to be a suburb of Babylon."[2]

This great city was built by Nimrod, the great Black king and hunter. The technology, government, architecture, astronomy, and astrology of Babylon was so advanced under Nimrod that Herodotus, the Greek historian, said that the Greek learned from Babylon the pole, the sundial, the division of the day into twelve parts. He goes on to say that the first lunar eclipse on record was accurately observed at Babylon on March 19, 721 B.C.

They built such great royal canals in Babylon that the waters of Babylon were navigable for merchant vessels and connected the city to the Euphrates and Tigris. No wonder the psalmist said:

> *By the rivers of Babylon, there we sat down, yea, we wept, when we remembered Zion* (Psalm 137:1).

Our subject of idolatry connects to Nimrod because the tower Nimrod built sought to make a name for Nimrod, to defy God's method of worship, to defeat the purpose of God of requiring that all men worship him alone. It was a tower that pointed up, which was defined as a self-deifying, God-defying boast. Possibly before the tower itself was ruined, Nimrod had built other temples in which planets and stars were worshiped. This was part of what the Greeks took from Babylon into their own civilization.

Sir H. Rawlinson, Jewish archaeologist, again quoted by the Fausset dictionary, found by excavation the tower consisted of seven stages of brickwork on an earthen platform, 3 feet high, each stage of a different color. The temple was devoted to the seven planets. The first stage as an exact square was 272 feet each way and 26 feet high. The bricks, black with bitumen, were probably devoted to Saturn. The second was probably elevated and devoted to Jupiter, the third to Mars with red bricks. The fourth painted gold and devoted to the sun. The fifth was 104 square and was probably dedicated to Venus, Mercury, and the moon, but they were too ruined for measurement.[3]

The critic might want to argue whether the Babylonians were advanced enough to have studied the planets and to eventually communicate to the Greeks; particularly during the last 3,000 years, the world owes its progress mainly to Semitic and Indo-European races. We must always remember that originally the Hamitic race, the Cushites, the Egyptians, the Canaanites, now so depressed were the ones who took the lead in arts, sciences, power, the first alphabet, sculpture, painting, astrology, history, navigation, agriculture, weaving, etc.

Some might also argue that there are several accounts of floods around the world, and why should we believe the Bible's account. Fausset again quotes, "A Babylonian historian called Berosus whose account of the flood and of the confusion of tongues at Babylon accords with the Bible in most points."[4] Berosus was said to also have recorded that Nimrod, the son of Cush, came over in ships to Lower Mesopotamia, possibly from Africa, to build the city of Ur on the Euphrates.

With his focus on planetary worship and self-deification, we have our first clear account of false worship. In the New Testament we have the mystical Babylon, the comparative of the idolatry of the church or the nation, a comparative of the apostasy of the Church of God from God Himself, thus drawing a parallel with the Old Testament showing us that Babylon being the origination of false religion is also a pointer to New Testament false Christianity.

Sadly Babylon, as in the building of the tower of confusion and self-deification and worship and the dragging of people away from serving the only true God, was the first major contribution of the man of color. With the dispersal of nations from Babel, this worship of heavenly bodies, which later included animals, was carried by Cushites, Egyptians, and Canaanites around the world.

Diodorus Seculus, a Sicilian Greek historian who lived from 90 to 21 B.C., wrote a world history in 40 books, ending near the Gallic Wars, said concerning the Ethiopians and their contribution to religion: "And they say they were the first to be taught to honor the gods and to hold sacrifices and processions and festivals and the other rites by which men honor deity; and that in consequence their piety has been published abroad among all men, and it is generally held that the sacrifices practised among the Ethiopians are those which are the most pleasing to heaven. As witness to this they call upon the poet who is perhaps the oldest and certainly the most venerated among the Greeks; for in the *Iliad* he represents both Zeus and the rest of the gods with him as absent on a visit to Ethiopia to share in the sacrifices and the banquet which were given annually by the Ethiopians for all the gods: For Zeus had yesterday to ocean's bound set forth to feast with Ethiop's faultless men, and he was followed there by all the gods."[5]

Egypt is where we might say idolatry was perfected, and in order to have a clear glimpse into the magnitude of idolatry in Egypt and

Ethiopia, followed by the consequences, we need at this point to quote Scripture and expound as we go on.

And I will set the Egyptians against the Egyptians: and they shall fight every one against his brother, and every one against his neighbour; city against city, and kingdom against kingdom (Isaiah 19:2).

DISUNITY

This verse in Isaiah first of all shows us that idolatry would result in demonic disunity among Blacks. In every major city of the world that has attracted people from various nationalities, it seems as if it does not take long for people who immigrate to be able to get assimilated into the system and/or be able to help one another to become economically strong.

An example are the Koreans of Los Angeles, the Jews that spread around the world, and the Asians in the United Kingdom who left East Africa following the problems with President Idi Amin.

Disunity among Blacks, however, is a major problem.

CIVIL WAR AND UNREST

Civil war and unrest characterizes many African nations; and in the case of the Caribbean, there is a lot of unrest because of apparent disparity between those who seem to have a certain degree of wealth and those who do not. In recent times, the violence on the streets of Kingston, Jamaica has risen beyond imagination.

KINGDOMS AGAINST KINGDOMS

Tribal conflicts are still a major problem across the whole of Africa. People's acquisition of education has not made them rise above the nepotism of their lands.

FAILURE

And the spirit of Egypt shall fail in the midst thereof; and I will destroy the counsel thereof: and they shall seek to the idols, and to the charmers, and to them that have familiar spirits, and to the wizards (Isaiah 19:3).

In spite of the efforts across Europe and the United States to give people equal rights, the Black community is still challenged with the apparent failure in its community.

YOUNG PEOPLE UNDERACHIEVING

"...I will destroy the counsel thereof..."

The word *counsel* here means "plans." It suggests failed plans. Several initiatives have been known to come forth among Black people to help them gain economic, political, and material emancipation. It is interesting that many of them have also ended in failure. This verse makes us understand why.

"...idols, and to the charmers, and to them that have familiar spirits, and to the wizards."

The pursuit of superstition is a curse of idolatry. People give up wisdom; they give up the pursuit of the Lord to go after unclean spirits. They are never satisfied with what the Lord can do in their life. It seems as if in every community where Blacks are, superstition runs high, whether it is in Africa or in the Caribbean. We shall see this in more detail.

COLONIZATION

And the Egyptians will I give over into the hand of a cruel lord; and a fierce king shall rule over them, saith the Lord, the Lord of hosts (Isaiah 19:4).

In the 1880s the King of Belgium invited five European powers to divide Africa among them so that over 50 countries fell under these European powers. Belgium itself colonized the Democratic Republic of Congo, which was 91 times more than its own size. Only Abbysinnia (Ethiopia) and Liberia were never colonized, and even Liberia itself was really a nation formed to accommodate ex-slaves.

EXECUTIVE UNEMPLOYMENT

Moreover they that work in fine flax, and they that weave networks, shall be confounded (Isaiah 19:9).

Egypt was known to have the finest linen on earth, but God said that because of idolatry, they would work and have no one to buy. Within the Black community, the man of color has known the worst discrimination on earth. Sometimes people with the highest education have found themselves either unemployed or employed because they were perpetually given an appraisal that made them look as if they were below average and could not perform beyond that.

An interesting story that caught my eye one time in the British press was about Sir Paul Condon who was the chief commissioner of police for the whole of the metropolitan police of London. At that time his Black mate at the police college when they started had only risen to the level of a sergeant.

ENTERTAINERS

Surely the princes of Zoan are fools, the counsel of the wise counsellors of Pharaoh is become brutish: how say ye unto Pharaoh, I am the son of the wise, the son of ancient kings? (Isaiah 19:11)

God predicated that the Egyptians who were known as great and wise people would not be acknowledged for their wisdom, but for their ability to entertain, to make themselves look like fools. While this is not intended to cast an aspersion at people in the entertainment industry, yet it is sad to note that across Europe whenever a Black person makes news in the national tabloids, newspapers, radio, or television, it is often people in the entertainment business. No wonder it becomes a continuous source of attraction to young people in the Black community.

CRUDE LEADERSHIP

...the counsel of the wise counsellors of Pharaoh is become brutish... (Isaiah 19:11).

God said because of the idolatry of Egypt, her wise counsellors, her leaders, shall become brutish and crude. Black Africa has produced many despots—crude leaders who think that by consulting witchdoctors, marabous, and wizards, they can perpetuate their leadership. They start by arguing for the gains of democracy, but perpetuate their place in the office through corruption, murderous acts, and siphoning money into accounts all over the world.

WITCHCRAFT

Where are they? where are thy wise men? and let them tell thee now, and let them know what the Lord of hosts hath purposed upon Egypt. The princes of Zoan are become fools, the princes of Noph are deceived; they have also seduced Egypt, even they that are the stay of the tribes thereof (Isaiah 19:12-13).

Noph is what is known today as the city of Memphis. It probably had more temples, sphinxes, and statues of pharaohs than any other Egyptian town. The Egyptians, though advanced in knowledge, writing, arithmetic, architecture, astronomy, ship-building, farming, and the shaping of the calendars, also became seduced into witchcraft to the point that they could not draw the line between the physical and the spiritual.

PERVERSION

The Lord hath mingled a perverse spirit in the midst thereof: and they have caused Egypt to err in every work thereof, as a drunken man staggereth in his vomit (Isaiah 19:14).

To be *perverse* means to be wrong, to err, to be unreasonable, to vary from the correct, or to use in an abnormal way. It is a disregard of morality and duty. Much of idolatry from ancient times was never practiced without a degree of sexual perversion or the perversion of all natural things.

UNEMPLOYMENT

Neither shall there be any work for Egypt, which the head or tail, branch or rush, may do (Isaiah 19:15).

Unemployment among Blacks is very high, whether in their own domain in the Caribbean or Africa and wherever they have migrated to, the majority of Black migration is economic. This verse says whether they be head or tail, branch or rush, there will be no work for them.

FEAR

In that day shall Egypt be like unto women: and it shall be afraid and fear because of the shaking of the hand of the Lord of hosts, which he shaketh over it (Isaiah 19:16).

A visit to most of the cities of Africa would convince you that the spirit of fear rules over a lot of African nations. People are not at liberty to move around as they would love to because of the low value placed on lives by burglars, armed robbers, and other dangers that confront you and bring you face to face with death.

And the land of Judah shall be a terror unto Egypt, every one that maketh mention thereof shall be afraid in himself, because of the counsel of the Lord of hosts, which he hath determined against it (Isaiah 19:17).

Blacks in the West face a different reason for fear. The chance of being stopped and searched as a Black person is much higher than other races. The chances of dying en-route to the police station or while in police custody for the flimsiest reason such as choking on your vomit and many other untenable reasons are major reasons for fear.

Oppression

And it shall be for a sign and for a witness unto the Lord of hosts in the land of Egypt: for they shall cry unto the Lord because of the oppressors, and he shall send them a saviour, and a great one, and he shall deliver them (Isaiah 19:20).

"...*For they shall cry unto the Lord because of the oppressors...*"

No race or group of people have suffered oppression like Black people have, either as people taken into slavery or in the lands of their original birth.

Defeat

And the Lord shall smite Egypt: he shall smite and heal it: and they shall return even to the Lord, and he shall be intreated of them, and shall heal them (Isaiah 19:22).

The Hebrew word for smite is *nagaph*, it means "to be struck, to push, to thrust, to be bitten or routed, to stumble." When it occurred in Exodus 21:22 it was delivered with malice and potentially capable of causing death. Whenever the Lord did it, He smote with a plague placed on the people, with sickness, or with death.

And the magicians of Egypt did so with their enchantments: and Pharaoh's heart was hardened, neither did he hearken unto them; as the Lord had said (Exodus 7:22).

And the Lord smote Benjamin before Israel: and the children of Israel destroyed of the Benjamites that day twenty and five thousand and an hundred men: all these drew the sword (Judges 20:35).

And when the people were come into the camp, the elders of Israel said, Wherefore hath the Lord smitten us to day before the Philistines? Let us fetch the ark of the covenant of the Lord out of Shiloh unto us, that, when it cometh among us, it may save us out of the hand of our enemies (1 Samuel 4:3).

This passage having declared that the Lord will smite the Egyptian, means many consequences which break out by way of plagues, ravages, or disease among people of color are the by-products of idolatry.

In that day shall there be a highway out of Egypt to Assyria, and the Assyrian shall come into Egypt, and the Egyptian into Assyria, and the Egyptians shall serve with the Assyrians (Isaiah 19:23).

The latter part of this verse says the Egyptians shall serve with the Assyrians—servitude even in his own land where he is in the majority and ruled by one of his kind. Idolatry has caused Blacks to be in perpetual servitude. The biggest business in the Caribbean is tourism, and the majority of the tourists are other races, while the people who are occupants of the land will gladly serve for a couple of dollars.

You are more likely the last to be served in a restaurant in Kenya, if your color is similar to the people serving, compared to people of other races who come to the same restaurant. It is so interesting that in Africa if anything works, really works well, the impression is that it must have been imported from the West.

So shall the king of Assyria lead away the Egyptians prisoners, and the Ethiopians captives, young and old, naked and barefoot, even with their buttocks uncovered, to the shame of Egypt (Isaiah 20:4).

Isaiah chapter 20 establishes idolatry as a major reason for the mass enslavement of Black people. Over 100 million were taken into the Arab world and 14 million into the new world. One of the worst atrocities that ever took place on our planet, the most inhumane treatment of one human being by another, was slavery; the magnitude to which it took place from the lands of Africa is too much to comprehend.

Having been pushed down into the forests following his idolatrous walk, the Black man was then exposed to a forceful kidnapping and carried away as a slave to various parts of the world.

And they shall be afraid and ashamed of Ethiopia their expectation, and of Egypt their glory (Isaiah 20:5).

Constant shame and embarrassing experiences have been prophesied to be what will follow Egypt and Ethiopia. Have you noticed the images on the television and how the West portrays Africa and the Caribbean or Black neighborhoods? They are images that are selective and are not totally representative of what happens.

And the inhabitant of this isle shall say in that day, Behold, such is our expectation, whither we flee for help to be delivered from the king of Assyria: and how shall we escape? (Isaiah 20:6)

This verse seems to indicate that even freed slaves who live on the isles, as in the Caribbean, would be as the Egyptians—wherever they went the burdens of the Black man still followed.

CONQUEST BY FOREIGNERS

So they came into the land of Egypt: for they obeyed not the voice of the Lord: thus came they even to Tahpanhes.

Then came the word of the Lord unto Jeremiah in Tahpanhes, saying, Take great stones in thine hand, and hide them in the clay in the brickkiln, which is at the entry of Pharaoh's house in Tahpanhes, in the sight of the men of Judah; And say unto them, Thus saith the Lord of hosts, the God of Israel; Behold, I will send and take Nebuchadrezzar the king of Babylon, my servant, and will set his throne upon these stones that I have hid; and he shall spread his royal pavilion over them (Jeremiah 43:8-10).

All African nations have gained independence from their colonial masters, yet that has not eradicated the impact of colonial presence and conquest by foreigners. Even now most of these nations survive on foreign aid and can almost not endure if there were no foreign investment, aid, and support. Certain parts of East Africa have their economy heavily dominated by foreigners who have chosen to settle. Blacks in the Diaspora, particularly in the Caribbean, sustain their economy in the majority on tourism and money transfers by citizens who work abroad.

LOW VALUE ON LIFE

And when he cometh, he shall smite the land of Egypt, and deliver such as are for death to death; and such as are for captivity to captivity; and such as are for the sword to the sword (Jeremiah 43:11).

The ravages of HIV/AIDS in Africa, the high rate of road accidents by drunken drivers, and the high rate of armed robbery in nations like Nigeria, make life look so cheap. Much of Africa's civil war is fought by the young and the old, boy soldiers who have not yet learned to value life are fighting a cause they do not understand.

DESOLATION AND DEFEAT

He shall break also the images of Bethshemesh, that is in the land of Egypt; and the houses of the gods of the Egyptians shall he burn with fire (Jeremiah 43:13).

Defeat follows people who place a low value on their life.

DEFEAT

Wherefore have I seen them dismayed and turned away back? and their mighty ones are beaten down, and are fled apace, and look not back: for fear was round about, saith the Lord (Jeremiah 46:5).

From the conquest of Egypt by its neighboring countries following its idolatry, to the conquest of the rest of Africa by almost every nation that invaded, it was obvious that the people seem to have been given to continuous defeat by their enemies. Defeat is a by-product of disobedience to God according to Deuteronomy 28:25.

The Lord shall cause thee to be smitten before thine enemies: thou shalt go out one way against them, and flee seven ways before them: and shalt be removed into all the kingdoms of the earth (Deuteronomy 28:25).

Facing the Vengeance of God

Let not the swift flee away, nor the mighty man escape; they shall stumble, and fall toward the north by the river Euphrates. Who is this that cometh up as a flood, whose waters are moved as the rivers? Egypt riseth up like a flood, and his waters are moved like the rivers; and he saith, I will go up, and will cover the earth; I will destroy the city and the inhabitants thereof. Come up, ye horses; and rage, ye chariots; and let the mighty men come forth; the Ethiopians and the Libyans, that handle the shield; and the Lydians, that handle and bend the bow. For this is the day of the Lord God of hosts, a day of vengeance, that he may avenge him of his adversaries: and the sword shall devour, and it shall be satiate and made drunk with their blood: for the Lord God of hosts hath a sacrifice in the north country by the river Euphrates (Jeremiah 46:6-10).

God used Nebuchadnezzar to defeat Tyre and promised him Egypt as a reward for being the one to humble Tyre.

And it came to pass in the seven and twentieth year, in the first month, in the first day of the month, the word of the Lord came unto me, saying, Son of man, Nebuchadrezzar king of Babylon caused his army to serve a great service against Tyrus: every head was made bald, and every shoulder was peeled: yet had he no wages, nor his army, for Tyrus, for the service that he had served against it: Therefore thus saith the Lord God; Behold, I will give the land of Egypt unto Nebuchadrezzar king of Babylon; and he shall take her multitude, and take her spoil, and take her prey; and it shall be the wages for his army. I have given him the land of Egypt for his labour wherewith he served against it, because they wrought for me, saith the Lord God (Ezekiel 29:17-20).

Egypt was to be defeated and handed over to this evil king because of her idolatry. The consequence of bowing to other gods for the man of color is immense because it provokes the vengeance of God. It takes attention from God who should be the center of our worship.

INCURABLE DISEASES

Go up into Gilead, and take balm, O virgin, the daughter of Egypt: in vain shalt thou use many medicines; for thou shalt not be cured (Jeremiah 46:11).

A controversial conclusion about HIV/AID's having its origin in Africa continues. Certainly idolatry results in incurable diseases. Out of Africa have also come forth many diseases including the Ebola virus.

FALL OF HER GREAT LEADERS

The nations have heard of thy shame, and thy cry hath filled the land: for the mighty man hath stumbled against the mighty, and they are fallen both together (Jeremiah 46:12).

In their heyday the Blacks, as Egypt and Ethiopia, seemed almost unconquerable; but with their defeat followed by their being thrown out of the land of their occupation, everyone who came in an aggressive way took them for easy pickings, from the North of Africa to the South.

Even today one of the tragedies of the Black community is when leaders rise, it does not take long before they fall. They seem unable to overcome the influence of power, sexual immorality, and financial impropriety.

CONTINUOUS CONQUEST OF EGYPT

Declare ye in Egypt, and publish in Migdol, and publish in Noph and in Tahpanhes: say ye, Stand fast, and prepare thee; for the sword shall devour round about thee (Jeremiah 46:14).

This verse predicts the continuous conquests of the people of color because of the problem of idolatry.

WASTAGE OF MEMPHIS

O thou daughter dwelling in Egypt, furnish thyself to go into captivity: for Noph shall be waste and desolate without an inhabitant (Jeremiah 46:19).

Noph in this verse is a reference to Memphis. The defeat of Egypt was so severe that even today the towns mentioned in this passage remain unoccupied and desolate.

MALE IRRESPONSIBILITY

Egypt is like a very fair heifer, but destruction cometh; it cometh out of the north. Also her hired men are in the midst of her like fatted bullocks; for they also are turned back, and are fled away together: they did not stand, because the day of their calamity was come upon them, and the time of their visitation. The voice thereof shall go like a serpent; for they shall march with an army, and come against her with axes, as hewers of wood (Jeremiah 46:20-22).

The biggest challenge for Blacks in the Diaspora is male irresponsibility—a product of bastardization which white slave masters used to perpetually keep slaves in check and to produce slaves. Male slaves were seen as studs. Women were made available for them to sleep with in order to produce more slaves. The men were not encouraged to stay home and raise their children. They were moved from one plantation to the other. Women had to stay home and raise their children. Three hundred years later, the consequences of this process was that within the Black community in the Caribbean and Europe, 50 percent of homes are led by a single parent, mostly women; and in the United States 70-75 percent.

FOREIGN PLUNDERING OF HER TIMBER

They shall cut down her forest, saith the Lord, though it cannot be searched; because they are more than the grasshoppers, and are innumerable (Jeremiah 46:23).

At the time this book was written, foreign companies were felling much of the timber in the Democratic Republic of Congo and all of Congo. The Iroko tree, which is used as a hardwood for much of building around the world, is found only in Africa.

DOMINATION FROM THE NORTH

The daughter of Egypt shall be confounded; she shall be delivered into the hand of the people of the north (Jeremiah 46:24).

The obvious "people of the north" of Africa are Western Europeans. This gives us a picture of who will come and take over the daughters of Egypt, the nations that shall go forth.

From the exploration of Portuguese travelers, like Bartholomew Diaz in 1488 when he traveled around the Cape of Good Hope, to their visit of the Midwest of Nigeria in the 15th century up until 1912, countries of Africa have been partitioned among the five European nations.

FROM THE NORTH TO THE SOUTH

France colonized Algeria, Morocco, Tunisia, Somalia, Togo, Madagascar, Benin Republic, Burkina Faso formerly known as Upper Volta, Ivory Coast, French Guinea, Mali, etc.

While the British conquered Egypt, Sudan, Uganda, Kenya, Tanzania (which was a combination of Tangayinka and Zanzibar), Rhodesia (which later was known as Zimbabwe), Swaziland, Gambia, Sierra Leone, Ghana, (formerly known as the Gold Coast), and Nigeria.

Though the Portuguese were the first in Africa, they only colonized Guinea Bisau, Angola, and Mozambique.

Belgium took over the Congo, Rwanda, and Burundi.

The Spanish only took over small islands that were known as the Spanish Guinea, (later changed to Principe and Saotome), the Spanish Sahara, and a part of Morocco.

Italy had a brief stint in Libya, Eritrea, and Somali land and tried to conquer Ethiopia.

Cameroon came under the French and the English.

The Netherlands took slaves from Africa to the Caribbean; the Netherlands, Antilles, and Surinam were founded as slave colonies.

No greater humiliation can come upon a people than to have their power, possessions, privileges, and beauty taken from them. The daughters of Egypt were truly confounded.

MASS SUFFERING

The Lord of hosts, the God of Israel, saith; Behold, I will punish the multitude of No, and Pharaoh, and Egypt, with their gods, and their kings; even Pharaoh, and all them that trust in him: (Jeremiah 46:25).

DEFEAT AND PLUNDERING

And I will deliver them into the hand of those that seek their lives, and into the hand of Nebuchadrezzar king of Babylon, and into the hand of his servants: and afterward it shall be inhabited, as in the days of old, saith the Lord (Jeremiah 46:26).

A FORESTATION OF ORIGINAL EGYPTIANS

And I will leave thee thrown into the wilderness, thee and all the fish of thy rivers... (Ezekiel 29:5).

Ezekiel 29:5 is the first clear indication of God making it known to the Black person that he will be sent into the wilderness and the bushes to live the rest of his life, if he does not repent of his sins. This would be the second time, the first being at the Tower of Babel.

DEMONIC DISUNITY

thou shalt fall upon the open fields; thou shalt not be brought together, nor gathered... (Ezekiel 29:5).

This reiterates what Isaiah told the Egyptians at the time when he walked the streets of Egypt prophesying to the man of color.

And I will set the Egyptians against the Egyptians: and they shall fight every one against his brother, and every one against his neighbour; city against city, and kingdom against kingdom (Isaiah 19:2).

EXPOSURE TO WILD BEASTS

...I have given thee for meat to the beasts of the field and to the fowls of the heaven (Ezekiel 29:5).

It seems as if nature reacts differently in Africa. The wildest beast is regarded as being African. African elephants are not easily tamed as are Asian. The list goes on and on.

RAVAGES OF CIVIL WARS

Therefore thus saith the Lord God; Behold, I will bring a sword upon thee, and cut off man and beast out of thee (Ezekiel 29:8).

As of this writing, almost one-third of Africa is being destroyed by internal conflict and civil wars, and there is hardly any African nation that has not had one.

DESERTIFICATION

Behold, therefore I am against thee, and against thy rivers, and I will make the land of Egypt utterly waste and desolate, from the tower of Syene even unto the border of Ethiopia (Ezekiel 29:10).

The Sahara, Kalahari, and Serengeti are three of Africa's large deserts. The Sahara desert is 8.6 million km,^{2} barren and almost uninhabitable. Only two million people occupy the whole of the Sahara.

And I will make the land of Egypt desolate in the midst of the countries that are desolate, and her cities among the cities that are laid waste shall be desolate forty years… (Ezekiel 29:12).

BLACKS, BLACKS EVERYWHERE

…and I will scatter the Egyptians among the nations, and will disperse them through the countries (Ezekiel 29:12).

Blacks can be found on all continents, including the Aborigines who probably were part of the first of the dispersal of humans following the confusion of language, as a result of Nimrod's self-worship and attempt to defy God and deify himself.

BEGGAR NATIONS

And I will bring again the captivity of Egypt, and will cause them to return into the land of Pathros, into the land of their habitation; and they shall be there a base kingdom (Ezekiel 29:14).

God said for his idolatry the Egyptian should become a beggar. Much of the aid circulated today goes to Africa. Africa is always carrying its beggar pan in hand to go after the International Monetary Fund (IMF), World Bank, and other charities.

The call to "Make Poverty History" was to help relieve mostly African nations of their national debt, what they owe the wealthier nations. Nearly all of Africa is part of HIPC (Highly Indebted Poor Countries).

CONTINUOUS DECLINE

It shall be the basest of the kingdoms; neither shall it exalt itself any more above the nations: for I will diminish them, that they shall no more rule over the nations (Ezekiel 29:15).

The Black man began what would be called civilization, but this prophecy declares that Blacks will always have the least of kingdoms and will never rise to their original prominence. If anything, they will only recover their individual dignity.

THE PLUNDERING OF THE WEALTH OF AFRICA

Therefore thus saith the Lord God; Behold, I will give the land of Egypt unto Nebuchadrezzar king of Babylon; and he shall take her multitude, and take her spoil, and take her prey; and it shall be the wages for his army (Ezekiel 29:19).

As we have established earlier, the continent that was most plundered by colonialists was Africa. With its boundaries partitioned and divided among Western nations, it became the basket for minerals for developing nations.

CONTINUOUS CONQUEST AND ENSLAVEMENT

And the sword shall come upon Egypt, and great pain shall be in Ethiopia, when the slain shall fall in Egypt, and they shall take away her multitude, and her foundations shall be broken down. Ethiopia, and Libya, and Lydia, and all the mingled people, and Chub, and the men of the land that is in league, shall fall with them by the sword. Thus saith the Lord; They also that uphold Egypt shall fall; and the pride of her power shall come down: from the tower of Syene shall they fall in it by the sword, saith the Lord God. And they shall be desolate in the midst of the countries that are desolate, and her cities shall be in the midst of the cities that are wasted. And they shall know that I am the

Lord, when I have set a fire in Egypt, and when all her helpers shall be destroyed (Ezekiel 30:4-8).

Here the prophet combines all the sons of Ham except for Canaan as those who would be taken in slavery and conquered.

SLAVERY AND COLONIZATION

In that day shall messengers go forth from me in ships to make the careless Ethiopians afraid, and great pain shall come upon them, as in the day of Egypt: for, lo, it cometh (Ezekiel 30:9).

This verse establishes the fact that a people shall come in ships to carry away the Black person.

THE DESTRUCTION OF CAPITALS AND KINGS

Thus saith the Lord God; I will also make the multitude of Egypt to cease by the hand of Nebuchadrezzar king of Babylon. He and his people with him, the terrible of the nations, shall be brought to destroy the land: and they shall draw their swords against Egypt, and fill the land with the slain. And I will make the rivers dry, and sell the land into the hand of the wicked: and I will make the land waste, and all that is therein, by the hand of strangers: I the Lord have spoken it (Ezekiel 30:10-12).

African capitals and kings were plundered. Heads and kings of various nations were carried away to exile. The king of Lagos, whose name was Kosoko, was carried to exile while the city was shelled by the British navy in 1861; the ship was called the HMS Beecroft.

The king of the Ashantis who resisted the military and colonial invasion of the British, the Ashantehene, was carried to the Seychelles. In March 2001 I had the privilege of meeting his last daughter who was born in the Seychelles. At that time she was almost 75.

King Cetshwayo was packed off on a mule wagon to Cape Town from his Zulu land by the British Pro-consular Wolseley.

LEADERSHIP CRISIS

Thus saith the Lord God; I will also destroy the idols, and I will cause their images to cease out of Noph; and there shall be no more a prince of the land of Egypt: and I will put a fear in the land of Egypt (Ezekiel 30:13).

One of the biggest challenges of the Black community worldwide is its inability to have an emergence of strong leadership. It is perpetually divided, particularly Blacks in the Diaspora. Each one who gains a certain degree of visibility and respectability tends to treat their new position with such delicateness that they do not know how to make disciples like others and raise a continuous trend of leadership among themselves.

WEAK LEADERSHIP

Therefore thus saith the Lord God; Behold, I am against Pharaoh king of Egypt, and will break his arms, the strong, and that which was broken; and I will cause the sword to fall out of his hand (Ezekiel 30:22).

Among Blacks where there is leadership, it is a weak one that serves its own vision and interest. African politics is in the majority a leaning toward corruption, nepotism, cronyism, and tribalism. There have been perpetual challenges among Africans for the emergence of leadership on the basis of merit.

Certain Black nations have gone as far as making a rule in their constitution for geographical representation at the helm of national leadership. In Nigeria it is more aptly called "the quota system."

SLAVERY AND IMMIGRATION

And I will scatter the Egyptians among the nations, and will disperse them through the countries (Ezekiel 30:23).

And I will scatter the Egyptians among the nations, and disperse them among the countries; and they shall know that I am the Lord (Ezekiel 30:26).

There have been several dispersals of Blacks from their land. The first great dispersal and the confusion of language, explains the onward journey of Black people into Asia, as in the Indian, and continuously into Australia, as in the Aborigines. The second dispersal follows the prophecies of Isaiah, Jeremiah, and Ezekiel, which resulted in people of color pressed into the deep forests of the jungles of Africa. The third and fourth being slavery, and in recent times becoming economic migrants so that Africans, people of color, are found in faraway places such as Japan, washing dishes and cleaning homes, and in Iceland and Norway—places that are geographically incompatible with his body metabolism.

PAY A HEAVY PRICE FOR PRIDE

And it came to pass in the eleventh year, in the third month, in the first day of the month, that the word of the Lord came unto me, saying, Son of man, speak unto Pharaoh king of Egypt, and to his multitude; Whom art thou like in thy greatness? (Ezekiel 31:1-2).

Therefore thus saith the Lord God; Because thou hast lifted up thyself in height, and he hath shot up his top among the thick boughs, and his heart is lifted up in his height; I have therefore delivered him into the hand of the mighty one of the heathen; he shall surely deal with him: I have driven him out for his wickedness. And strangers, the terrible of the nations, have cut him off, and have left him: upon the mountains and in all the valleys his branches are fallen, and his boughs are broken by all the rivers of the land; and all the people of the earth are gone down from his shadow, and have left him (Ezekiel 31:10-12).

The refusal to repent from idolatry, which is the core challenge of the man of color, underpins the reason why God allowed the Negro to be a prey for conquest for everyone who has turned against him.

WASTED LAND

Upon his ruin shall all the fowls of the heaven remain, and all the beasts of the field shall be upon his branches (Ezekiel 31:13).

Africa also has the richest forestation, quality of land for agriculture, and yet has not been able to bring its agricultural system into sync with modern times.

BONDAGE (FINANCIAL, PHYSICAL, SOCIAL)

Son of man, take up a lamentation for Pharaoh king of Egypt, and say unto him, Thou art like a young lion of the nations, and thou art as a whale in the seas: and thou camest forth with thy rivers, and troubledst the waters with thy feet, and fouledst their rivers. Thus saith the Lord God; I will therefore spread out my net over thee with a company of many people; and they shall bring thee up in my net (Ezekiel 32:2-3).

By the swords of the mighty will I cause thy multitude to fall, the terrible of the nations, all of them: and they shall spoil the pomp of Egypt, and all the multitude thereof shall be destroyed (Ezekiel 32:12).

This is the lamentation wherewith they shall lament her: the daughters of the nations shall lament her: they shall lament for her, even for Egypt, and for all her multitude, saith the Lord God (Ezekiel 32:16).

Son of man, wail for the multitude of Egypt, and cast them down, even her, and the daughters of the famous nations, unto the nether parts of the earth, with them that go down into the pit (Ezekiel 32:18).

God said He would spoil the pride, the pomp of Egypt. A people lesser than her came to dominate her. Their great pride in navigation was taken from them. God told them, "Then will I leave thee upon the land." They became strangers in their own land as France, Britain, Belgium, Germany, Portugal, Italy, and Spain divided the spoils. Their land became the land of buffalos, rhinoceros, hyenas, monkeys, leopards, lions, giraffes, hippos, jackals—wild animals took over the land.

The same Egyptians who gave us a 30-day calendar and the observation of the stars, are now banished to the bush. They will never again impress the world as a nation or as a people group with their great wisdom and knowledge. There will be individual emancipations, there will be individuals who will shine, but first there has to be a breaking of the conformation of idolatry.

Mizraim, or Egypt, who settled by the River Nile became the greatest power of the ancient world, along with his brother Ethiopia. Mizraim delved into the world of mysticism, magic, astrology, and philosophy, everything to draw him away from God.

The method of Egyptian mythology was to have things in triads. The most famous gods of the Egyptians were Osiris, Isis, and Horus. Osiris was the father god, the sun god. Isis was the goddess, the moon, while Horus was their son. In addition to this, the Egyptians worshiped animals, nature, and humans.

The ten plagues God sent in the days of Moses were to humiliate the ten major gods of Egypt.

1. The plague of the blood (Exodus 7:20) was to humiliate the Egyptian deity, Hapi.

    And Moses and Aaron did so, as the Lord commanded; and he lifted up the rod, and smote the waters that were in the river, in the sight of Pharaoh, and in the sight of his servants; and all the waters that were in the river were turned to blood (Exodus 7:20).

2. The plague of frogs (Exodus 8:6) was to humiliate the Egyptian deity, Hecht. Hecht was believed to be wife of the god Khum. Frogs to Egyptians were images of resurrection and fertility.

    And Aaron stretched out his hand over the waters of Egypt; and the frogs came up, and covered the land of Egypt (Exodus 8:6).

3. The plague of the lice (Exodus 8:17) was to humiliate Hathor/Nut. This was to make the priests unclean and impure in doing their service to the various gods of the land, particularly Hathor who had to be worshiped in purity.

    And they did so; for Aaron stretched out his hand with his rod, and smote the dust of the earth, and it became lice in man, and in beast; all the dust of the land became lice throughout all the land of Egypt (Exodus 8:17).

4. The plague of flies (Exodus 8:24) was to humiliate Shu and Isis.

    And the Lord did so; and there came a grievous swarm of flies into the house of Pharaoh, and into his servants' houses, and into all the land of Egypt: the land was corrupted by reason of the swarm of flies (Exodus 8:24).

5. The plague of diseased livestock (Exodus 9:6) was to humiliate Apis. Apis was the Egyptian god of the lower world in the form of the dead Apis. It was symbolized by a bull.

    And the Lord did that thing on the morrow, and all the cattle of Egypt died: but of the cattle of the children of Israel died not one (Exodus 9:6).

    Pharaoh, in Exodus 9:7, sent someone to check if the livestock of the Jews did not die.

    And Pharaoh sent, and, behold, there was not one of the cattle of the Israelites dead. And the heart of Pharaoh was hardened, and he did not let the people go (Exodus 9:7).

6. The plague of boils (Exodus 9:10) was to humiliate the Egyptian deity, Sekhmet.

    And they took ashes of the furnace, and stood before Pharaoh; and Moses sprinkled it up toward heaven; and it became a boil breaking forth with blains upon man, and upon beast (Exodus 9:10).

7. The plague of hail (Exodus 9:23) was to humiliate the Egyptian deity, Geb.

    And Moses stretched forth his rod toward heaven: and the Lord sent thunder and hail, and the fire ran along upon the ground; and the Lord rained hail upon the land of Egypt (Exodus 9:23).

8. The plague of locusts (Exodus 10:13) was to humiliate the Egyptian deity, Serapis. Serapis was related to Apis.

    And Moses stretched forth his rod over the land of Egypt, and the Lord brought an east wind upon the land all that day, and all that night; and when it was morning, the east wind brought the locusts (Exodus 10:13).

9. The plague of darkness (Exodus 10:22) was to humiliate Rah, the sun god. This was the most major deity of the Egyptian triad of the sun, the moon, and Horus.

    And Moses stretched forth his hand toward heaven; and there was a thick darkness in all the land of Egypt three days: (Exodus 10:22).

The sun god was believed to provide warmth and sunshine from day to day. Utter darkness meant that their daily worship was interrupted and rituals could not take place to any other god.

10. The death of the firstborn (Exodus 12:29). This had a greater implication for the Egyptians because it meant that since the firstborn of the pharaoh must die, continuity of the lines of rulership must have suffered. This probably was one of the reasons for the immediate decline of the Egyptian dynasties, following the death of Rameses II, who most probably was the one who died in the Red Sea at the pursuit of the Israelites.

And it came to pass, that at midnight the Lord smote all the firstborn in the land of Egypt, from the firstborn of Pharaoh that sat on his throne unto the firstborn of the captive that was in the dungeon; and all the firstborn of cattle (Exodus 12:29).

Many of the kings of Egypt also were deified, a habit already started by Nimrod in Babylon. Ritually the pharaohs were identified in the solar hierarchy as the sons of Rah, the supreme god of the Egyptians. In some cases some pharaohs were regarded as the incarnation of Horus, the elder son of Rah. Osiris, Isis, and Horus, the triad gods, were carried by Egyptians into several cultures, thus the worship of mother and son as in the case of Nimrod and his mother. Later Osiris, Isis, and Horus were carried into Roman religion and various other parts of the world.

Israel, the first born of Jehovah, had been exposed to Egyptian idolatry; this probably accounts for God's attempt to sanitize them from it as He gave them the Ten Commandments. God told them, "Thou shalt have no other gods before Me." Unlike the Egyptians whose lives were dominated and influenced by their religious belief, the scientific advancement of Egypt was unfortunately lost in its metaphysical pursuit. All the streets of Egypt were lined with monuments and sculptures, pharaohs who from the fifth dynasty (2494-2345 B.C.) had been deified and worshiped. The Egyptians with their supposed discovery of eternal life and pursuit of it tried to perpetuate the life of dead souls by embalming their bodies.

The idolatry of Egypt became such a major abomination to God that God sent prophets to warn him on different occasions, but Egypt rather pursued after idols, charmers, and familiar spirits even further.

And the spirit of Egypt shall fail in the midst thereof; and I will destroy the counsel thereof: and they shall seek to the idols, and to the charmers, and to them that have familiar spirits, and to the wizards (Isaiah 19:3).

God warned Pharaoh and Egypt that if they did not change and turn from their idolatry, all the prophecies He had given would come to pass. Much of the spread of the worship of satan and the practice of black magic was later to be carried by Blacks to the corners of the world. Slaves from West Africa took their strange gods to Haiti, Cuba, the United States of America, Brazil, Central America, the Caribbean, and Panama. They pioneered the practice of voodoo in these lands. In some cases the exact names of the nature gods they worshiped were carried with them.

- ❖ Yemoja - the mermaid goddess of the sea was carried from Western Nigeria to Brazil.

- ❖ Shango - the god of thunder who was believed to spit fire was from Nigeria and carried to Brazil.

- ❖ Ogun - the god of iron was also carried from Yoruba land in Nigeria to Brazil.

- ❖ Voodoo - was carried from Benin Republic, the next door neighbor to Nigeria, where it was called vodum, to Brazil and Haiti.

- ❖ Olokun - the god of the sea, also worshiped by Western Nigerians, was carried to Brazil.

Just like the Scripture indicates, they will seek idols, talisman, necklaces, amulets, candlesticks, and charmers (witchdoctors) and those who deal with familiar spirits, fortune tellers, spiritists, wizards (medicine men), witches, and warlocks. For the space of three years God made the prophet Isaiah walk the streets of Egypt naked and barefooted. Prophesying to the whole of the Black nations that just as he, Isaiah the prophet, had walked naked, they would be carried in slavery and be made to walk naked by those whom they would serve.

In the year that Tartan came unto Ashdod, (when Sargon the king of Assyria sent him,) and fought against Ashdod, and took it; At the same time spake the Lord by Isaiah the son of Amoz, saying, Go and loose the sackcloth from off thy loins, and put off thy shoe from thy foot. And he did so, walking naked and bare-foot. And the Lord said, Like as my servant Isaiah hath walked naked and barefoot three years for a sign and wonder upon Egypt and upon Ethiopia; So shall the king of Assyria lead away the Egyptians prisoners, and the Ethiopians captives, young and old, naked and barefoot, even with their buttocks uncovered, to the shame of Egypt. And they shall be afraid and ashamed of Ethiopia their expectation, and of Egypt their glory. And the in-habitant of this isle shall say in that day, Behold, such is our ex-pectation, whither we flee for help to be delivered from the king of Assyria: and how shall we escape? (Isaiah 20:1-6).

The passages quoted previously give us insight into some of the things happening in Black communities around the world and their reasons. The original sin of the Black man, which also continued in spite of warnings from Isaiah, Jeremiah, and Ezekiel, was idolatry. This provoked his being scattered all over the world, and even then it did not stop him from the pursuit of idolatry.

From Isaiah chapter 19 we see God saying that because of idolatry, Blacks will know perpetual disunity.

And I will set the Egyptians against the Egyptians: and they shall fight every one against his brother, and every one against his neighbour; city against city, and kingdom against kingdom (Isaiah 19:2).

As a writer who lives in the United Kingdom, I have witnessed an immigration of people into the United Kingdom, either as a people group or as individuals. Whenever they have come as a people group, their resilience and unity has worked for them. The close of the 19th century saw the Jewish pogrom in Russia, and many Jews fled and settled in the United Kingdom. Settling in East London, they worked together as tailors, builders, carpenters, painters, and rose in society moving from East London to the North, changing their human geography.

They were followed closely by other communities as in the Asian community that was expelled by General Kaka Idi Amin from Uganda. They too were settled particularly in East London, and although they are still in the majority there, they have managed to help one another and have emerged as a political force and an economic power. Blacks in the United Kingdom are still perpetually marginalized.

And the spirit of Egypt shall fail in the midst thereof; and I will destroy the counsel thereof: and they shall seek to the idols, and to the charmers, and to them that have familiar spirits, and to the wizards (Isaiah 19:3).

This is a big problem within the Black community even today. Sophisticated Blacks on the streets of London pay tremendous amounts to marabous (witch doctors), just as it is done in Africa. The same problem applies on the streets of New Orleans,[6] at least so writes Reverend Earl Carter in his book, *No Apology Necessary.*

And the Egyptians will I give over into the hand of a cruel lord; and a fierce king shall rule over them, saith the Lord, the Lord of hosts (Isaiah 19:4).

This passage talks of the slavery that shall come upon the Black community—one of the conformations or the things that has shaped certain Blacks and has left incredible damage on their lives.

And the waters shall fail from the sea, and the river shall be wasted and dried up (Isaiah 19:5).

This passage talks of drought, one of the biggest problems of Africa on a continuous basis.

And they shall turn the rivers far away; and the brooks of defence shall be emptied and dried up: the reeds and flags shall wither (Isaiah 19:6).

Talk of people of great skill and ability! In the previous chapter you read about the great wealth of Africa, yet unfortunately the Black community has almost an innate inability to excel or to invent. It perpetually remains a consumer rather than a producing society.

Surely the princes of Zoan are fools, the counsel of the wise counsellors of Pharaoh is become brutish: how say ye unto

Pharaoh, I am the son of the wise, the son of ancient kings?
(Isaiah 19:11).

In Europe it is often thought that the greatest contributions Blacks can ever make are entertainment, music, and comedy. It seems as if there is a deliberate attempt not to acknowledge key leaders in the Black community in the Western hemisphere. Some of the actions that have come out of the Black community give the impression that the devices and the thoughts of the Black community are perpetually brutish.

The fishers also shall mourn, and all they that cast angle into the brooks shall lament, and they that spread nets upon the waters shall languish (Isaiah 19:8).

Establishing the fact that Blacks introduced the first civilization shows that they are not sons of Kunta Kinteh, but descendants of kings; idolatry has made them brutish and banished them into the bush.

The Lord hath mingled a perverse spirit in the midst thereof:.. (Isaiah 19:14).

Sometimes some of the magazines and newspapers that come out of the Black community, particularly in Europe, seem to portray them as a people who prefer self-degradation and walking in nakedness, instead of appreciating the beauty and excellence of their community.

Neither shall there be any work for Egypt, which the head or tail, branch or rush, may do (Isaiah 19:15).

The degree of unemployment in the Black community was already predicted in this verse. Blacks do not only face unemployment, they face underemployment, and even in places where their rights are protected legally by equal opportunity laws, there is still a deliberate discrimination.

Time does not permit a look at each person in this chapter now, however the idolatry of Egypt continued in spite of warnings from God that He would punish her by sending kings to invade. Nebuchadnezzar, the king of Babylon, was sent to smite the land of Egypt.

And say unto them, Thus saith the Lord of hosts, the God of Israel; Behold, I will send and take Nebuchadrezzar the king of Babylon, my servant, and will set his throne upon these stones that I have hid; and he shall spread his royal pavilion over them. And when he cometh, he shall smite the land of Egypt, and deliver such as are for death to death; and such as are for captivity to captivity; and such as are for the sword to the sword (Jeremiah 43:10-11).

They were told that a people would come and carry them away in ships, which predicted the European invasion, yet idolatry did not stop.

Egypt is like a very fair heifer, but destruction cometh; it cometh out of the north. The daughter of Egypt shall be confounded; she shall be delivered into the hand of the people of the north (Jeremiah 46:20,24).

Ezekiel was the last great prophet God sent to issue warning to the Pharaoh. Four chapters in Ezekiel (29–32), deliver a strong and stern message to the pharaohs who lived in his time. In her book *Bible Legacy of the Black Race*, Joyce Andrews establishes the dates of the prophecies of Isaiah to be 713 B.C., Jeremiah 586 B.C., while Ezekiel was 585 B.C., a year after Jeremiah.

Although Egypt was not at this time in its great height of power, its streets were still lined with various statues, sphinxes, phalanxes, and idols. God warned them that if they did not repent, He would throw them into the wilderness, He would make them desolate, they would be the lowest of nations, and slavery would come upon them suddenly. Their power and glory would be taken from them. Their banishment to the bush was predicted in Ezekiel 29:5; it sounded unbelievable and impossible to the Egyptians and Ethiopians who had occupied such grandeur and beauty.

ENDNOTES

1. *Fausset's Bible Dictionary* (Grand Rapids, MI: Zondervan, 1984).

2. Ibid.

3. Ibid.

4. Ibid.

5. Diodorus Siculus, *The Library of History*, Books 11.35-4.58, trans. C.H. Oldfather (Cambridge: Harvard University Press, 2000).

6. Reverend Earl Carter, *No Apology Necessary: Just Respect* (Lake Mary, FL: Charisma House, 1997).

CHAPTER 7

Superstition

And the spirit of Egypt shall fail in the midst thereof; and I will destroy
the counsel thereof: and they shall seek to the idols, and to the charmers,
and to them that have familiar spirits, and to the wizards (Isaiah 19:3).

The evolution of false religion in Babylon, which was subsequently
carried around the world by Black people, came along with superstition.
The intricacy of superstition and religion is that there is sometimes hardly
a dividing line between the superstitious and the supernatural. However,
superstitions have become a major force in inhibiting, limiting, debasing,
and belittling the person of color.

What Is Superstition?

The *International Webster's Comprehensive Dictionary of the English
Language: Encyclopedic Edition* defines superstition:

It is a belief founded on irrational feelings, especially of fear
and marked by credulity.

Any rite or practice inspired by such belief. Specifically a belief
in a religious system regarded by others than the believer as

without reasonable support also any of its rites. Credulity regarding irreverence for the occult or supernatural, as belief in omens, charms and signs, loosely any unreasoning or unreasonable belief or impression.

Superstitions are not limited to Black people, but are in the majority very influential in the decision-making process within their community. From Angola to Zimbabwe, from Jamaica to Antigua, superstitions hold sway all across. Some of them convey their impression of the world, God, and the future. A lot of superstitions are built around luck or ill luck.

From Sierra Leone comes the following:

1. A bride should not look in the mirror, otherwise she will die or go mad.

2. The child of a woman getting married should not see the mother in the bridal attire, or she will go mad.

3. You must not whistle at night or you may unknowingly call things passing, specifically, a particular devil known as Rhon-sho (Rown-sho.)

4. Do not leave footwear overturned; it brings bereavement, particularly the death of one's mother or father, in that order.

5. Do not answer if you hear your name called at night; a devil could be calling you, resulting in death.

6. Do not walk backward as it brings the death of your parents—mother and father, in that order.

A superstition in one place may be thought to be a bringer of blessing or luck in another place; unfortunately, this has hindered people and limited their scope.

1. He who fishes on Sunday will be turned into a monkey.

2. If a man eats the head of a rat, he will become a thief.

3. If a woman dreams of being bitten by a snake, she has conceived.

4. A wife who calls the name of her mother-in-law will evoke an earthquake.

5. A person who found money must give half of it as alms, or he will lose more than what he found.

6. One who eats and walks is eating with the devil.

7. If you eat from the same pan or plate with a woman, she will sap your strength.

8. You will be in perpetual debt if you shave your head on Saturday.

9. The devil urinates in an uncovered yawning mouth.

10. If a boy or man is hit with a woman's headgear, he will not find a wife.

11. If a girl or a woman is hit with the trousers of a man, she will not find a husband.

In Antigua they say you must not look in the mirror with a candle in the dark, it is considered an invitation for spirits to appear to you.

1. Never sweep the house at night, you might raise dead spirits.

2. When going home at night, walk into your house backward, in case something is following you into the house.

These superstitions have led to the loss of life, livelihood, and premature death of people. For example, prior to Christianity in Cross River State Nigeria, twins were considered taboo and therefore they were killed. Mary Slessor, the Scottish missionary, helped to stop the practice.

In another part of Nigeria, twins were considered to be very powerful and the parents had to do whatever the twins required or requested. In some cases parents have been said to be instructed by their twins to go begging.

The Fan people of the Congo believe in a god called Nzame who had two sons. His two sons were a Black man and a gorilla. His two sons offended him; Nzame sent them to the bush and went to live with a White man. That sounds like a justification for someone else's domination.

Various West African people worship Buku, a sky god, sometimes known also as a goddess who was said to create everything.

Danh is the rainbow snake that encircles the world. The worship of this deity was carried to Haiti by the slaves and is known in Haiti as Dan Pedro.

A god among the Ewes of Ghana is known as Nana-Bouclou; the same deity was carried along by slaves to Haiti, known by the same name, but remembered there as the god of herbs.

Because the Yorubas of Nigeria and their neighboring culture in Dahomey, now Benin Republic, could not understand the devastating power of the small pox disease, they worshiped the god of small pox, Shanponna.

Some of these beliefs also reflect bastardized understandings of the antediluvian era, the flood that destroyed the first world. The Kikuyus of Kenya have their version; the Yorubas of Nigeria have their version of the flood. In the Ivory Coast, they believe a charitable man gave away everything he had, and the god Awunde rewarded him with riches, advised him to leave the area, and sent six months of rain to destroy his selfish neighbors. The Bakongo people of the western part of Congo have their own version. The Cameroonians also have their version of the flood.

As you read earlier, it is sometimes difficult to know where to draw the dividing line between simple superstitions, the occult, and the supernatural.

Among the Yorubas, they have superstitions like "egungun." Originally the "egungun" were believed to be spirits that were sent from Heaven to visit the people of the earth until there was a disaster when one day the face of one masquerade was exposed. The same superstition was carried to Sierra Leone by ex-British slaves of Yoruba ancestry who were released there.

One interesting superstition among the Yorubas of Nigeria is the Oro. The word *Oro* could also mean "fierceness, tempest, provocation," but it is purely and simply what among the English is known as the Bull-Roarer. It is said to haunt forests and towns by the strange and roaring noise it makes. Oro is produced by the whirling round and round of a thin strip of wood something like two and a half inches broad, 12 inches long, more like a standard ruler with a string attached to it. This practice may have possibly started in Babylon or Egypt because it was later carried into Ancient Greece. Remember, people such as Pythagoras the mathematician came from Greece to study in Egypt for 21 years. The Oro Bull-Roarer superstition was carried to Australia, New Mexico, New Zealand, and South Africa.

The Yorubas believe no woman must see the Bull-Roarer. The same thing is practiced in Australia and known as the Boomerang. The practice of the Oro in the way it goes among the Yorubas of Nigeria is very similar to the Kurnani of Australia.

It would be impossible to state fully all of the superstitions that are believed around the world, but certainly among Blacks, whether it is the Caribbean, the United States, Africa or Australasia, the list could go on and on.

1. Don't bring an axe into the home because it presages the death of a family member or close friend.

2. A bat falling on you or hitting you may be bad luck.

3. Killing a bat may shorten your life.

4. It may be bad luck if bees fly into your house.

5. Who you see early in the morning matters; you may or may not sell.

6. Giving someone a purse or wallet is not good unless you put a coin in it.

This even influences the choice of what to do with the days of the week. The Yorubas of Nigeria believe Monday is the day to start a business; Tuesday is the day to start a battle if you must win, because it is the day that predicts victory.

Certainly God said the counsel of the Egyptian would come to nothing. If Blacks ruled more by superstition than reasoning, it meant that some things did not make sense when elevated beyond reason and Scripture. Take, for example, tree-spirits. This was a belief held strongly by Blacks; it was even carried back by the Greeks, possibly from their visit of Black civilization in Egypt.

Among the Harma-dryads of Ancient Greece, there was the belief that trees had spirits in them. The Akan tribes of Ghana also believed that certain spirits animate the gigantic silk cotton trees. The same people believe that an evil spirit inhabits mahogany trees. Again, among the Yorubas in Nigeria, the bigger the tree, the greater the chance that a whole family of spirits live in such a tree; instead of the Black person studying nature and understanding it, he turned it into an object of worship.

THE COUNSEL OF EGYPT FAILS

And the spirit of Egypt shall fail in the midst thereof; and I will destroy the counsel thereof: and they shall seek to the idols, and to the charmers, and to them that have familiar spirits, and to the wizards (Isaiah 19:3).

Before trees are cut in some parts of Africa, libations and sacrifices have to be observed. Even the most cultured and educated Blacks find themselves bound by these superstitions, and unless a person knows the transformation of the Holy Spirit, it could be controlling to the mind.

Superstition is a leftover of the false spirits and a religion carried from Babylon to Egypt and Ethiopia and subsequently into every place the Black person is. There are superstitions among other peoples of the world, but the one person whose destiny has been greatly influenced by superstition is the man of color. First, because his traditions perpetuate it, in any attempt to try to disbelieve them, he is immediately accused of not keeping the traditions of his fathers. These superstitions have therefore conformed and shaped the world of Black people and controlled their ability to produce, achieve, or succeed.

For young Blacks in the Diaspora, this has resulted in confusion, particularly when there are first- and second-generation immigrants holding to such superstitions, and their children do not hold the same view.

Superstition has perpetuated fear within the Black community; it has inhibited our ability to be inventive or to break out of the mold and achieve greatness.

From the Republic of Benin come the following:

1. A pregnant woman must not have her shower by night in a bathroom with an open ceiling, or wicked spirits could disturb her and the child.

2. You must not whistle at night as it attracts snakes.

3. You must not call someone by their name at night as the demons could hear it.

4. You must not sweep or pour hot water on the floor at night, in order not to disturb wandering spirits of nature—you must warn them before doing such a thing.

5. Every child who is born inherits the totem of the family.

6. You must not do the washing up at night, or it brings evil.

7. The aunties on your father's side of the family must be revered and feared; they have the power of life and destiny over their nieces. Their blessing is indispensable for marital happiness.

8. You must not cut nails on the floor because it might bring fights and unrest in the home.

CHAPTER 8

Witchcraft

The third conformation of Black people is witchcraft.

And I stayed in the mount, according to the first time, forty days and forty nights; and the Lord hearkened unto me at that time also, and the Lord would not destroy thee. And the Lord said unto me, Arise, take thy journey before the people, that they may go in and possess the land, which I sware unto their fathers to give unto them (Deuteronomy 10:10-11).

The dictionary defines witchcraft as "the practices or powers of witches or wizards, especially when regarded as due to dealing with evil spirits or the devil."

One dictionary goes on to say, "A witch doctor therefore is among certain primitive people of Africa, a medicine man skilled in detecting witches and counteracting evil spells, hence any medicine man or magician, one who professes to heal or cure by sorcery."

And the spirit of Egypt shall fail in the midst thereof; and I will destroy the counsel thereof: and they shall seek to the idols, and to the charmers, and to them that have familiar spirits, and to the wizards (Isaiah 19:3).

The first practice of witchcraft was in Babylon, and with the subsequent scattering of humanity, the sons of Ham in particular, carried it with them. The Mongoloid sons of Ham carried it into China, and other parts of Asia. The Ethiopians and Egyptians brought it into Africa and perfected it. Today the use of the power of sorcery and witchcraft still pervades the whole of the community where Blacks can be found.

It shapes their views, world, lifestyle, convictions, and how they perceive the future. In Egypt we see the apogee of witchcraft as they tried to outperform the miracles of Jehovah that He did through the hands of Moses, His servant. Today the witchdoctor still holds sway in the Black community; whether it is on the streets of Lagos or on the corners of Brixton, London, or among the Aborigines of Australia, the witchdoctor still has great powers.

Even in certain parts of Africa where people have been converted to Christianity, there still remains an indigenous belief in the practice of witchcraft to an extent.

> *And Moses and Aaron went in unto Pharaoh, and they did so as the Lord had commanded: and Aaron cast down his rod before Pharaoh, and before his servants, and it became a serpent. Then Pharaoh also called the wise men and the sorcerers: now the magicians of Egypt, they also did in like manner with their enchantments* (Exodus 7:10-11).

There certainly will be a degree of deception in a place where there is a belief in the supernatural. However, in light of the encounter of Moses and Aaron with the Egyptian sorcerers and witches, the power of witchcraft cannot be underestimated, particularly as we see it trying to counter the work of Moses as God led him.

> *And Moses and Aaron did so, as the Lord commanded; and he lifted up the rod, and smote the waters that were in the river, in the sight of Pharaoh, and in the sight of his servants; and all the waters that were in the river were turned to blood. And the fish that was in the river died; and the river stank, and the Egyptians could not drink of the water of the river;...and the magicians of Egypt did so with their enchantments: and Pharaoh's heart was*

hardened, neither did he hearken unto them; as the Lord had said (Exodus 7:20-22).

Moses turned water into a blood-like color, and the Egyptians with their magical power did it also. The rod of Moses became a snake, and the Egyptians also had their rod turned to a snake. When God therefore threw them out of Egypt into the forests of Africa, they carried these powers with them. They became people who had charms to protect themselves, who made charms to protect them from evil spirits, wild beasts, sicknesses, and diseases; obviously they also capitalized on the fears of the people by attributing the supernatural to things that just might be environmental.

In cases where diseases were not understood and therefore were unable to be cured, they were attributed to spirits.

...And they shall seek to the idols, and to the charmers, and to them that have familiar spirits, and to the wizards (Isaiah 19:3).

Blacks were given over to the practice of sorcery following idolatry and today it has shaped our worldview and has become one of the most major conformations of Black people. Voodoo was carried to Latin America, so there is a lack of progress because there is more fear of witches than fear of God. Sometimes no attempt is made to understand things scientifically, once they are looked at with a supernatural eye.

This conformation has shaped Black views to the point that there is a practice of inhumanity to fellow humans. Listen to young boys who are soldiers in the jungles of Africa; when they meet their enemies, they tear out their hearts and eat it because they believe that such cannibalistic acts give them boldness and the ability to defy death. These are legacies of witchcraft.

It is interesting to note that in nations where witchcraft is given prominence, social and economic advancement is deficient among the practitioners. Take Latin America, particularly Haiti and Brazil where voodoo is given prominence; voodoo dolls are made, and voodoo libation bottles are used. The dolls are made to represent individuals they want to attack, and they are stuck with pins and sharp objects for the person to have pain wherever such piercing takes place.

Haiti ranks among the poorest nations of the world, and the degree of poverty among the Blacks of Brazil is almost unimaginable. There are even whispers that in churches where they mention the name "Jesus," there could be practitioners of witchcraft who use powers other than the anointing of the Holy Spirit in an attempt to be seen to be powerful. What characterizes this church is often times the fact that they exploit people's fears and put more emphasis on evil spirits.

African politics also has not been without its own measure of witchcraft. A good number of African leaders are said to consult witch doctors, or marabous, to retain their longevity in power and to perpetuate the victory over the opposing candidates. Because of our conformation to the view of Africans on witchcraft, sometimes certain people are not challenged. Until Africa and Blacks, whether on the streets of New Orleans or any place where they consult with witches, recognize that it is still dabbling in idolatry and spirits that undermine, they will be perpetually conformed, strangulated, and held down.

God forbids us to practice witchcraft, and He forbids us to allow witches to continue to perpetuate.

Thou shalt not suffer a witch to live (Exodus 22:18).

It will be difficult for the Black man to drop his burden until he comes to the point when he realizes that he may have allowed witchcraft and its power to shape and control him more than necessary.

CHAPTER 9

Slavery

*And the Egyptians will I give over into the hand of a cruel lord;
and a fierce king shall rule over them, saith the Lord, the Lord
of hosts* (Isaiah 19:4).

Of all the pathologies that conformed people of color, the greatest is
probably slavery. The enslavement of people of color may be classified
into internal, Arabic and Western enslavement.

Internal slavery based on intertribal wars and conquests has been in
Africa since A.D. 600.

Arabic slavery has existed from about A.D. 1000, while the Portuguese
invasion of the West Coast of Africa and some parts of South Africa in the
14th and 15th century began the trading of slaves from Africa to the West.

*And I will scatter the Egyptians among the nations, and will dis-
perse them through the countries* (Ezekiel 30:23).

The enslavement of Blacks and their carriage to the West has had
tremendous impact on their lives 300 years on. It has shaped every aspect of their lives and perspectives, particularly, those who now live and
have no contact with the place of origin of their forefathers. Of course

this argument is not to create an atmosphere of determinism, as if individual choice and volition could not shape their future. Slavery has been known to be global, but no people experienced it on the scale that Africans have known it.

In the book *Breaking the Chains of Psychological Slavery*, Naim Akbar writes, "The protracted and intensive atrocities of slavery had a lingering effect and the pain of times past continues to call out from the genetic memories of those whose ancestors survived the test of slavery."[1]

The shackles that were put on the wrist, neck, and legs of the people, damaged their physical body, but the consequence reached beyond the flesh and affected their motivation, aspirations, sense of dignity, personal identity, and perception of self. It generated a perpetual desire for self-destruction. If anything, one of its dehumanizing effects is that it created a process and a sense of inferiority in Africans, particularly the ones who have left the shores of the Continent.

This process of dehumanizing was effectively achieved as slave drivers flogged people into submission. Families were separated at slave markets, mothers were separated from their sucklings, and husbands were deprived of their wives. Every aspect of human dignity was attacked by those who enslaved.

In the book *The Adventures of Huckleberry Finn*, Mark Twain puts it this way, "Good gracious, anybody hurt? No, killed the nigger. Well it's lucky because sometimes people do get hurt."[2]

The dehumanization of the Black person was captured in that succinct expression.

The first account of Africans as slaves in North America dates back to 1619.[3]

Prior to this, Blacks have been present in Central and South America for over 100 years in Spanish and Portuguese plantations.

WHY?

The burden of Egypt. Behold, the Lord rideth upon a swift cloud, and shall come into Egypt: and the idols of Egypt shall be moved at his presence, and the heart of Egypt shall melt in the midst of it. And I will set the Egyptians against the Egyptians: and they shall fight every one against his brother, and every one against his neighbour; city against city, and kingdom against kingdom. And the spirit of Egypt shall fail in the midst thereof; and I will destroy the counsel thereof: and they shall seek to the idols, and to the charmers, and to them that have familiar spirits, and to the wizards. And the Egyptians will I give over into the hand of a cruel lord; and a fierce king shall rule over them, saith the Lord, the Lord of hosts (Isaiah 19:1-4).

The question on every Black lip is, why the Black person? Because he has been the human commodity most shipped in shackles to the four corners of the earth—Central America, South America, North America, the Caribbean Islands, Virgin Islands, and far away places like China and India.

Why? Again we must remember that Blacks pioneered idolatry, which God looks at as the worst sin to commit. Egypt and Ethiopia were the central domain of Blacks in Bible times. Because Egypt was advanced in idolatry, God sends the prophet Isaiah to warn her that if there is no repentance they will go into enslavement. God asks the prophet Isaiah, who was both a prince and a prophet, to humble himself and walk naked on the streets of Egypt prophesying for three years to the Egyptians on the consequence of their idolatry. (See Isaiah 20:1-6).

They were warned that they would be handed over to cruel masters; fierce kings would rule over them.

And the Egyptians will I give over into the hand of a cruel lord; and a fierce king shall rule over them, saith the Lord, the Lord of hosts (Isaiah 19:4).

He tells them that the young and the old will be carried away unless they repent and totally turn to God. This prophetic action of Isaiah was to stand against the people of God if they did not repent and stop idolatry. And as if the matter was already concluded, since there was no obvious sign of repentance, God speaks.

And the Lord said, Like as my servant Isaiah hath walked naked and barefoot three years for a sign and wonder upon Egypt and upon Ethiopia; (Isaiah 20:3).

The stage was set for the slave trade that would thrive for 400 years. The stage was set for this people who were once wise and great to be auctioned like animals in slave markets, to be carried naked, barefoot, uncovered, diseased, and sick wherever they were taken to be used and abused. A people who were said to be like the gods by Herodotus were now to expose their buttocks, as they are scattered by God.

The prophet Isaiah was followed by Jeremiah and later by Ezekiel. Egypt and Ethiopia hardened their hearts and would not repent of their idolatry. So Ezekiel predicts that they will be carried by the shipload. (See Ezekiel 30:6-9.)

The extent of their scattering would be all over the world and truly Blacks were shipped to places as far as Turkey, Belize, and Brazil. So far beyond that they could never travel back to their original homeland.

> *And I will scatter the Egyptians among the nations, and will disperse them through the countries* (Ezekiel 30:23).

One might argue why God places such a harsh judgment on idolatry. Remember Deuteronomy 28:14-15 makes it clear that if you turn to gods other than Him, the curses in the same chapter (from verses 16 to 68) will alight on the people. Take the time to read Deuteronomy 28:16-68, and you will see how many of these things are manifest where people of color are.

Before you take offense, it is important to remember that when we looked at idolatry as a major conformation of Black people, we established historically, biblically, and practically that Blacks started, perpetrated, and promoted idolatry; even in their enslavement, the very slaves carried those gods with them to the places of their castrations.

> *Therefore shalt thou serve thine enemies which the Lord shall send against thee, in hunger, and in thirst, and in nakedness, and in want of all things: and he shall put a yoke of iron upon thy neck, until he have destroyed thee* (Deuteronomy 28:48).

Outside of Scripture there is no other way therefore to explain the fact that the most scattered people have been Blacks, and it is because of no reason other than the fact that the hand of the Lord is in it.

> *Why are thy valiant men swept away? they stood not, because the Lord did drive them* (Jeremiah 46:15).

INTER-AFRICAN SLAVERY

Africans enslaved one another, and on occasions when external slave drivers wanted to stop because of the abolition, chiefs who had profited from it fought hard to keep it going. Slavery was widespread from antiquity in Africa. In certain cultures, as in the death of the kings of Dahomey, slaves were executed to commemorate the death of their monarch.[4]

The great Mansa Musa of West Africa was known to have many slaves.[5] Certainly people did not frown at the idea of having domestic slaves. However, domestic slaves were more often bond servants, people who had been given over by their own families to serve as an indirect payment for monies borrowed.

In the case of the Ibos of Nigeria, they even had a slave community made up of those known as the Osu, ex-slaves who had now settled in their own community, albeit near those who were their captors. The fact that slavery brought cheap and free labor and advanced the work of the captors meant that tribal leaders fought hard to see that the slave trade continued.

On different occasions slave traders and drivers of the Congo, Dahomey, and some other African nations sent delegations to London and Paris to fight against any form of abolition.[6]

One of the inter-African slave routes was from Kanemi, a city that encompassed the Northeast of Nigeria, the Chad Republic, and a little of Niger Republic. Slaves were taken from here to as far as Egypt for sale. A 19th century slave of Hausa origin captured by the people of Kanemi in Borno remarked, "The country of Borno, I am telling the truth, is a country of slaves."[7]

The demand for Black slaves, particularly the Nubians from the Sudan, was very high in the Muslim world as the king of Borno would have thousands of them in readiness for exportation.

ARABIAN SLAVERY

The biggest exportation of Black people as slaves was more to the Arab world than to the West. The reason for a lower presence of Blacks in Arab lands compared to the West was the survival rate en route. A 19th century writer attested to the fact that many lives were lost during the slave raids; many old people, children, and the feeble were lost during the journeys.[8] Gustav Nachtigal, a German doctor who also traveled in Africa in the 19th century, gave an eye witness account of the treatment of slaves in the yards of Abu Sekkin, the ruler of Bagirmi (today's Nigeria). The slaves were shackled in chains with most of them feeling weak and unable to move.[9]

In over a thousand years, about 14 million Blacks were sold across the Sahara, Sudan, and across the Red Sea, the three major routes for slaves to leave the African continent into Arab lands.[10]

As early as the second century, Greek historians have recorded the lifting of Blacks from the horn of Africa. The Greek records also indicate the presence of Arab slave drivers.[11]

While slavery to the new world was essentially economic, much of slavery to Arab lands was domestic and military, i.e., slaves who were castrated to meet the high demand for slave eunuchs. The castration of slaves was itself a life-wasting venture. A.B. Wylde who was a British consul at Jedda at one time and who widely traveled in the Middle East, said, "say there are 500 eunuchs in Cairo today: 100,000 Soudanese had died to produce these eunuchs."[12]

Gustav Nachtigal also gave a vivid eye witness account of the process involved when castrating the eunuchs. The castrators "being sufficiently devoid of conscience to collect from time to time hundreds of boys, and to subject them to castration, condemned though this is by Islam. Under the pretext of wanting to circumcise the boys, the barbers who perform the operation are accustomed with a quick grip to grasp the whole of their external genitals in the left hand, and with the right hand to amputate them with a sharp knife. Boiling butter is kept in readiness and poured on the flesh wound to staunch the bleeding of the unfortunate boys."[13]

Female slaves were used as concubines, in some cases thousands of them to one man. There was also a specialized market for homosexual slaves. Certain men who wanted them for pederasty reasons also sought boys.[14]

It must be observed here that, while the Koran upholds the distinction between a slave and a slave owner, yet it sees the freeing of a slave as an act of piety. This also runs parallel with Paul's letter to Philemon in which he had pleaded for clemency for the slave Onesimus, although he had not asked for the freedom of the young slave.

Arabs raided African lands for slaves on a regular basis. From 1391 to 1392, King Uthman Ibn Idris, who ruled the Bornu, sent a letter of protest against the regime of Egypt because their tribes had come and raided his land and carried away free men and women as slaves.[15]

If someone could catalog several of thousands of harems and rulers who owned thousands of slaves of Black origin, the harem of Abdul Al Rahman III (912-61 B.C.) in Cordoba, Spain—a part of Spain that was conquered by Arabs around this time—contained 6,000 concubines.

According to Ronald Segal in his book *Islam's Black Slaves*, there was one particular palace, the Fatimid palace in Cairo, that had 12,000 concubines.[16] Tradesmen, people of lower social skills, also kept Black people as slaves in Arab lands.

The Caliph in Baghdad at the beginning of the 12th century had 7,000 Black eunuchs in his palace.[17]

Arab lands were a place where males were preoccupied with their masculine honor. To be a slave, therefore, in such a place was to lose all dignity. Through the Red Sea, the people of Zanzibar, known as Zanj, were brought in thousands into the Arab land to work in various places, goldmines, salt mines, and to serve in the private army of some of the Caliphates.

Muslim law required that slaves be treated properly and female slaves, when possible, should be educated, released, and helped to get married or be married by the owner. They were not to be marked according to the Koran, or any part of their body cut. Strong protection laws were established by Prophet Mohammed who said, "Whoever cuts off the nose of a slave, his nose will be cut off, and whoever castrates a slave, him shall we castrate."

The Koran also stipulates that a slave who wants to buy his freedom must be allowed to do so: "those your right hand own who seek emancipation, contract with them accordingly, if you know some good in them, and give them of the wealth of God that he has given to you."[18]

One wonders how Mohammed would have reacted if he knew that corroborated stories were still tracing slavery to Mecca even as late as 1962. During this same period, Saudi princes, who were possibly backed by President Nasser's government, alerted the world to the ongoing slavery in Saudi Arabia.

"We consider it our sacred duty to make the international public aware of the question of negro and white slavery in Saudi Arabia...Agents go as far afield as Africa, Iraq, and Iran to find their human merchandise, which they bring back to Saudi Arabia. The slave is often put to work for oil companies and his wages paid to his master."[19]

One of Prophet Mohammed's ten closest so-called companions was said to have freed no fewer than 30,000 slaves when he died in A.D. 652.[20]

Slave dealers were notorious; they did not respect the Islamic law they purported to believe in. They looked down on the slaves and approved of the large-scale importation of slaves from Africa, and the menial jobs they performed must have influenced Arab perspectives of Blacks.

The belittling of Blacks may have been influenced, among other things, by the writings of an Arab eminent writer al-Masudi who died in A.D. 956. He was a student of Roman writer Galen who lived in the second century and held the view that Black males in particular were lazy and only given to merriment. Galen said "merriment dominates the Black man because of his defective brain, whence also the weakness of his intelligence."[21]

However, Ronald Segal quotes the prophet Mohammed as having said in one of his last sermons, "No Arab has any priority over a non-Arab and no White over a Black except in righteousness."[22]

One Arab thinker, however, deviates from the teaching of Mohammed by claiming "That the Negro nations are as a rule submissive to slavery" because, according to him, they "have attributes that are quite similar to those of dumb animals."[23]

Pre-Islamic Arabia did not place any stigma on Blackness according to Bernard Lewis.[24] However, the large-scale importation of Blacks into the Arab lands, particularly through the doors of slavery, began to change attitudes toward them.[25]

Furthermore, the culture of Islamic nations placed high value on intellectual acuity and less emphasis on physical prowess. On the other hand, the majority of Blacks were brought to the land for physical and menial jobs; this method of entry into the land made the Arabs look at Blacks as being intellectually inferior.

By the close of the 19th century, every regard and respect for slaves as it relates to those shipped to Arab lands had disappeared. Slavery became violent; survival became less. Slavery to Arab lands was of a higher volume than to the West. There was a high death rate; but after they got to the land, they were probably better treated than the slaves who arrived in the West. Much of the pain and brutality they may have suffered in the hands of the slave drivers and the slave traders was not always directly attributable to the color of their skin; however, it dented their sense of dignity.

Once the slaves reached the Arab lands, Black women were highly priced, obviously since they were used as concubines. One of the 12th century geographers, an Arab man, Al Idris, 1110-1165, eloquently describes them, "Their women are of surpassing beauty, they are circumcised and of fragrant smelling. Their lips are thin, their mouth small and their hair flowing...it is on account of these qualities of theirs that the rulers of Egypt were so desirous of them and outbid others to purchase them afterwards fathering children from them."[26]

The magnitude of Black importation into Arab lands and their influence there has not been fully studied or reported. This book may not do justice to it either since it is intended to show conformations, and in this particular chapter as it relates to slavery. Concerning Black slaves, another author has this to say of the men; "The male Nubians in Egypt as well as in Arabia are preferred to all others for labor: they bear a good character and sell at Shandy in Nubia and in Egypt twenty percent dearer than the Negroes. The male Abyssinians on the contrary are known to be little fit for bodily work, but they are esteemed for their fidelity and make excellent house servants and often clerks, their intellects being certainly much superior to those of Blacks. The Nubians are said to be of a healthier construction and to suffer less from disease than the Abyssinians (today's Ethiopians). The greatest part of them are exported to Egypt, but some are sent to Suakin, the Red Sea port for shipment to Jidah on the Arabian coast."[27]

In effect there was a higher rate of social assimilation of Blacks into the Islamic world, with the Blacks rising to high positions.

On the matter of social assimilation, and its contrast with the plight of Blacks, H.J. Fisher writes: "It is arguable that a considerable majority of the slaves crossing the Sahara were destined to become concubines in North Africa, the Middle East, and occasionally even farther afield. And it may be this, in turn, which helps to explain why a flow of slaves possibly greater in total than that across the Atlantic has not led to any comparably dramatic racial confrontation in North Africa society, although distinctions there of course are."[28]

Raymond Mauvy gives us a figure of 14 million for slaves taken into the Arab world.[29]

Although we deal here with slaves taken to Arab lands, we must mention that Blacks were carried to other places that have not been given much attention. Blacks were carried as slaves as early as the 12th century to China to work. They were called wild men and were described as being, "Black as ink with teeth white and their hair curly." Their language was described as unintelligible, and people described them as "devil slaves."[30]

WESTERN SLAVERY

England's aspiration to gain a colonial foothold on the North American continent influenced its commitment to slave trade. The first Africans to that part of the world were brought as indentured servants, although the Spanish and Portuguese had been involved in elaborate slavery, creating slave plantations a century earlier.[31]

Slaves were taken by the Portuguese on the Guinean coast for sale in Lisbon as early as 1444.[32]

Following the importation in 1619 of indentured slaves to America which boosted the economy, a new race-based slavery system developed. The majority of Africans and African Americans who were to end up in that part of the world were to be held as slaves for life. Laws were to be promulgated that perpetuated slavery. The State of Massachusetts became the first colony in 1641 to legalize slavery while Virginia in 1663 passed a law that a child born in slavery like the mother is also a slave.

This unjust law was to be passed by almost every one of the states in North America with Georgia being the last of the British North American colonies to legalize slavery in 1750.

The kind of slavery the people were introduced to, according to Basil Davidson in his book *The African Slave Trade*, was different from that which was practiced on the continent of Africa. Slaves on the continent of Africa owned property and sometimes owned slaves themselves. Slaves were never passed from one generation to the other except for a few rare cases. By the start of the 16th century, almost 200,000 Africans had been transported to Europe and islands in the Atlantic. They were to become workers for the new slave masters in Spain and Caribbean islands. This was because the Native Americans they met on most of these islands were resistant and therefore fled from the Europeans. With the boom in the production of cotton, the Europeans saw the African slave as the answer to the shortage of labor.[33]

The African continent provided cheap labor. The trading of humans from particularly the West coast of Africa continued for 300 years. The Europeans made more than 54,000 voyages to trade human beings and sent at least 10-12 million Africans to the Caribbean and the Americas.

The slave trade devastated the continent of Africa and the Africans in general. People were taken with disregard for their culture and traditions, families were fragmented, people were abducted, friends told on friends, and guns were introduced into the culture of these people. Men and women were unwillingly captured and made to walk a long way, sometimes from the hindermost place of Africa to the coastal regions where the slave masters, in collaboration with the coastal chiefs, had built forts. Some of these walks from the hinterland were close to 1,000 miles and when they were packed on slave ships, they were packed ankle-to-ankle, wrist-to-wrist and chained in pairs.

The women provided sexual satisfaction for the ship owners. When diseases like dysentery broke out on the ships, it killed many as they wallowed in their own feces and urine. They were treated in the most inhuman way. Whenever a ship was overloaded, live slaves were thrown overboard.

Slave history grew larger as the invention of the cotton gin and the booming southern economy of the United States fueled the push for more slaves. Every uprising by the slaves was quelled. The Haitian revolution of 1791-1804, the Gabriel's revolution of 1800, the Denmark Vesis plot of 1822, and Nat Turner's revolt of 1831 are reminders of the desire of every man, bond or free, to taste and live in freedom.

The death rate among slaves was very high, and to replace their losses, plantation owners who had bought the slaves encouraged the slaves to have more children. After all, children who were born in slavery were slaves themselves. Women were encouraged to sleep with many men so that children would be born. They gave the women the false hope that they would gain freedom after they produced 15 children. The world of Southern United States was built on the backbones of these African slaves.

The large landowners who would usually own well over 100 slaves relied heavily also on slave drivers who supervised the slaves. It is estimated that by 1850 about 1,000 families who owned slaves and plantations had an income of about $15 million, while another 660 families who owned between 15 or more slaves had an income of $60 million. This kind of money certainly was very high for the 18th century.

SLAVE DRIVERS

Slave drivers were overseers who were employed to run plantations on behalf of slave owners. These overseers were given production levels that had to be achieved in order to maximize profits. The onus rested on the slave driver to keep the punishment going on until the slaves produced to capacity. They used cat whips to tie slaves upside down in the hot sun, then tied burning hog flesh over them so that the melting hot fat fell on them to subdue the slaves to carry out what they wanted.

Moses Grandy wrote about his overseer in his autobiography, *Life of a Slave*. "They were flogged, pork or beef brine was put on their bleeding backs to increase the pain. He sitting by, resting himself and seeing it done. After being thus flogged and pickled the sufferers often remained tied up all day. The feet were just touching the ground, the legs tied and pieces of wood put between the legs." He said furthermore "thus exposed and helpless, the yellow flies and mosquitoes in great numbers would settle on the bleeding and smitten back and put the sufferer to extreme torture."[34]

Various methods were used by McPherson, the slave driver in the case of Moses Grandy. Moses Grandy goes on to say, "sometimes he would increase his misery by blustering and calling out that he was coming to flog again, which he did not. The slave would sometimes be tied with his shirt over his head that he might not flinch when the blow was coming. Sometimes this increases the misery. Slaves were flogged until their entrails were visible and in other cases the sufferers died on the spot."

Some slave drivers kept their own personal jails and whipping posts, and whatever cruelty was perpetrated there was passed without comment as carried out by the well-paid overseers. After all the wealth of the slave owner was made to increase.

SLAVE MARKETS

With the demand for crops from the Caribbean and America by Europe, slave markets were established and people were sold at auctions.

William Wells Brown in "The American Slave Trade," published in *The Liberty Bell*, tells about some of the experiences at such slave markets. "Several slave speculators who are always to be found at auctions where slaves are to be sold were present. The man was first put up and sold to the first bidder. The wife was next ordered to ascend the platform. I was present. She slowly obeyed the order. The auctioneer commenced and soon several hundred dollars were bid. My eyes were intensely fixed on the face of the woman whose cheeks were wet with tears but a conversation between the slave and his new master attracted my attention. I drew near them to listen: the slave was begging his new master to purchase his wife said he: "Master, if you would only buy Fanny, I know you would get the worth of your money, she is a good cook, a good washer and her last mistress liked her very much. If you only buy her, how happy I shall be." The new master in this case replied that he did not want her but if she sold cheap he would purchase her."[35] In this way, husband and wife would be parted, never to see each other again. No matter how strong a man's composition, such cruel separations leave an indelible mark on any person.

Henry Bibb in *The Life and Adventure of an American Slave*, gives us an insight on how a slave may respond when he is being sold like an ox. "He is bound in chains and hands and foot and his sufferings are hundredfold by the terrible thought that he is not allowed to struggle against misfortune, corporal punishment, insults and outrages committed upon himself or family. He is not allowed to help himself, to resist or escape the blow which he sees impending over him."[36]

SLAVE MARRIAGES

Most slave owners encouraged their slaves to marry. This was not because the welfare of the man was sought but because a child born in slavery was himself a slave, an addition to the stock of slaves owned by the master. What slaves had could not really be described as marriage because a slave could not pledge to protect, care for his wife, or stand for her. He himself being without rights could not argue for his wife's rights. Childbearing started around the age of 13 for most slaves, and by 20 the women slaves would expect to have had four or five children.

Henry Bibb gives us an insight into what happens once a slave marries, "If my wife must be exposed to the insults and licentious passions of wicked slave drivers and overseers, heaven forbid that I should be compelled to witness the sight."[37] This certainly was the experience of slaves.

Moses Grandy agrees and says that, "No colored man wishes to live at the house where his wife lives for he has to endure the continual misery of seeing her flogged and abused without daring to say a word in her defense."[38]

Not only was she flogged or abused, on occasions the master would tell the husband that tonight he wishes to sleep with the slave's wife. The only response must be, "Yes Sir." So slave masters have gone as far as requesting that the slave sit by the door to hear the passionate response of their wives. There was no vow of marriage. A man and woman intending to marry were only requested to jump over a stick as the sign that they were now one flesh and if no child was born within the year, the slave master separated them.

Bethany Veney, in her book *A Slave Woman*, gives the picture of what happened at her marriage. "One day there was a colored man, a peddler with his cat on the road and Jerry brought him in and said he was ready to be minister for us. He asked us a few questions which we answered in a satisfactory manner and then he declared us husband and wife. I did not want him to make us promise that we would always be true to each other because I knew that at anytime my masters would compel us to break such a promise."[39]

SLAVE CHILDHOOD

Pregnant slaves were expected to continue working until their child was born. Only a month's rest was allowed before the woman must be back to the cotton or sugar cane fields as the case may be. An old slave mother was made to watch over all the slaves' children while the mothers worked on the farm.

The great ex-slave and abolitionist Frederick Douglass claimed that, particularly in the State of Maryland where he was born, it was common "to part children from their mothers at a very early age frequently before the child had reached its twelfth month. Its mother is taken from it and hidden out on some farm, a considerable distance off and the child is placed under an old woman too old to go to field." Thus the child grows without knowing who his mother is. On other farms children were made to work from the age of five.

The separation of the mother and child must be very cruel and certainly conforms a person to not in turn have affection or have the ability to communicate affection to their own children. Frederick Douglass would say further, "What this separation has done I do not know, unless it be to hinder the development of the child's affection toward its mother and to blunt and destroy the natural affection of the mother for the child. This is the inevitable result."[40]

HOUSE SLAVES VERSUS FIELD SLAVES

Every possible method of dividing and breaking the spirit of the slaves was employed. Field slaves were treated differently from the ones who worked in the house. The slaves who were of mixed race—products of the forceful copulation between the slave master, slave drivers, overseers, and the slave women—were given a higher status on grounds of the lightness of their color. Seeds of discord were sown to keep them perpetually at one another's neck.

And I will set the Egyptians against the Egyptians: and they shall fight every one against his brother, and every one against his neighbour; city against city, and kingdom against kingdom (Isaiah 19:2).

In 1712 Virginia slave owners invited a military general from the West Indies, William Lynch, to speak to them on the method of management of slaves as it is carried out in the Caribbean. The following is the speech he gave in 1712:

Gentlemen:

I greet you here on the bank of the James River in the year of our Lord, one thousand seven hundred and twelve. First, I shall thank you, the Gentlemen of the Colony of Virginia for bringing me here. I am here to help you solve some of your problems with slaves. Your invitation reached me on my modest plantation in the West Indies where I have experimented with some of the newest and still the oldest methods for control of slaves. Ancient Rome would envy us if my programme were implemented. As our boat sailed south on the James River, named for our illustrious King, whose version of the Bible we cherish, I saw enough to know that your problem is not unique. While Rome used cords of wood as crosses for standing human bodies along its old highway in great numbers, you are here using the tree and the rope on occasion.

I caught the whiff of a dead slave hanging from a tree a couple of miles back. You are not only losing valuable stock by hangings, you are having uprisings, slaves are running away, your crops are sometimes left in the field too long for maximum profit. You suffer occasional fires and your animals are killed. Gentlemen, you know what your problems are: I do not need to elaborate. I am not here to enumerate your problems. I am here to introduce you to a method of solving them.

In my bag here I have a foolproof method for controlling your Black slaves. I guarantee every one of you that if installed correctly it will control the slaves for at least 300 years. My method is simple and members of your family or any overseer can use it.

I have outlined a number of differences among the slaves and I take these differences and make them bigger. I use fear, distrust, and envy for control purposes. These methods have worked on my modest plantation in the West Indies and it will work throughout the South. Take this simple little list of differences and think about them. On the top of my list is 'age', but it is there only because it starts with 'a'; the second is 'color (or shade)'; there is intelligence, size, sex, size of plantation, status on plantation, attitude of owner, whether the slaves live in the valley, on a hill, east, west, north, south; have fine hair or coarse hair, or is tall or short. Now that you have a list of differences, I shall give you an outline of action, but before that I shall assure you that distrust is stronger than trust and envy is stronger than adulation, respect or admiration.

The Black slave after receiving this indoctrination shall carry on and will become self-refuelling and self-generating for hundreds of years, maybe thousands.

Don't forget you must pitch the old Black versus the young Black male and the young Black male against the old Black male. You must use the dark skin slaves versus the light skin slaves and the light skin slaves versus the dark skin slaves. You must also have your white servants and overseers distrust ALL Blacks, but it is necessary that they trust and depend on us. They must love, respect and trust ONLY us.

Gentleman, these kits are your keys to control: use them. Have your wives and children use them, never miss an opportunity. My plan is guaranteed, and the good thing about this plan is that if used INTENSELY for one year, the slaves themselves will remain perpetually distrustful.

Thank you gentlemen.[41]

How Slavery Affected People of Color

Imagine a happy family who live according to the culture, customs, and civilization of their environment, who suddenly find themselves plucked by raiders who carry them away and sell them to a strange land. Imagine such a family taken on a ship but separated because of their gender; put side by side with strangers they have never met and who do not speak their language, so tight that in the course of the journey, the person beside them probably dies and nobody comes for the corpse. When they get to the end of the journey, they have to separate the dead who have been frozen stiff as well as stuck to the living.

Imagine such a person now living in a manacled state in a hole where he is held down by others. But one day he is brought out and made to be bathed by someone else. Polished and creamed, unknown to him, it is his turn to be sold in a public market scantily covered with only a piece of rag to cover his genitals. They haggle over how much he is worth. People come and press his body, check his health, and finally the price is paid. He is taken on the back of a wagon through many difficult roads and given a piece of bread and cheese to eat. He finally feels happy at least to be given such decent food—at least he thinks it is.

He reaches a plantation where he is introduced to a dark, dank, dull room that will be his. It is built out of wood, and he meets other slaves who work for this master. They now could babble a few words which the master understands. He does not; he probably is from another tribe. He is woken early in the morning to join others at the cotton fields and every time he stands to gain a little rest, he fells a whiplash on his back by the slave driver. His first day at the farm is not pleasant at all. When he returns home in the darkest of night, he longs for the shores of Africa, for the freedom he once knew. He weeps, for tomorrow is another day to work.

He is probably 30 years old, but he is called "boy." He is shoved around. The boss has probably noticed that he may be sexually virile; he is given a woman who may not be from his tribe, and as soon as he has had enough children by her, he may be moved to another plantation where they have another woman ready for him to raise some more "home-grown" slaves. So his life takes the turn of being a sexual stud. He is deprived of the dignity of raising a family.

How does slavery affect such a person?

1. Slavery brings a devaluation of the person.

   Once you have been devalued, you hate your person and want to look like someone else. Dark skin has often been looked down upon as unattractive, and black hair has been called kinky. This is the worst thing one can do—self-rejection.

2. Physical and mental handicap.

   Blacks found themselves denied the opportunity as slaves to be educated and were deliberately kept from learning how to read or write. That in itself began to shape Black attitudes toward information.

3. Economic handicap.

   Slavery conformed people of color because of the way it was used. Legislations were firmly promulgated to ensure that Blacks were economically deprived.

   In 1686 the Carolina Trade Law barred Blacks from all trades.

   In 1619 the Maryland Segregation Policy recommended that Blacks be socially excluded.

   In 1705 the Virginia Public Office Law prohibited Blacks from holding or assuming any public office.

   More of these legal restrictions are found later in this chapter.

   Slaves were not permitted to run their own trade, they were not given land on which they could farm; and if they were given any land, it was limited. If they were made promises of economic freedom, they were never fulfilled, and the same system turned around and blamed them and called them lazy.

4. Devaluation of race.

   Black became a "B" word. The value they placed on each other became less and less. Slave owners knew they needed to argue that slaves were lesser than themselves in order to justify keeping of such stock.

   Joseph L. Graves said, "was not the African a beast of burden, delivered by providence to labor for the benefit of the noble and Christian European?"[42] In the search for further justification for the enslaving and maltreatment of Blacks, southern Europeans searched for the answer in religion: with the likes of Giordano Bruno and early Italian scientist Lucilio Vanini arguing along with the likes of French cleric Isaac de la Peyrere, concluding that Blacks and people who are Asiatics (another expression of Hamites) are all descendants from a pre-Adamic race.

Eminent members of the ruling class in the 18th century, Americans like Thomas Jefferson for example, held the view that Blacks were childlike and lazy, therefore needing supervision, or else they would starve to death. They held the view that the men were emotionless and unloving, while the women were like monkeys in the sun, wanton and needing sex to calm down, so sex with a Black woman, to them, was no rape.[43]

5. Self-hatred.

Physical slavery was promulgated as having ended but Black identity is still crushed, particularly those who generations later have a carryover from their forebears. Racist stereotypes still exist, particularly the ones that were started by the slave owners to make their slaves feel and think less of themselves. In the words of Cornel West, African Americans are consumed with self-contempt, self-hatred, self-affliction, and self-flagellation.[44]

Some others argue that this self-hatred, having its root in slavery, is a major reason for chronic homelessness, single parenthood, and the degree of violence within the Black-American community.

6. Rape.

In another chapter bastardization is discussed as a form of conformation that has affected the Black community and has its root in slavery. However, it all boils down to the view of the slave owners as it relates to the slaves. How slave owners view their property called the slave person is seen in William Goodell's book, *The American Slave Code*.[45]

The slave woman was expected to accept the sexual exploitation of the slave masters, his relatives, and his friends without resistance. Because, as Goodell documents it, "Forced concubinage of slave women with their masters and overseers often coerced by the lash, contributed an underclass of facts equally undesirable. Rape committed on a female slave is an offense not recognized by law and the reason it is not recognized by law is really because technically even if the slave woman were married, a slave in marriage is still a commodity, a property."[46]

Goodell continues these arguments, "The obligations of marriage are evidently inconsistent with the conditions of slavery, and cannot be performed by a slave. If a husband promises to protect his wife and provide for her, the wife promises to be the only helpmeet of her husband. They mutually promise to live with and cherish each other until parted by death. What can such promises by slaves mean? The legal relation of master and slaves renders them void. It forbids the slave to protect even himself. It clothes his master with authority to bid to inflict deadly bows on the woman he has sworn to protect. It prohibits his possession of any property wherewith to sustain her. It gives the master unlimited control and full possession of her own person and forbids her on pains of death to resist him if he drags her to his bed. It severs the plighted pair at the will of their master's occasionally and forever."[47]

It is this atmosphere that gave birth to a sense of irresponsibility in the case of the man who is therefore unable to truly keep the vow of marriage. This in itself perpetuated the big problem of 75 percent single parenthood in Black American society and 50 percent single parenthood with British Blacks.

7. Cruelty.

Earlier we quoted Mark Twain in his book, *Huckleberry Finn*. A Black person had been shot and was treated like he was nothing. Since slaves were considered legally as property, there were lots of contradictions. When slaves committed acts that were illegal, their humanity came to play and they were held accountable. When slaves were treated badly, in the words of Nathan Huggins, "A pig in the corn was not a thief, a slave in the smokehouse was. A horse that trampled the life from a cruel master was no murderer, a slave who struck out against brutality was."[48]

8. Inferiority.

Slave drivers, masters, owners had to justify to abolitionists and the rest of the West their reasons for holding captive men and women.

The argument put forward was often that their act, as a matter of fact, helped these African natives whose lifestyle in their original countries was very subsistent and lacking in any form of dignity, and that their exportation to the new world gave them a lifestyle they could never have had. It was further argued also that they were perpetually in intertribal war and therefore were inferior to all societies.

In a debate between Abraham Lincoln and Steven Douglas, the latter puts his argument this way, "The civilized world has always held that when a race of men have shown themselves to be so degraded by ignorance, superstition, cruelty and barbarism as to be utterly incapable of governing themselves, they must, in the nature of things, be governed by others, by such laws as are deemed to be applicable to their conditions."[49]

BOUNDARY SAFEGUARDS AND RESTRICTIONS IN SOUTHERN STATES [50]		
Year	State's Legal and Social Restrictions	Purpose of Restriction
1619	Maryland Segregation Policy	Recommended that Blacks be socially excluded
1642	Virginia Fugitive Law	Authorized branding of an 'R' in the face of runaway slaves
1686	Carolina Trade Law	Barred Blacks from all trades
1691	Virginia Marriage Law	Prescribed banishment for any White woman marrying a Black

1705	Virginia Public Office Law	Prohibited Blacks from holding or assuming any public office
1710	Virginia enacted Meritorious Manumission	Rewarded slaves with freedom for informing on other slaves
1712	South Carolina Fugitive Slave Act	Criminalized runaway slaves to protect owner's investments
1715	North Carolina Anti-interracial Marriage Law	Forbade and criminalized Black-White marriages
1717	South Carolina Anti-interracial Marriage Law	Forbade and criminalized Black-White marriages
1723	Virginia Anti-Assembly Law	Impeded Blacks from meeting or having a sense of community
1723	Virginia Weapons Law	Forbade Blacks from keeping weapons
1740	South Carolina Consolidated Slave Act	Forbade slaves from raising or owning farm animals
1775	Virginia Runaway Law	Allowed sale or execution of slaves attempting to flee
1775	North Caroline Manumission Law	Forbade freeing slaves except for meritorious service
1790	First Naturalization Law	Congress declares United States a white nation
1792	Federal Militia Law	Restricted enrollment in peace time militia to Whites only

1793	Fugitive Slave Law	Discourages slaves from running away; protected planters' invested capital
1793	Virginia Migration Law	Forbade free Blacks from entering the State
1806	Louisiana Migration Law	Forbade immigration for free Black males over 15 years old
1809	Congressional Mail Law	Excluded Blacks from carrying U.S. mail
1811	Kentucky Conspiracy Law	Made conspiracy among slaves a capital offense
1813	Virginia Poll Tax	Exacted a $1.50 tax on Blacks who were forbidden to vote
1814	Louisiana Migration Law	Prohibited free Blacks from entering the State
1815	Virginia Poll Tax	Required free Blacks to pay a $2.50 tax so Whites could vote
1816	Louisiana Jury Law	Provided that no Black slave could testify against a White person
1819	Missouri Literacy Law	Forbade assembling or teaching Black slaves to read or write
1820	South Carolina Migration Law	Prohibited free Blacks from entering the State
1826	North Carolina Migration Law	Forbade entry of free Blacks; violators penalized $500

1827	Florida Voting Law	Restricted voting to Whites
1829	Georgia Literacy Law	Provided fines and imprisonment for teaching a Black person to read
1830	Louisiana Expulsion Law	Required all free Blacks to leave State within 60 days
1830	Mississippi Employment Law	Forbade Blacks employment in printing and entertainment
1830	Kentucky Property Tax Law	Taxed Blacks; forbade their voting or attending school
1831	North Carolina License Law	Required all Black traders and peddlers to be licensed
1831	South Carolina enacted Licensing Prohibition	Free Blacks were denied any kind of a business license
1831	Mississippi Preaching Law	Forbade free Blacks to preach except with permission
1832	Alabama and Virginia Literacy Laws	Fined and flogged whites for teaching Blacks to read or write
1833	Georgia Employment Law	Prohibited Blacks from working in reading or writing jobs
1833	Georgia Literacy Law	Provided fines and whipping for teaching Blacks
1833	Kentucky Licensing Prohibition	No free person of color could obtain a business license

1835	Missouri Registration Law	Required the registration and bonding of all free Blacks
1835	Georgia Employment Law	Prohibited employing Blacks in drug stores
1837	South Carolina Curfew Law	Required Blacks to be off streets by a certain hour
1838	Virginia School Law	Forbade Blacks who had gone North to school to return
1838	North Carolina Marriage Law	Declared void all interracial marriages to 3rd generation
1841	South Carolina Observing Law	Forbade Blacks and Whites from looking out the same windows
1842	Maryland Information Law	Felonied Blacks demanding or receiving abolition newspapers
1844	Maryland Color Tax	Placed a tax on all employed Black artisans
1845	Georgia Contracting Law	Prohibited contracts with Black mechanics
1846	Kentucky Incitement Law	Provided imprisonment for inciting slaves to rebel
1847	Missouri Literacy Law	Prohibited teaching Blacks to read or write
1848	Virginia Incitement Law	Provided death penalty for advising slaves to rebel

1850	Fugitive Slave Law Enacted	Stronger enforcement provisions
1852	Georgia Tax Law	Imposed annual $5 per capita tax on free Blacks
1853	Virginia Poll Tax Law	Levied tax on all free Black males 21 to 55 years old
1856	Virginia Drug Law	Forbade selling poisonous drugs to Blacks
1857	Dred Scott Decision	Supreme Court dehumanized and disenfranchised Blacks
1858	Maryland Recreation Law	Forbade free Blacks and slaves from boating on the Potomac
1868	Southern Black Codes	Deprived Blacks of right to vote and hold public office
1883	Civil Rights Law of 1875 Weakened	Supreme Court challenged the constitutionality of the Law
1898	The Grandfather Clause	Deprived Blacks of the right to vote in Louisiana

BOUNDARY SAFEGUARDS AND RESTRICTIONS IN NORTHERN STATES

Year	States' Legal and Social Restrictions	Purpose of Restriction
1660	Connecticut Military Law	Barred Blacks from military service

1664	Maryland Marriage Law	Enactment of the first anti-interracial marriage statutes
1667	British Plantation Act	Established codes of conduct for slaves and slave holders
1705	Massachusetts Anti-Miscegenation Law	Criminalized interracial marriages
1705	New York Runaway Law	Prescribed execution for recaptured runaway slaves
1721	Delaware Marriage Law	Forbade marriage between White women and Black men
1722	Pennsylvania Morality Statement	Condemned Blacks for sexual acts with Whites
1722	Pennsylvania Anti-Miscegenation Law	Criminalized interracial marriages
1784	Connecticut Military Law	Forbade Blacks from serving in the militia
1800	Maryland Agricultural Laws	Prohibited Blacks from raising and selling agricultural products
1804	Ohio Anti-Mobility Law	Enacted "Black Laws" that restricted Blacks' movement
1804	Ohio Registration Law	Required Blacks to register and annually post a bond
1805	Maryland Licensure Law	Forbade Blacks from selling tobacco or corn without license

1807	Maryland Residence Law	Limited residence of entering free Blacks to two weeks
1810	Maryland Voting Law	Restricted voting rights to Whites only
1811	Delaware Migration Law	Forbade migration of Blacks; levied $10 per week fine
1818	Connecticut Voting Law	Disenfranchised Black voters
1821	District of Columbia Registration Law	Required Blacks to register annually and post bonds
1827	Maryland Occupation Acts (Petition to Legislature)	Prohibited Blacks from driving or owning hacks, carts, or drays
1829	Illinois Marriage Law	Forbade Black and White marriages
1831	Indiana Mobility Law	Required Blacks to register in order to work and post bond
1836	District of Columbia Business License Law	Prohibited licensing Blacks for profit-making activities
1844	Maryland Occupation Acts	Excluded Blacks from the carpentry trade

BRAINWASHING

Slave masters recognized that it was necessary to brainwash and control the mind of the slaves, getting them to the place where they believed that they deserved what they were experiencing.

Every act or step taken was therefore carried out with the mind to make the slave feel less than human. The house of the master was called the "big house." The master had to be called "master." Slaves, no matter their age, could not talk back to White children. Slaves were required to obey every White man, no matter who they were or how mean they were. A slave girl was available to be sexually exploited by the master, his friends, and relations.

These techniques in other subtle ways were elements of colonial rule later in most of Africa; and although all of Africa has now gained independence, Africans are so conformed by the brainwashing process which took place, nothing is thought to be superior or good enough, unless it is imported or brought from the West.

DESTABILIZATION

Prior to his capture from his African roots, cultural anthropologists have observed that most African cultures had developed their own forms of government, high discipline, matters of morality, a positive self-concept, the importance of dignity and integrity. This is revealed in several African cultural mores, proverbs, and sayings. Slavery decapitated people from their family roots, planting them in strange lands where having no spiritual, cultural, and social roots, made them culturally incompetent. And having traveled through a valley of consistent devaluation, they became confused as to their own identity and value. The treatment they received left them with deep, physical scars in the beatings, emotional scars by the bastardization, and psychological scars by the deliberate act of putting them down.

Slavery disrupted the expectations in various cultures. Childhood was suspended. Children were suddenly exposed to traumas they did not know before; and instead of their simple and friendly culture, in place of the civilization they knew, they found themselves in a hostile culture. The reverberations of the trauma has meant that a people have had to develop a culture within a culture; however, this time, a culture was being built out of fragments of the slave masters' leftovers.

Slavery has, to a great extent, conformed a lot of Blacks who ended in the West and who were carried to far places.

THE DESTRUCTION OF THE "AFRICAN VILLAGE" NETWORK

"It takes a village to raise a child."

My experience of being raised in Africa, albeit in cities, is such that when you offended, it was not only your parent who drew lines of discipline in your life, other parents in the neighborhood felt it was their duty to contribute to your upbringing. This was in cities of Africa; and if it was that strong in the cities, how much more in rural settings? The plundering of the African continent and the carriage of the people into slavery, particularly slaves who ended up in the new world, was the destruction of the socializing elements necessary for preparing people for their future.

Slavery, although it was abolished, created a situation where the influence of the parents and the other adults had been weakened. The result was a generation who lacked discipline and when discipline was applied, it was regarded as abuse. The right of passage introduced and encouraged in the African setting where a young man or woman is prepared for adulthood by certain rites carried out was denied them. If you were ever introduced to any rite of passage, it was by the "boyz in the hood," whose idea runs counter to any civil society.

Within this African village concept, a young man was expected to conduct himself properly, and if he were to be in courtship with a girl, he was to treat her right. The Yorubas of Southern Nigeria, from where a good chunk of slaves were exported, would not allow a young man to visit his fiancée alone in the old days. There had to be a middleman, an arbitrator who was present at all meetings of these two people in courtship, sitting albeit in a place slightly distant to allow them to have privacy without undue intimacy.

The Yorubas celebrated the virginity of a girl to the day of her wedding. The husband was required to compensate her parents after the first night of sexual relationship if the girl were a virgin. It was the greatest joy of the parent as their daughter had brought them honor.

Slavery treated the men as sexual studs and the girls as tools in the hand of the masters when more slaves needed to be raised. An ex-slave, Linda Brent, puts it this way, "These God-breathing machines are no more, in the sight of their masters than the cotton they plant or the horses they tend."[51]

ENDNOTES

1. Naim Akbar, *Breaking The Chains of Psychological Slavery* (Jersey City, NJ: Mind Productions, 1996).

2. Mark Twain, *The Adventures of Huckleberry Finn* (New York: Bantam Books, 1981).

3. Salmon Rushdie, *Imaginary Homelands* (New York: Penguin Books, 1991), 145.

4. Suzanne Miers and Igor Kopytoff, *Slavery in Africa: Historical and Anthropological Perspectives* (Madison: University of Wisconsin Press, 1977).

5. Ibid.

6. L.H. Gann and Peter Duignan, *Africa, South of the Sahara* (Stanford, CA: Hoover Institution Press, 1981), 4.

7. J.F. Schon, *Magana Hausa: Native Literature of Proverbs, Tales, Fables and Historical Fragments in the Hausa language* (London, 1885), 52.

8. Hourst, *Mission hydrographique du Niger*, cited in Fisher and Fisher, op. cit., (1896).

9. Gustav Nachtigal, *Sahara and Sudan* (Amherst, NY: Humanity Books, 1987), 652-53.

10. Thomas Sowell, *Race and Culture* (New York: Basic Books, 1994), 188.

11. Murray Gordon, *Slavery in the Arab World* (New York: New Amsterdam Books, 1989).

12. A.B. Wylde, *'83 to '87 in the Soudan, Vol. 2* (London: Remington & Co., 1888), 257.

13. Nachtigal, *Sahara and Sudan.*

14. Lewis, *Race and Slavery in the Middle East* (New York: Oxford University Press, 1990), 11-12, 48, 75-76.

15. H.R. Palmer, *The Bornu, Sahara and Sudan* (London, 1936), 218.

16. Ronald Segal, *Islam's Black Slaves* (New York: Farrar, Straus, and Giroux, 2002).

17. Lewis, *Race and Slavery in the Middle East*.

18. *The Koran*, translated by Arberry, op. cit., 356.

19. John Laffin, *The Arabs as Master Slavers* (Englewood, NJ: SBS Publishing, 1982), 69-70.

20. I.P. Petrushevskii, *Islam in Iran*, tran. Hubert Evans (London: Athlone Press, 1985), 158.

21. *Works of Galen,* presented as Masudi's *Muraj al-Dharab wa Ma'adin al'Jawahar*, ed. and trans. Charles Pellat (Paris: 1962), 69.

22. Segal, *Islam's Black Slaves*.

23. Ibn Khaldun, *The Muqaddimah*, trans F. Rosenthal, Vol. 1 (New York: Pantheon Books, 1958), 301.

24. Lewis, *Race and Slavery in the Middle East*.

25. Ibid.

26. J.O. Hunwick, "Black Africans in the Islamic World: An Understudied Dimension of the Black Diaspora," *Tarikh* 5, No. 4, (1978), 27.

27. Burckhard, *Travels in Nubia*, 278-279.

28. H.J. Fisher, *The Cambridge History of Africa,* ed. Oliver, and his other work, *Slavery in the History of Muslim Black Africa* (New York: Doubleday, 1971).

29. Raymond Mauvy, *The African Slave Trade from the Fifteenth to the Nineteenth Century* (Paris: Unesco, 1979), 169-170, 173.

30. Segal, *Islam's Black Slaves*.

31. Audrey Smedley, *Race in North America* (Boulder, CO: West View Press, 1993), 95.

32. Barnet Litvinoff, *The Decline in Medievalism and the Rise of the Modern Age* (New York: Avon Books, 1991), 28.

33. Basil Davidson, *The African Slave Trade* (New York: Back Bay Books, 1988).

34. Moses Grandy, *Life of a Slave* (Boston: O. Johnson, 1844).

35. William Wells Brown, "The American Slave Trade" *The Liberty Bell* (Boston: National Anti-slavery Bazaar, 1848).

36. Henry Bibb, *Henry Bibb, an American Slave* (London: 1851).

37. Ibid.

38. Grandy, *Life of a Slave*.

39. Bethany Veney, *A Slave Woman*, 1889.

40. See autobiographies by Frederick Douglass: *A Narrative of the Life of Frederick Douglass, an American Slave* (1845); *Autographs for Freedom*. ed. Julia Griffiths (Boston: Jewett and Company, 1853); *My Bondage and My Freedom* (1855); *Life and Times of Frederick Douglass* (1881, revised 1892).

41. Speech by Willie Lynch, 1712, http://www.freemaninstitute. com/lynch.htm.

42. Joseph L. Graves Jr., *The Emperor's New Clothes: Biological Theories of Race at the Millennium* (New Brunswick, NJ: Rutgers University Press, 2001), 25-26.

43. Thomas Jefferson, *Notes on The State of Virginia* (1781-82). *Writings*, 264.

44. Cornel West, "Philosophy and the Urban Class," Bill Lawson, *The Underclass Question* (Philadelphia: Temple University Press, 1992), 195.

45. William Goodell, *The American Slave Code* (New York: American Foreign Anti-slavery Society, 1835), 105.

46. Ibid.

47. Ibid.

48. Nathan Huggins, *Black Odyssey* (New York: Vintage, 1990), 116.

49. Cited by Harry Jaffa, *Crisis of the House Divided* (Chicago: University of Chicago Press, 1959), 32.

50. Claud Anderson, *Black Labor, White Wealth: The Search for Power and Economic Justice* (Maryland: PowerNomics Corporation of America, 1994).

51. Harriet Jacobs, *Incidents in the Life of a Slave Girl* (New York: Dover Publications, 2001).

CHAPTER 10

Distorted Family Values

Family, according to the *Shorter Oxford English Dictionary*, is:

a. The body of persons who live in one house or under one head, including parents, children, servants, etc.

b. The group consisting of parents and their children whether living together or not.

c. In a wider sense, all those who are nearly connected by blood or affinity.

Pan-Africanist Oba Tshaka defines a family as the central economic unit, the base for local and national economic development and the foundation of our community, organizations, churches, and social organizations.[1]

Within the Black community, the phrase "extended family" also comes into play. This notion is taken from the African setting where a family embraces more than the nuclear make-up of a father, mother, and children. This concept of extended family continued even into slavery. In spite of the harrowing experiences of the passage of such people into an unknown world, the extended family concept gives the reason why June Jordan advocates for a revival of African kingship and an extended family system as a possible solution for the breakdown of marriage within the African-American community.[2]

The Bible's view of family possibly takes the nuclear and extended family onboard. When Abraham was instructed to leave Ur of the Chaldeans, it was said that he was to leave his extended family. And in the case of Israel who went to live in Egypt in the land of Goshen, his family was the polygamous or extended one.

Originally, God saw that it was not good for Adam to be alone and He made him a helpmeet, and blessed him with children—immediately constituting a family. That pattern was maintained in Scripture. The extended family may be a method that creates more ranks of protection for the marriage and children.

However, once the man of color had disobeyed God—one of the key areas which suffered the consequence of idolatry, one of the key pathologies of the Black community has been "distorted family values." From the polygamous homes in Africa to the one-parent situations in almost every Black community, and from the incestuous relationships described by Barrington Brennen as being prevalent in the Bahamas and the Caribbean,[3] it is very clear and obvious that this pathology is destroying the Black person's future and causing incredible problems.

It is so widespread that certain Black sociologists are beginning to think that we should accommodate some of the distorted values. Asnon Belahooks, for example, argues that female-headed households are part of a tradition of "meaningful and productive lifestyles" that do not conform to White societal norms.[4]

This immediately reduces the nuclear family to a White idea and not a Bible idea.

So are the distortions a product of the enslavement and victimization of the person of color?

Slave women became prey to the slave master, sex toys for them to use, breaking down the dignity and culture of Black people, and the sacred, romantic, and loving approach they gave to sexual relationships.

Largely within the Black community in Africa, even in modern times, the degree of promiscuity which came out of slavery, and has since been propounded, was never present. Other family patterns were to follow which stem from the degradation of slavery, i.e., the prevalence of single parenthood.

And although today it is a big challenge, Alice Walker thinks differently. She argues that single motherhood is a beautiful thing to experience as it is time for Blacks to jettison the European tradition of a nuclear family.[5]

What are some of these distortions?

1. Polygamy

   The first, which comes to mind, is polygamy. "Please allow the young men to get married too!" were the words of President Yahya Jammeh, the President of Gambia, at a speech celebrating the ninth anniversary of his regime. The seriousness in his voice conveyed a major reaction even though his audience burst into laughter. He made his comment because the country of Gambia is faced with a high level of polygamy.[6]

   What is polygamy?

   The dictionary defines it as "marriage with several or more than one at once, plurality of spouses, the practice or custom according to which one man has several wives."

   This tradition was not considered to be a distortion within the Black African community, rather it was viewed as a custom for giving a man adequate support for his business and family, giving him status within the community and protection for the children. Polygamy was to become one major reason for the resistance to Christianity and its advocacy for the nuclear family.

   Emmanuel Twesigye, Professor and Director of Black World Studies, at Ohio Wesleyan University, gives insight about why Africans considered polygamy to be of high value:

   ❖ A man's wealth was measured by the number of wives he had.

   ❖ It was prestigious to have many wives.

   ❖ The more wives one had, the more political alliances one could form, and therefore, become a very powerful power broker.

- Polygamy produced wealth, at least for the man, as well as the whole group which the patriarch supported.

- Women and children were safer in larger households where they were better protected from aggressors.

- Men also preferred polygamy because it gave them sexual gratification.

- Polygamy also provided a form of birth control.

- Polygamy insured that most marriageable girls were married off.

- In most of traditional Africa, there was a custom of levirate or widow inheritance.

- In modern times when some workers live in the city, they may prefer to have two wives and two families, one in the city and the other in the rural areas on the ancestral land.[7]

Downsides of Polygamy

What the professor did not do was look at the downsides of polygamy and the distortion of the values of marriage.

Polygamy immediately measures the wealth of the man and associates his wives and children on the same parameter with his cattle. Although some of the women who married kings may think that it gave them a name and status in society; however, it reduced the power of such status since they had to share it with many others.

In the case where women were passed on to various chiefs and kings to form alliances, the women and the children they bore became goods and services for furthering the man's egotistic and chauvinist views.

Wives were treated as mere laborers to increase the productivity of the farm and, in most cases, never enjoyed the benefits.

The professor argues that the women and children were safer in a larger setting but omitted the apparent chances of jealousy, bitterness, and subsequent consultations with witch doctors and witchcraft to attempt to destroy or limit the children of other women.

Polygamy seems to have provided a lot of sexual gratification for the man and possibly served as a form of birth control. However, no birth was controlled because the consequence of so many children and so many women depending on the same land or business the man had. In effect there was an increase in demand from the number of children but no increase in supply by the economic base of the man.

The sexual frustration of some such women, having to wait their turn, meant that they often turned to extra-marital affairs which placed them, and subsequently the entire polygamous family, at risk of HIV/AIDS. This may account for the extremely high number of HIV/AIDS cases in certain parts of Africa.

The professor also did not highlight the fact that once sexually transmitted diseases invade the family and destroy the mothers and father, the number of orphans in society increases dramatically.

One of the forms of polygamy dealt with by the professor— rural and city families—creates even more distortions. One set of children will suffer from the absence of the father and in effect will have a diminishing return on society.

2. Incest

In his article titled, "Dad, You Are Hurting Me Again," Barrington Brennen, writing on incest says, "in the Bahamas and the Caribbean, incest is very common and the majority of the population denies that it is a problem or that it really exists at all."[8]

Incest is the crime of sexual intercourse or co-habitation of persons too closely related to be legally married. It is one of the most painful, dark secrets which carries along with it shame, guilt, or threat from the perpetrator. Brennen argues that within the society of his reference, incestuous relationships have reached a proportion that makes them as frequent and as popular as heterosexual promiscuous relationships.

What has made it prevalent within the Black culture and family is the habit of silence; in other words, nobody asks, no one discusses, and it is carried out surreptitiously. The consequence, according to Brennen, is obvious in the medical problems and dilemmas which the social agencies and the medical agencies are handling.

3. Baby-Fatherism

Along with polygamy and incest come other distorted family values such as baby-fatherism.

Baby-fatherism is the practice of men having children by women within the Black community, without the intention of marrying them. In some cases the men see it as a possible opportunity for making money from the women because in the Western hemisphere, the social security system guarantees welfare money to the mother of such a child. Her payday becomes a day of visitation for some young men who go and take the money she has just collected.

4. Baby-Motherism

Where there are baby-fathers, there will be baby-mothers. These are girls as young as 13 within the African and Black community who deliberately look to be pregnant, to have children, in spite of their age, without intent or desire to marry.

For the highly acclaimed author, Toni Morrison, the problem is not baby-motherism but society's refusal to recognize women as heads of households. In Morrison's opinion, we should abandon societal restraints and return to the elemental urge of nature. If it feels good, do it, so she thinks.

She argues, "The little nuclear family is a paradigm that just doesn't work. Why we are hanging on to it, I do not know. I do not think a female running a house is a problem. It is perceived as one because of the notion that a head is a man. The child is not going to hurt the woman. Who cares about the schedule? What is this business that you have to finish school at eighteen? The body is ready to have babies. Nature wants it done then. I want to take them all in my arms and say 'your baby is beautiful and so are you…and when you want to be a brain surgeon, call me—I will take care of your baby.'"[9]

5. Live-in Lover

The "live-in lover" is a very common scenario within the Black community and a distortion of family values; where two people, because it feels good, live together, having a lifestyle that married people have, without the covenant and commitment therein.

In most cases, the woman wants the relationship consolidated while the man does not, or rather in the words of one such man when asked why he would not wed the lady, he said, "Why buy the cow if the milk is free?"

6. Common Law Wife

This scenario is similar to the live-in lover except for the fact that the two people who live together share life, buy things together, and act as if they are a couple. Again, the legal implication is that upon the death of one of the spouses, neither have rights over what the other person owns.

Because living together is popular does not mean it is approved by God.

You cannot say because there is a multiplication of wrong it makes it right. No, the standard of God stands sure.

To get it right, you have to do it right.

Living together pulls you away from the Lord.

Living together clouds your opinion of the partner.

Co-habiting is a major reason for a lot of heartbreak.

Co-habiting may result in unwanted pregnancy.

It is likely to hurt the children caught up in this mess.

It is likely to eventually destroy the relationship.

Being with this person may be a hindrance to meeting the right person.

It will hinder your marital hopes and dreams.

Everyone you co-habit with leaves a bit of themselves with you.

You cannot feel totally secure in the relationship.

Male and female reasons for co-habitation are often different.

If you eventually marry each other, the unhealthy dynamic in that relationship will stay.

The price of heartbreak is more than the challenge of celibacy.

When children are involved, they cannot be guaranteed a stable home.

Children from previous relationships can be badly hurt.

In most cases, people living together cannot claim married couple's tax allowance.

Married people have obligations to maintain the other person despite separation; no law binds co-habitants.

Gifts between husband and wife may be free from capital tax gains, but not with co-habitants.

Your co-habitant cannot insure your life; married people can.

If a married person dies intestate, most of his or her estate goes to a spouse, but a co-habitant is not legally entitled to anything.

Widows may claim Widowed Mother's allowance. Bereaved co-habitants cannot claim extra state benefits.

Statistics show that the divorce rate is high among co-habitants.[10]

7. One-night Stands and Casual Sex

Prevalent within the Black community nowadays is one-night stands and casual sex. People who hardly know each other, who met within a short time, have dragged themselves to the nearest available couch, car, or corner. The lyrics of the musicians encourage it, the boundaries that no longer exist within certain families inspire it, and the fact that some such people were raised in the atmosphere where mother brought an uncle home every night makes it look normal.

Other distortions for which we may not give a full comment at this time include poor parenting skills—children raising children. Inadequate parenting skills mean a deficient upbringing. In most cases, the very children who birthed such children were themselves victims of inadequate parenting.

8. Children Raised by Others

    In the African community, the desire to live in the West may mean sending their children to live with a relation abroad. Such children raised in totally strange atmospheres with their parents not being around become victims of incest, molestation, and social alienation, unable to connect to their parent or their culture. They are lost in limbo.

9. Multiple Fathers

    In the one-parent atmosphere, where there are no sexual boundaries, ethics, or abstinence by the mother, the children experience a "multiple uncle syndrome." The word "uncle" is loosely used within the Black community; it stems from a universal Black culture where younger people tend not to call older people by name but respectfully use the word "uncle."

    However, the word is abused when it is introduced in the home and used in a blanket way whenever men visit and sometimes stay overnight. Children in this home with a distorted value are introduced to a different uncle almost every other night.

MANIFESTATION OF DISTORTED VALUES

There is a phenomenon within the Black community—inevitable when it comes to family values. Suddenly, there is a higher rate of criminal activity; and a predominance, particularly in the West, of single-parent families—75 percent in the United States and 50 percent in the United Kingdom. There is hostility to academic achievement, the treatment of illegitimacy as normal, family abandonment by men, high unemployment rate, the predominant atmosphere of adultery, and a scarcity of major enterprises, industries, or businesses within the Black community anywhere in the world. Most of the thriving businesses in Africa are foreign investments.

Along with the aforementioned is the absence of role models in different spheres of society other than music and sports, the increase in youth rebelliousness, the breakdown of law and order within the Black community, the absence of discipline, and an attitude of liberalism toward family values.

In addition to this, there is a culture of over-celebration. We have almost become the people who entertain themselves to death. We have replaced meaning with music. Even our children laugh at the ones who are keen about education, the sciences, technology, etc.

Over-celebration is probably one of the greatest weaknesses of the Black Africans. Thousands of pounds of sterling will be spent in the celebration of the birth, wedding, or burial of a relative, compared to what would be invested in their life.

Within the African community also, the distortion is magnified by an open-house mentality whereby cousins, nephews, nieces, and even non-relatives are invited to come and live in the home for years. This truly may be the extended family syndrome which has its positive side, but its impact on the nuclear family has not been properly measured.

Certainly the children are unable to bond with their parent as much as they would want to. The privacy required in raising children is eroded. The opportunity for children to observe their parents who should be their first role model for homemaking is reduced. The behavior pattern, weaknesses, and challenges of the home from which the relatives come immediately impact on the host person's home.

Three hundred years of slavery, along with the social and mental slavery which followed the declaration of the end of slavery in the United States in 1865, still leaves the Black family vulnerable. The family has been left deeply hurt and caught in the quagmire of distorted family values. We must bear in mind the fact that the slave master effectively separated father and mother, creating an atmosphere where the mother led the home and the man was reduced to a mere work tool in the farm. He was also used as a sexual predator or a sexual stud for raising more slaves.

Once such pathology had been created, it has been very difficult to reverse. African-American scholars are discussing it and leaders are talking about it.

Haki Madhubuti, in the book *Black Men: Obsolete, Single, Dangerous*, describes the destructive pattern of behavior of the African-American who, "buys few books, gravitates towards incompetence and medioc-rity...has a welfare conscious/get-it-for-nothing attitude...loves sexual conquests...does not want children or responsibility of home life...actively fights against discipline...is involved in Black on Black crime...rejects criticism and is drug dependent."[11]

Reverend Jesse Jackson agrees with this observation, "We talked 30 years ago about genocide. It is now fratricide. At this point, the Klan is not nearly the threat that your next door neighbors are."[12]

Maybe admission is the first sign of ill health and prognosis is an at-tempt to understand and cure the problem.

Marian Wright Edelman of the Children's Defense Fund said, "We have a Black child crisis, worse than any since slavery."[13]

This catastrophe still dates back not only to slavery but also to the consequences of slavery. Beyond that, laws we propagated shackle, limit, and withhold Blacks from excelling.

Illegitimate births account for 60 percent of children born to Black people within the United States of America.[14]

The irony of American society today is its acceptance of illegitimacy and its viewing of it as being morally right. The rate of tolerance of ille-gitimacy within the Black community is far higher here than any other part of the Western societies.

Ninety-five percent of Black teenage mothers in the United States are unmarried compared with 55 percent of their White peers.[15]

The level of illegitimacy and single parent situation is heightened by the fact that many boys within these communities consider sexual grati-fication, sexual conquests, as things to boast about. It is like earning one more star. The more girls they conquer, the faster they rise on the ladder of sexual generals. A boy's inability to rise within that rank makes his friends describe him as a sissy.

The ones who decide to raise their children in a morally upright man-ner are ridiculed. In their book *The Endangered Black Family*, Dr. Nathan and Julia Haye argue that the Black family is now suffering by a sustained campaign led by the government of the United States.[16]

In 1970, the Nixon administration established a commission on population growth; part of their responsibility was to argue that continued growth would aggravate social and economic problems. They were to argue that varying combinations of non-marriage or childlessness were necessary. They said this was a matter of free choice. They offered abortion and birth control as a way to prevent or terminate unwanted pregnancies on grounds that it would help to reduce this fast growth.

Among many other conclusions of the commission was that there was a concentrated and unwanted fertility within the Black community; therefore, they were advocating discouragement of youthful marriage, an increase of access to abortion/contraception, especially for the Black and poor, and the downplay of traditional sex roles as in husband and wife.

In addition, the commission encouraged the transformation and denigration of motherhood, childbearing, and social values; and when men were ready, the commission encouraged the payment for such men to go through trainings and operations, making them transsexual.[17]

The by-product of all this was an external influence on the home: teenage pregnancies, which meant babies running the home, a ghettoized lifestyle, a lack of desire for the pursuit of excellence in education, achievement, work, etc.

Turning it all around—what is the way out? How can the man of color reverse this pathology?

We must first face the realities. The most serious Black pathology may be distorted family values. Once it is wrong in the home, every other area becomes wrong.

In order to reverse this negative situation, there has to be an understanding of the purpose, the role of the family. What did God have in mind when he created the family?

And the Lord God said, It is not good that the man should be alone; I will make him an help meet for him (Genesis 2:18).

We must recognize the standard God has for the family.

Wives, submit yourselves unto your own husbands, as unto the Lord. For the husband is the head of the wife, even as Christ is the head of the church: and He is the saviour of the body. There-fore as the church is subject unto Christ, so let the wives be to their own husbands in every thing. Husbands, love your wives, even as Christ also loved the church, and gave Himself for it; That He might sanctify and cleanse it with the washing of water by the word, That He might present it to Himself a glorious church, not having spot, or wrinkle, or any such thing; but that it should be holy and without blemish. So ought men to love their wives as their own bodies. He that loveth his wife loveth himself (Ephesians 5:22-28).

Children, obey your parents in the Lord: for this is right. Hon-our thy father and mother; which is the first commandment with promise; That it may be well with thee, and thou mayest live long on the earth (Ephesians 6:1-3).

When these Scriptures are violated, and many others relating to the home, distortions become inevitable.

The African person has to recognize that the dignity of the woman and the children in a polygamous atmosphere has been eroded; although it may satisfy the sexual urge and economic desire of the man, it raises the chances of a child being deficient economically, physically, and spiritually if the atmosphere of his upbringing was polygamous. Sibling rivalry is higher, and the chances of a spiritual attack on each other is increased.

What Is the Way Out Again?

Not only must we understand the purpose and the strong tie of the nuclear family which is positive, communication skills must be reintroduced in homes. That way, the home becomes the source of affirmation for the child, where he is taught to treat authority figures with deference, and to walk within the boundaries of morality. It becomes the room where we teach that a good name and a good reputation is absolutely important.

Restoring the value of the home includes an understanding of male and female needs. Within the Black community there is a need to use the wisdom and insight of experts to raise young people. We must teach young people to abide by the law, and that would be first by example for them to see that the law was made in order for society to run properly.

Parents cannot be pilfering at work, breaking the law, driving through red lights, and at the same time challenging their children to respect law and order. You cannot put down law enforcement agents, whatever prejudices you have about them, and imagine that it will not have a consequence on your children.

Talking about law enforcement agents, Black parents must recognize that they cannot hand over the responsibility for raising their children to teachers, the police, or employers. Part of the establishment of family values should include teaching children to recognize the power of generational wealth.

> *A good man leaveth an inheritance to his children's children: and the wealth of the sinner is laid up for the just* (Proverbs 13:22).

The Black family today is known for being notoriously in debt, spending the money of generations to come, very much into downward investment—buying liabilities and not gathering things that increase in value.

Having said that, generational wealth needs to be perpetuated, yet balance must also be there so that the emphasis is not on material wealth. Once the measurement of the children or family is based on what they own, it becomes inevitable that the child will again turn around to want to own in illegitimate ways.

Children must be exposed to the Word of God and to training in the principles of Scripture.

> *And that from a child thou hast known the holy scriptures, which are able to make thee wise unto salvation through faith which is in Christ Jesus* (2 Timothy 3:15).

Restoring family values would include training ourselves and children in what we consider to be positive Black values, i.e., respect for elders, respect for our history, communityhood, familyhood, and nationhood.

Restoring family values includes taking responsibility for our failures as well as our successes, teaching our children to recognize, "If it is going to be, it is up to me."

Let me close this pathology by giving you seven positive values a family can adopt to begin to turn around the distorted images within the Black family. I take them from Joyce Ladner's book, *The Ties That Bind: Timeless Values For African American Families.*[18]

1. Show that you believe a good reputation is critical.

2. Treat authority figures with deference.

3. Teach morality.

4. Put your family first.

5. Show that you believe money is not everything.

6. Show that manners and grooming are important.

7. Minimize negative influences.

ENDNOTES

1. Oba T'Shaka, *The Art of Leadership, Vol. 1* (Richmond, CA: Pan-African Publishers, 1990).

2. June Jordan, *Technical Difficulties: African-American Notes on the State of the Union* (New York: Vintage Books, 1994), 22, 73-74.

3. www.soencouragement.org.articlelist.htm.

4. B. Hooks, *Yearning, Race, Gender and Cultural Politics* (Boston: Southend Press, 1990), 76.

5. Alice Walker, *In Search of Our Mother's Gardens* (San Diego: Harcourt Grace Jovanovich, 1983).

6. "Gambian Freeze on Polygamy" by Demba Jawo, July 22, 2003, http://news.bbc.co.uk/2/hi/africa/3088315.stm.

7. http://www.inform.umd.edu/EdRes/Topic/Diversity/Specific/Race/Specific/African_American_Resources/Issues/Heritage/polygamy.html.

8. Barrington Brennen, "Dad, You Are Hurting Me Again," http:// www.soencouragement.org/incest2.htm.

9. Toni Morrison, *Beloved* (New York: Plume, 1994), and Bonnie Angelo, "The Pain of Being Black," *Time*, May 22, 1989.

10. Matthew Ashimolowo, *Singles 707*, Vol. 3 (London: Mattyson Media, 2001), 123-136.

11. Haki Madhubuti, *Black Men: Obsolete, Single, Dangerous?* (Chicago: Third World Press, 1990), 9.

12. "Jackson urges Blacks to Excel in Government Jobs," *Washington Post*, August 24, 1993.

13. Barbara Vobedja, "Black Adults are Pessimistic about Prospects of Children," *Washington Post*, May 27, 1994, A2.

14. "The American Community—Blacks 2004" issued February 2007 by the U.S. Bureau of the Census, http://www.census.gov/prod/2007pubs/acs-04.pdf.

15. U.S. Bureau of the Census, "Fertility of American Women," *Current Population Report*, Washington DC, June 1993, Table B, P.X.

16. Dr. Nathan and Julia Hare, *The Endangered Black Family: Coping with Unisexualization and Coming Extinction of the Black Race* (San Francisco: Black Think Tank, 1984).

17. T'Shaka, *The Art of Leadership*.

18. Joyce Ladner, *The Ties that Bind: Timeless Values For African American Families* (New York: John Wiley & Sons Inc., 1998), 164-171.

Black Disunity

And I will set the Egyptians against the Egyptians: and they shall fight every one against his brother, and every one against his neighbour; city against city, and kingdom against kingdom (Isaiah 19:2).

Since 1876 when the scramble for Africa was started by King Leopold of Belgium, one of the pathologies which made it easy for the man of color to be plundered, which has also caused a major problem to the economic, social, and political landscape of Africa and subsequently wherever Black people live, is disunity.

Someone has said that while every dollar which enters the Jewish community may touch seven Jewish hands before it exits, it is safe to conclude that if a dollar enters the Black community, it exits within 24 hours.

In Isaiah chapter 19, the mournfully inspired prediction given to the prophet was to predict the things that would befall Black people, particularly because of their commitment to idolatry and disobedience.

One which stands strongly above other pathologies is disunity. "Everyone against his neighbour—everyone against his brother."

This disunity seems to have manifested itself in all facets of life—religious, economic, physical, mental, locational, educational, etc. The list could go on and on.

For example, one of the strongest areas for people of color is worship, yet in the words of Martin Luther King, "11 o'clock on Sunday morning is the most segregated hour in America." It is not only in America, but also all around the world.

If people worship in different churches on grounds of differences, Blacks have perfected their reasons for separation of churches. In the end, they become irrelevant because they are unable to address the ills of society. After all, in their division they become weak; in their division they speak different spiritual language, and therefore are unable to convince the world.

WHY ARE WE SO DIVIDED

Let us go back to the church again, and you will find that many different opinions, tastes, clichés, approaches, or previously hurt feelings account for the reasons why storefront churches or large churches of people of color exist in towns and cities around the world. In that scenario, unity becomes virtually impossible.

First there is the big preacher versus the small one. The big-size ministries versus the small size. It is difficult, but if the truth be told, a lot of Black-led churches are, in a great measure, personality driven. It seems as if congregants attend some churches not because of the content and depth of the Word received, but because of the power of associating with the name that graces the pulpit on Sunday morning.

Along with general problems regarding the ability to accept leadership, comes what the Bible calls the manifestations of the flesh—gossip and backbiting. These things further divide the church.

Disunity among Blacks probably accounts for why slavery was easy to establish and Black African nations became easy pickings for colonial masters. After all, the "divide and rule" system of placing smaller tribes on top of the bigger and educating the smaller tribe so that it produced the technocrats or the politicians, worked in several instances.

This scourge and curse of disunity, as predicted by Isaiah, accounts for the destruction of African empires that once existed—the Shongaï, Ghanaian, Oyo, and the Egyptian empires.

Disunity was used effectively to manage and keep the slaves. This therefore meant that house slaves and field slaves had nothing in common. So they thought.

Disunity fueled the slave trade so that brothers sold brothers and cousins; neighbors rose against neighbors and ensured they were sold to points of no return.

There is disunity among Blacks; it has caused acute dislike among them. Part of this disunity is fueled by the multiple ethnic situations in Africa. This multiplicity led to what was otherwise known as tribalism.

Tribalism worked effectively to keep the people perpetually disunited and at war with one another. Tribal loyalties therefore meant that the good of the nation was not sought first, but rather watching to ensure that one's tribe had the upper hand.

Joyce Andrews argues in her book *The Bible Legacy of the Black Race*, that "The ability of five million whites in South Africa to rule over twenty eight million Blacks could not be, were it not for the spirit of disunity that exists and the inability to come together as one nation."[1]

This certainly was a fulfillment for Isaiah's prophecy that brother would be against brother. Disunity encouraged continuous war among the tribes, and that factor worked in favor of the Europeans who had agreed at the Berlin Conference of 1885 called by King Leopold, to divide off the continent.

Almost every sub-Saharan country has suffered the consequence of disunity. The dominance of other tribes was always at the back of each tribe.

Take for example the rise of Shaka Zulu whose kingdom spanned Zimbabwe and South Africa. His reign was cruel and notorious; he pillaged nations, and his soldiers were held accountable for the least of acts of insubordination. However, he was murdered by his half brothers.

Following in the footsteps of Shaka Zulu were other Zulu kings who went against the Xhosas. The Zulu-Xhosa war spanned 200 years and even influenced the politics of South Africa as Nelson Mandela's African National Congress (ANC) was working to unseat the White-ruled government. It was confronted by the strong Zulu-backed kingdom of Chief Buthelezi.

Within certain cultures, another pathology which has encouraged disunity is the absence or the lack of quality leadership among Blacks—take the pathology on leadership problems which was already highlighted, and imagine who might stand today as a leader for the African American.

When people have no leadership, they become easy to pillage and divide. Black disunity is encouraged by the young/old dichotomy. Gerontocracy seems to be a unifying view of leadership within the Black community.

Check it out in Africa, the Caribbean, and Black Britain or among African Americans, and it seems as if there is a global agreement that only the eldest should lead. This further encourages disunity because young people become agitated, feel unappreciated, unheard, and misunderstood.

Talking about the young and the old, disunity is further strengthened by the lack of appreciation for history, be it African Caribbean or African American. In Africa the young do not particularly appreciate the struggle of the older ones to gain independence from colonial masters. The same applies in the Caribbean where much of the struggle for independence started in the late 1940s, except for Haiti which has had over 200 years of independence.

It is now 39 years since the death of Dr. Martin Luther King, Jr. In the United States, the old often feel that the younger generation does not appreciate what they had to go through, the price they had to pay for the seeming freedom and advancement the young enjoy.

This age gap plays a major role in that the perspective of the old seems to be different from that of the young. In an African American setting, the old want some form of reparation for slavery and pain of the past while the young are agitated because they want whatever the future holds.

The use of race segregation and prejudice is viewed differently today. The older Blacks had to ride at the back of the bus or stand up for a

White person while the young today seem to have overt and subtler prejudices to deal with. In effect, approaches are different resulting in further disunity.

What divides the Black community the most, wherever they live, is their socio-economic status, political beliefs, lifestyles, and the aspirations of the young and old—perhaps and perhaps not.

For a graphic picture of what is meant, take for example a city like Los Angeles where Blacks have lived, possibly since slavery, and some are still at the bottom of the economic ladder. While on the other hand, there has been a new immigration of oriental people; Vietnamese and Koreans coming in with nothing, barely hoping for a foothold. Suddenly they own properties and businesses, and the Black residents are the consumers while the new immigrants are the providers.

Most of the Asian immigrants tend to help one another set up; the banks in their communities are user friendly. But within the Black community, there is a spirit of disunity, a strong discord, a continuous carry over of the prophecies: "The Egyptian against the Egyptian—everyone against his brother."

Disunity is further strengthened by the commitment of different age groups and social economic groups when it comes to fighting for Black rights, Black opportunities, or issues that affect the community.

Social and political activism, such as the anti-war protest marches of the '60s in the United States, or the strong political fights of the '40s and '50s by the activists who defeated the colonialists in Africa, is not met with the same passion, excitement, or vision by the young of today.

Three hundred years of Blacks spread around the world, having different languages in Africa, and accents either in America or the Caribbean has created all kinds of classifications; and the irony of classifications is that once you can be classified you can also be nullified sociologically.

Thomas Sowell puts the argument about multiple languages in Africa in particular, in a better perspective. He writes, "...Africans are less than 10 percent of the human race, their many languages are one-third of all the languages in the world." To buttress its impact on Black unity he said, "the great number of languages and dialects...constitute as well a severe handicap in themselves, inhibiting effective economic or political consolidation of numerous separate peoples." It is his opinion that it is a major barrier to any form of interchange for sub-Saharan Africa.[2]

Take Blacks in the United States for example; when the chief executive officer of the National Association for the Advancement of Colored People (NAACP) speaks, is he representing the Caribbean Blacks, Africans of African descent, and those who are new generation immigrants—80 percent of which were not born in the United States but now live there?

We may not conclude this matter without also referring to the fact that when Blacks raise Black issues in Europe it immediately raises questions. Which Black? The African Black, the Caribbean Black, or Blacks born in Europe? The same applies in the United States of America.

This kind of disunity, therefore, makes the community unable to speak as one and unable to advance as a people.

THE EFFECT OF DISUNITY AMONG BLACKS

What effectively made Black disunity work was when brothers rose up against brothers verbally and physically. Brothers were willing to put down each other before their masters—slave masters, colonial masters—to gain advancement.

Joyce Andrews writes, "It was common for one Black to inform against his other Black brother in the days of slavery in spite of the fact that they were all in the same boat."[3]

In most colonial missions—that is nations colonized by the United Kingdom, Germany, France, Belgium, Denmark, the Netherlands, etc.—once permission was given for political parties to be formed, the disunity among the people became apparent.

African political parties have essentially been geopolitical and tribal. People of a certain tribe tend to be in the majority.

In that time shall the present be brought unto the Lord of hosts of a people scattered and peeled, and from a people terrible from their beginning hitherto; a nation meted out and trodden under

162

foot, whose land the rivers have spoiled, to the place of the name of the Lord of hosts, the mount Zion (Isaiah 18:7).

With their people scattered and their language confused, disunity becomes the order of the day. Africa has over 3,000 languages, with thousands of tribes. The knowledge of the cause of an argument with another tribe was enough to set them against each other. Once their power was broken in Babylon, they were scattered and did not find solace until they hid in the bushes of Africa.

In the first chapter of Ula Taylor's *The Veiled Garvey,* dealing with the formative years of Pan-Africanism in the U.S., the division of the slaves of Jamaica on grounds of color gives insight into the disunity it brought.[4]

Color and class systems were used effectively by the slave masters. The initial division of the whole island was whites versus slaves; later, it was to include freed men and women who were former slaves but who lacked the full rights of a free person.

Slave masters placed the whites of Jamaica at the top of the hierarchy, occupying the role of masters. They had a preference for color. They were obsessed with the pigmentation of the people and considered it as an indicator of one's level of intelligence.

Your phenotype determined the category they placed you in, the job you got and the people you could move with—it determined how you were treated. You were either African or European or somewhere in between.

At some point, they created further divisions and subdivisions, which were in the following categories according to Ula Yvette Taylor:[5]

- ❖ Negro – Child of a Negro and Negro
- ❖ Mulato – Child of a White and Negro
- ❖ Sambo – Child of a Mulato and Negro
- ❖ Quadroon – Child of a White and Mulato
- ❖ Mustee – Child of a White and Quadroon
- ❖ Mustifino – Child of a White and Mustee

❖ Quintroon – Child of a White and Mustifino

❖ Octoroon – Child of a White and Quintroon

All these people were regarded as colored. In the Caribbean, particularly in Jamaica, colored people outnumbered the Africans, that is the dark skinned, and they were more skilled in trade and were underrepresented in the fields.

Your level also determined how much money you had. Some of the colored people inherited wealth from their forebearers. At the bottom were the African Blacks—the ones without a mixed birth.

These differences kept the Jamaican society effectively divided. To know "how much" White or Black a person was, categories were assigned:[6]

	Black	White
Negro – Child of a Negro and Negro	1	0
Mulato – Child of a White and Negro	1/2	1/2
Sambo – Child of a Mulato and Negro	3/4	1/4
Quadroon – Child of a White and Mulato	1/4	3/4
Mustee – Child of a White and Quadroon	1/8	7/8
Mustifino – Child of a White and Mustee	1/16	15/16
Quintroon – Child of a White and Mustifino	1/32	31/32
Octoroon – Child of a White and Quintroon	1/64	63/64

If anything reflects how Black disunity has been effectively carried out, either by white supremacists or slave masters, it is in a letter purported to have been written by a Caribbean plantation owner named William (Willie) Lynch. This letter has generated a lot of controversy as to its authenticity. I will not be drawn into the debate, rather, I presented the letter in Chapter 9 because it in effect reflects the very things that have divided and caused disunity within the Black community.

The letter is purported to be five years short of being 300 years old; however, today, as we look at it, every description of the letter fits what is happening within the Black community.

The programming of Willie Lynch has worked effectively. Blacks have been as divided as ever on grounds of color, sex, nationality, tribe, shades of color, age, the places we live in or don't live in, etc.

What is the way out? What can our community do to break free from this scourge of disunity that has kept us divided, therefore weak?

The root of all racial disunity is Babel, where men ganged up to defy God and started their own worship. What was separated at Babel can only be united at Calvary.

However, if Calvary must unite us, the church must change. This means letting old feuds, wounds, and differences, whether doctrinal or emotional, give way to the unity of the Spirit. Unity does not mean unification; however, imagine if the churches pulled together their resources and did something for the community, not minding who got the accolade or who floated the idea.

What a change we would make!

The church must always remember it could be the social hub of the community, the rallying point for bringing a broken people together to find hope, help, and direction. What name or label the church bears that carries out such initiative should matter less to us.

It is true, we may not be homogeneously categorized as one big Black family; however, in our differences of status and class, there are things that unite us more. The unity of our heritage, background, our Hamitic origin, and the fact that we all come from the same continent should be a major rallying point and not a point of difference.

The statistics are not readily available to me of Black response to disasters; for example the hurricanes in the Caribbean, disasters in Africa, or the volcano eruption of Montserrat. The response of Blacks to help is either under-reported by the press or does not exist.

At the root of Black disunity is a certain kind of hatred for one another. There has to be a re-orientation in our thinking for us to realize that hatred only divides and destroys our community.

Fears and phobias we have of different people, color, class, and nations must be put behind; and if we observe weaknesses of any strand of the Black community, it is only in our coming together that we strengthen one another.

There is no one solution to the things that divide us—gender issues, generation gaps, class distinctions—we must comfort ourselves with the fact that we know that unity is not uniformity. It is a people pulling together in spite of their differences to achieve and overcome.

We refer to gerontocracy as one of the weaknesses and reasons for disunity; however, regard and respect for the elderly, which is popular within the Black community must itself be seen as strength.

ENDNOTES

1. Joyce Andrews, *Bible Legacy of the Black Race: The Prophecy Fulfilled* (Bensenville, IL: Lushena Books, Inc., 2000), 5.

2. Thomas Sowell, *Race and Culture: A World View* (New York: Basic Books, 1994).

3. Andrews, *Bible Legacy of the Black Race.*

4. Ula Yvette Taylor, *The Veiled Garvey* (Chapel Hill: University of North Carolina Press, 2002).

5. Ibid.

6. http://uncpress.unc.edu/chapters/taylor veiled.html.

CHAPTER 12

Black on Black Crime

And I will set the Egyptians against the Egyptians: and they shall fight every one against his brother, and every one against his neighbour; city against city, and kingdom against kingdom (Isaiah 19:2).

The last few decades have ushered in unprecedented crime within the Black community and the majority of it is "Black on Black"—a Black person acting in criminal activity against other Blacks.

It makes the previous threats to Blacks—for example the Ku Klux Klan—to be child's play compared to the challenges of today. The worrying phenomenon is its effect on the coming generations, making it a negative roller coaster problem which seems to want to stay around us long-term.

THE STATISTICAL PICTURE

In the District of Columbia, United States, Black residents are more likely to be killed than are people in war-torn regions such as Northern Ireland and the Middle East.[1]

The life expectancy of Black men in Harlem, a neighborhood in New York City, particularly central Harlem, is shorter than that of men in Bangladesh.[2]

In 1992 the violent crime rate for Blacks was the highest ever recorded by John Dilulio Jr.[3] An estimated 12 percent of African American men aged 20-34 are in jail, compared to 1.6 percent of White men in the same age category, according to a U.S. Justice Department report.[4] The same report noted that almost 7 percent of all Black male adults were in jail or in prison in 1995.[5]

Of non-fatal firearm injuries from mid-1992 to mid-1993, 59 percent of the victims were Black.

One quarter of all those shot were Black males between the ages of 15 to 24.[6]

One quarter of the crime victims who were shot are young Black males.[7]

In 1992, half of all murder victims were African American; 94 percent of murdered Blacks were killed by other Blacks.[8]

The Bureau of Justice and Statistics for the United States has calculated that 28 percent of Black men will be sent to jail in their lifetime.[9]

In Cincinnati, Ohio, where there has been a spate of shooting and crimes committed by Blacks or Black on Black, the *Cincinnati Enquirer* newspaper published an infographic of shootings.

❖ 41 shootings were reported (compared with 3 such shootings in Mountain Spring), in 2000.

❖ 34 percent of the shootings had indications of gang activity including multiple suspects and multiple getaway cars.

❖ In total, 59 people ended up on the wrong side of a gun, and all except one were Black.

❖ The 22 known and arrested suspects were Black males.

Black on Black shootings noticeably rose after April 7, 2001, when a Cincinnati police officer shot an unarmed 19-year-old African American, Timothy Thomas, in an area known as "Over the Rine," a predominantly Black neighborhood, known for violence and shootings.

In a report posted by Angela May on BBCNewsFour.com titled "City Working to Find Solution for Black Crime," she reports that in Charleston, South Carolina, Blacks accounted for 71 percent of the city's 45 homicide victims in the past three years, since March 8, 2004. At least one Black person has been charged in every case where there has been an arrest. This is in a city where Blacks make up 34 percent of the 97,000 population.[10]

Back to the city of Cincinnati. On January 1, 2004, the *Enquirer* posted on its Website the following statistics:

Of the 75 percent of people killed in Cincinnati in 2003, 84 percent were Blacks. That 75 percent constituted a 12 percent increase over the 2002 record of 66 deaths. Another newspaper for the same city, the *Cincinnati Post*, in a report by Jennifer Edwards titled, 'Black on Black Crime Increasing' claims that 80 percent of the murders in the city since 1995, 188 of 238 homicides involved Black victims and Black offenders according to law enforcement statistics.[11]

While reviewing Jared Taylor's book, *Paved with Good Intentions: The Failure of Race Relations in Contemporary America*, Peter Brimelow gives indication of the crime wave in the city of New York and its environment.[12] By the 1970s Blacks made up over 60 percent of those arrested for violent crime though being only 20 percent of the city's population. Black men have been responsible for over 85 percent of the felonies committed against New York City taxi cab drivers.

Nationwide, Blacks account for 64 percent of all violent crimes and arrests and 71 percent of all robbery arrests even though they only make up 12 percent of the population.[13]

In the United Kingdom, according to the article, "Breaking out of the Black Gangster Ghetto" by Lee Jasper, 45 percent of London's unemployed are Blacks.[14]

The Black prison population in Britain has doubled since 1994. Young Black men occupy more than 44 percent of the psychiatric beds in London. Teenage pregnancy rates are the highest in Europe, and the number of single parents is going through the roof.

In another article on the scenario in London and the Home Counties titled "Police to Build on Success in Black on Black Crime Initiative" by Hugh Muir, indicates that 9 percent of the shootings among Blacks occurred because of an argument over issues of "disrespect." Eighty percent were attributed to drugs and 12 percent were related to robbery.[15]

In the same kind of shooting within the United Kingdom involving Jamaicans, 2 percent were predominantly caused by gang activity, 16 percent followed an argument about "disrespect," 25 percent were related to drugs, and 23 percent were related to robbery.

In the Caribbean, the picture of Black on Black crime is exacerbated by the police response to the spate of crime. There have been 1,400 people shot dead by the police over the past ten years in Jamaica, according to Amnesty International as posted on their Website.[16]

Black on Black crime probably reaches its greatest height when one considers the case of genocide in Africa committed by fellow Africans. The nations of the world agreed over 50 years ago that genocide is a crime against humanity.[17]

Despite this agreement, modern genocides have increased, particularly among Blacks and Africa in particular. Only a handful of the perpetrators have ever been brought to justice. In Uganda, during Idi Amin's regime from 1972 to 1979, over 300,000 lost their lives in this way.[18]

In Angola, the genocide war which started in 1975 between the government of that nation and Unita led by Jonas Savimbi, claimed 550,000 lives. Of that number, over 300,000 died between 1992 and recent times.[19]

The Washington Post on December 15, 1998, puts the number at 300,000 between 1975 and 1991, and an additional 500,000 during the renewed fighting between 1992 and 1994, bringing the total number to 800,000 people killed. Of this number, non-combatants were close to 400,000 according to Ingrid Tvedten in her writing, "Angola, Struggle for Peace and Reconstruction."[20]

Idi Amin, in Uganda, lost another 300,000 during the fight between the government and the National Resistance Army.

In Liberia, the National Patriotic Front fought the government of the country until it collapsed, and created a situation of chaos and anarchy resulting in the loss of about 200,000 lives.[21]

Somalia, between 1991 and recent times, experienced a civil war which claimed 400,000 lives. Of this number, only 50,000 died in fighting compared to over 300,000 who died of starvation in the months following January 1991.[22] The War Annual 8 of 1997 puts the number at 500,000 people.[23] On December 14, 1998, the *Vancouver Sun* newspaper recorded the number at 400,000 dead from war, famine, and disease.[24]

In the Democratic Republic of Congo, civil war broke out in 1997. *Agence France Presse,* dated February 20, 1998, puts the number of refugees at 200,000 who were unaccounted for. Seven hundred thousand fled east when the war began, 400,000 fled west; 125,000 eventually returned to Rwanda; 53,000 remained in the Democratic Republic of Congo; and 222,000 people disappeared.[25]

One of the biggest cases of genocide in Africa was brother against brother between the Hutus and the Tutsis. The loss is estimated at close to a million people.

Why?

That is a question raised all the time when Blacks rise against each other. The words of Isaiah 19:2 are very far reaching as you can see its manifestation in our days. Blacks just can't seem to get together since they were scattered after Babel.

Isaiah's prophecy has followed Cushites, or Egyptians, wherever they have been. The irony of it is that we have already said that people of Negroid and Mongoloid descent and some Asiatic, are all Hamitic people. The one who has struggled the most has been the Black man, particularly because of the pathologies that keep shaping his community.

Black men are busy destroying each other in record numbers all around the world. The value placed on life is so low. A record number of wars continue decade after decade in Africa. Blacks hurt each other. While hurts do come from other people, the worst and most difficult to take in is from Blacks.

It is very difficult to lay the blame for the pathology of Black against Black at somebody else's doorstep. Some Black writers argue that in America, for example, the prison system becomes a breeding ground for certain kinds of Black men who prey on their own communities.

While true prison reform has not been addressed worldwide, to blame Black on Black crime on some White system is probably unjustifiable. We must still ask the question: Why is there such a high Black on Black crime rate?

One person blames it on the fact that every system seems to be against him compared to other nations. American gang leader Lil Monster appeared on the ABC television program "Night Line," and told Ted Koppel that while Asians come into the United States of America and get instant credit and instant bank loans, African Americans born in the nation must battle to even get a mere account opened.[26]

Many angry Black young people, whether on the streets of the United Kingdom, Jamaica, Africa, or the United States, consider themselves as being set up by society, especially when society parades before them unaffordable material wealth on television and in exhibitions.

They feel, particularly young African Americans, that the system has no room for them to live the American dream. Talking about the challenges of the economy and the American dream, Alvin Poussaint, in his book, *Why Blacks Kill Blacks*, argues that "Economic and psychological survival has often meant that Blacks have had to participate in anti-social acts." He argues further that we need "to distinguish deviant behavior from what is in fact different behavior."[27] He therefore sees the reaction of Black America as an understandable response to White racism and White marketing which leaves the young Black person unfulfilled.

Consider the cases in Cincinnati, Ohio, where 75 people were killed and 84 percent of them were Blacks. The perpetrators themselves in the majority were Blacks. According to the chief of police, 90 percent of the killings in that city were drug related.

Blacks have truly become a house divided against itself that cannot stand. Of all the pathologies considered in this book, Black on Black crime is probably one of the worst. When a people decide to turn on themselves, they make it justifiable for others to hurt them.

Crime against anybody is bad, but when criminals pick on their own because they are weaker, easier to target, and easier to hurt, that is very destructive. In an article titled, "It is No Longer a Black on Black Problem," the newspaper reports that Ibor Etienne, program controller at Choice FM and other radio stations based in South London was taking comments on Black on Black crime. One of the responses was, "We are not looking after our young children and teaching them the proper values. It is a family issue."[28]

Scripture cannot be broken, and once parents forfeit or fail to train their children to obey the law and be responsible, then there is a challenge.

> *Righteousness exalteth a nation: but sin is a reproach to any people* (Proverbs 14:34).

> *Train up a child in the way he should go: and when he is old, he will not depart from it* (Proverbs 22:6).

Some people also advance the argument that it must be a result of a profound lack of self esteem. The same article refers to Elaine Sihera, magazine publisher, commentator, and founder of the British Diversity Awards and the Windrush Achievement Awards, who said, "When people fear that they cannot advance because they are discriminated against or are deprived of power, you find a sub-culture developing. Guns are associated with power, allowing someone with low self-esteem to feel they can make an impression and be someone significant."[29]

That sense of significance is what is missing in the United Kingdom where there is 5 percent unemployment among the White community but between 18-25 percent unemployment among minorities, according to the *Observer* newspaper.[30]

In effect, these young people turn to music and activities to handle their anger. Once people are excluded, they act also in an excluded way. They become alienated; they alienate their minds on the actions they carry out.

However, Hugh Muir's report on Black on Black crime which gave a huge 16 percent of British Jamaicans carrying out Black on Black crime because of disrespect, minimizes the value of the life of the person against whom it was committed.[31]

Eighteen percent of the shootings in the cases reported occurred in private dwellings. Sixteen percent in night clubs, 16 percent in the street, and 14 percent involved someone sitting in or firing from a vehicle. In 13 percent of the cases, shots were fired between two rival people in vehicles.[32]

Dianne Abbott, the Black member of Parliament for Hackney North in London, brings out the fact that "Operation Trident," the police initiative to curb Black on Black crime, struggles because the criminals are so organized, constantly on their mobile phones between London, Birmingham, and Manchester telling one another what next to do.

That in itself shows that the man of color is not ignorant, foolish, or stupid. But he needs to direct his energy to that which builds other Blacks, not destroys. Black on Black crime is not justifiable. It is a pathology people must break free from as they put value on other human beings whom God has created and whom He values.

> *Thank you for making me so wonderfully complex! It is amazing to think about. Your workmanship is marvellous—and how well I know it. You were there while I was being formed in utter seclusion! You saw me before I was born and scheduled each day of my life before I began to breathe. Every day was recorded in your book!* (Psalm 139:14-16 TLB).

However, Lee Jasper, in the article titled "To Breaking Out of the Black Gangster Ghetto," gives years of unemployment, poor housing, 45 percent unemployment in London among Blacks, and failure rate among Black kids in the schools as some of the reasons for these reactions to society.[33]

According to the Operation Trident Website, the reason for having such a squad is because, "The majority of these crimes were being perpetrated by Black criminals on members of the Black community and the incidents were made harder to investigate because of the unwillingness of witnesses to come forward through fear of reprisals from the criminals involved."[34]

In Jamaica, reasons for killing fellow citizens could be as little as suspecting someone of being a police informer.[35]

That leaves one with the feeling that if you were to stand for righteousness, our community—the Black community—is tempted to tear you down. At least that is the reason why Black on Black crime in general seems to be committed.

The economic challenges young Black people face with the level of unemployment in their community cannot be downplayed. In fact some of them argue that if young White men were to face the same problems that young Black men face, they would carry guns too.

Many of the young Afro-Caribbeans who live in London, according to *The Guardian* newspaper, were born in the United Kingdom, but found themselves, having emerged from the school system, feeling disenfranchised, on the outside looking in. In frustration, they turned to the sin culture because the first place where they should have found help, other than their parents, is the school system; particularly in the United Kingdom is filled with teachers who too often give up on Black kids and resign to them leaving school. Thus the kids resign to leaving school without qualifications.

Norma Holts Davis of the Cincinnati Chapter of the NAACP said it succinctly when she said, "It should not be surprising that crime among African Americans is so high—they face a disproportionate share of poverty, poor housing in high crime areas and unemployment." She continued, "We are working on improving the economic, political, social and educational situation for persons of color. That in our opinion will certainly include not harming each other. But we do not have any solution for reducing crime. That is what we pay police for."[36]

Everywhere people of color live, where there has been a low value placed on human life, they of course have reasons to give from poverty and depravation to ethnic/tribal differences. The honor and dignity people have lost in Christ is now manifest in this terrible Black pathology. That is why a young person, trotting London, Birmingham, Nottingham, Bristol, Manchester, and elsewhere with a gun in his pocket thinks violence is a way to get respect. At the slightest problem between him and someone else, he pulls an Uzy Kalashnikov or a Magnum 45.

On top of this, the British police force has it wrong. They thought it was a bunch of people who were coming from the backyards of Jamaica, so they called them the Yardies; later to find that three out of every five victims are British born, and the majority of the perpetrators are also Black British.

The anger is not just with Jamaica, it is with the inefficiency and the deficiency the Black people have in their lives. All crimes are wrong, and some even think it is idiomatic purposelessness to call it Black on Black crime. God didn't think so when he allowed it.

And I will set the Egyptians against the Egyptians: and they shall fight every one against his brother, and every one against his neighbour; city against city, and kingdom against kingdom (Isaiah 19:2).

Black on Black crime is a hard and unavoidable fact. It is happening all over Africa where the police overreact at the slightest action from members of the public and most times justice is not done.

Black on Black violence—killing, stabbing, shooting—is so characteristic of and so predominant among Black people. Black on Black crime is human sinfulness at its core, the disobedience of the sons of Ham; it is a perpetuation of an evil from father to sons for generations.

THE PROBLEM DEEPENS

Within our community, when people have information about a crime or a criminal, they are frightened to speak up or give evidence. In the United Kingdom the police publish the name and address of the one who gave the evidence. We have become so cowardly that we are unable to confront another one of the negative pathologies.

Some of the scholars within the Black community would even want us not to admit that these things do exist. The magazines, radio stations, television stations that represent the Black community do not help either.

Maybe this is the reason why Lee Jasper writes, "This has been the reality of London's Black community for the past twenty years, resulting in a huge erosion of any restraining moral framework."

THE WAY OUT?

When God brought Israel out of Egypt, the first thing He did was to try to get Egypt out of them. He gave them the Ten Commandments.

Four had to do with their relationship with God, not serving the gods of Egypt any longer; but six had to do with their relationship with their fellow human beings.

God told them, "You must love your neighbor, do not kill, do not covet your neighbor's property or wife." You must teach those who belong in our community that you cannot destroy what you call precious. Jesus said to love your neighbor as yourself. One of the scourges of our times is just teaching people to look for jobs. It is not enough for governments to talk about what is going on; neither should the older people in the community merely make comments.

Maybe part of this pathology is self-hatred; and because of that self-hatred, the people who are caught in the web of Black on Black crime are easy prey.

It takes a loving person to give love and a hateful person to spread hatred. An end has to be put to it; and to find an end, we must react like Laketa Cole, one of four city workers in the city of Cincinnati, who reacted to the spate of Black on Black crime by seeking financial help to fight Black on Black violence.[37]

Our disgust for hatred, for the loss of young, vibrant, promising lives must be obvious to all men and we must speak out where we see Black on Black crime or any form of criminality.

Young people should be taught to understand that you do not tear society down because you do not like what you are getting from it. To fight this scourge within the Black community, businesses need to get onboard, to take significant steps to find jobs for these young people, but above everything, people must be confronted with the truth that only Jesus can bring a transformation, only He can change lives.

> *I beseech you therefore, brethren, by the mercies of God, that ye present your bodies a living sacrifice, holy, acceptable unto God, which is your reasonable service. And be not conformed to this world: but be ye transformed by the renewing of your mind, that ye may prove what is that good, and acceptable, and perfect will of God* (Romans 12:1-2).

ENDNOTES

1. "From Uncivil Wars," *The Economist*, October 7, 1989, p. 38.

2. "Who will help the Black man," *New York Times Magazine*, December 4, 1974, p. 74.

3. John Dilulio Jr, "The Question of Black Crime," *The Public Interest*, Fall 1994.

4. Fox Butterfield, "Jail Rate for Young Blacks Hit Peak in U.S. Prison Boom," *New York Times*, April 8, 2003.

5. U.S. Department of Justice, Bureau of Justice, Statistics, "State and Federal Prison Report Record Growth During the Last 12 Months," Press Release, December 3, 1995.

6. Ibid.

7. U.S. Department of Justice, Press Release, April 11, 1996.

8. U.S. Department of Justice, United States, Crime Reports, 1993, Washington D.C., p. 17.

9. Fox Butterfield, "Jail Rate for Young Blacks."

10. Angela May, "City Working to Find Solution for Black Crime," BBCNews4.com.

11. *The Enquirer*, www.theenquirer.com, January 1, 2004.

12. Jared Taylor, *Paved with Good Intentions: The Failure of Race Relations in Contemporary America*, (Long Beach, CA: New Century Books, 2004), 416.

13. Vdare.com.

14. Lee Jasper, "Breaking out of the Black Gangster Ghetto," *The Observer*, Sunday, February 17, 2002.

15. Hugh Muir, "Police to build on success in Black on Black crime initiative," *The Guardian*, September 20, 2003.

16. www.amnesty.org/web/wire.nsf/may2001/jamaica.

17. Convention on the prevention and punishment of the crime of genocide, www.preventgenocide.org/law/convention/text.html£ 82rummelr.

18. Encarta Encyclopedia, Source: Dictionary of 20th Century World History puts the number at 250,000.

19. *Agence France Presse*, March 8, 2002.

20. *The Washington Post*, December 15, 1998.

21. *Chicago Tribune*, April 17, 1996; *Boston Globe*, March 29, 2003; *Time* Magazine, July 28, 1997; *The War Annual*, Vol. 8, 1997; and *The Times of London*, July 22, 2003.

22. *The Washington Post*, February 12, 1993.

23. *War Annual 8* of 1997.

24. *Vancouver Sun*, December 14, 1998.

25. *Agence France Presse*, February 20, 1998.

26. "Night Line" in South Central, Transcript, ABC News, May 4, 1992, p. 9.

27. Alvin Poussaint, *Why Blacks Kill Blacks* (New York: 1972).

28. "It is no longer a Black on Black problem," *Sunday Observer*, United Kingdom, January 5, 2003.

29. Ibid.

30. *Observer* newspaper.

31. Hugh Muir, *The Guardian*, Saturday, September 20, 2003.

32. Hugh Muir, "Police to build on success in Black on Black crime initiative," *The Guardian*, September 20, 2003, Website: www.society.guardian.co.uk.

33. Lee Jasper, "Breaking out," *The Observer*.

34. www.met.police.uk/trident.

35. Horace Hence, "Murders Rocks Blacks Town Jamaica, 2nd Killing in 24 hours leaves quiet district in fear," *Zebra Correspondent* or www.jamaicaobserver.com/new/hotmail.

36. www.cincipost.com/2001/may/12/crime0151201.html.

37. www.enquirer.com/editions/2004/01/01/loc.

CHAPTER 13

Economically Challenged

The United Nations (UN) Development Program, Human Development Report of 2003, lists 175 nations and the levels of their development.[1]

Of the 31 at the bottom, 30 are from sub-Sahara Africa. This includes nations already listed as being very rich in mineral resources including the Democratic Republic of Congo, Nigeria, and Madagascar. Another report of the same organization dated July 2003 goes on to say, "most of the countries that were poorer in [the year] 2000 than in 1990 are in sub-Sahara Africa."[2]

A UN administrator said of the report's findings that poverty can be a political problem. The report shows that there are many countries whose income levels are high enough to end absolute poverty, but pockets of deep poverty remain, often because of discrimination in the provision of basic services.

This trend is not only reflective of Blacks on the African continent. The same goes for African Americans. In 1860, 98 percent of Black people in America were enslaved and owned only 1.5 percent of the nation's wealth. Some 140 years later, when Blacks are supposed to be free, they still only have 1.5 percent of the nation's wealth.[3]

For Black America it is not a case of the lack of income, rather an inability to generate and perpetuate wealth. In the article "Black Buying Power Up, Savings Still Lag," by Stacey Gilliam of BET.com, it was reported that "in 1990 Blacks held a buying power of $318 billion compared to $688 billion this year."[4]

Black spending dollars have grown by 17 percent while White spending dollars have only grown by 14 percent. Gilliam's report indicates that though Blacks may have not fared as well as they should in all of the states, things have become better for them in places like Georgia, Minnesota, Nevada, and Delaware.[5]

However, Blacks are economically challenged. Why?

First, there seems to be an inability or a lack of culture of generational wealth.

A good man leaveth an inheritance to his children's children: and the wealth of the sinner is laid up for the just (Proverbs 13:22).

Whether it is on the continent of Africa or in the United States or the Caribbean, it is hard to find Blacks who have been able to break into the wealth zone and to perpetuate it for generations. In Africa, apart from a few tribes such as the Bamileke of Cameroon, the Yorubas, the Ibos of Nigeria, and the Ashantis of Ghana, most other African tribes put emphasis on what the African person *is* rather than what the African person *has*.

Daniel Etounga-Manguelle argues it best when he writes, "In Africa, what classifies man is his intrinsic value and his breath. If the African is not very thrifty it is because his vision of the world attributes very little importance, too little to the financial and economic aspects of life. Other than some groups like the well-known Bamilekes of Cameroon or the Kamba in Kenya, the African is a bad homo-economicos."[6]

The question still is: "Why are Blacks economically challenged apart from the fact that poverty is a general curse that rests upon a people who violate the principles of God?"

The stranger that is within thee shall get up above thee very high; and thou shalt come down very low. He shall lend to thee, and thou shalt not lend to him: he shall be the head, and thou shalt be the tail. Moreover all these curses shall come upon thee, and shall pursue thee, and overtake thee, till thou be destroyed; because thou hearkenedst not unto the voice of the Lord thy God, to keep his commandments and his statutes which he commanded thee (Deuteronomy 28:43-45).

The truth is that Blacks:

1. Have a habit of collecting liabilities. The collection of liabilities is focusing your spending primarily on things that do not increase in value. Research was done a couple of years ago on Black spending habits within the United States, and it showed a disproportionate amount of trainers and leather jackets bought by young African-Americans, "Black females spend a lot more than white females on cosmetics, shoes and hair care."[7]

2. Are economically challenged because they do not invest. Why? African-American households have a shorter financial planning horizon; they spend more rather than less of their income. They do not invest, and if they do, it is not regularly. And even if they save, it is in places where it can be easily accessed, not in long-term investments.

    The added burden for the African who is trying to save is the expectation from his extended family to have to finance the studies of brothers, sisters, cousins, nephews, nieces, and sometimes people who are not related but come from the same geographical location.

3. Do not practice group economics. "The Buying Power of Black America" was recently released by Target Market New Inc., TMN, a Chicago-based research group. The analysis of the spending power of African-American showed $631 billion flowing through Black hands. This would have made African Americans the 11th richest nation in the world.[8]

    However, there has been no effort by the Black community to work together, join hands together, and practice what Claud Anderson calls *PowerNomics* in his book by that title. He argues in his book that in a capitalist society, producers, distributors, and sellers have power over the consumers. And Black Americans are exactly where they were in 1860 on the eve of the civil war.[9]

This is purely because of the chronic disunity among Blacks, as predicted by Isaiah in chapter 19, which also affects the ability of Blacks to be a people of economic might.

4. Have been shaped by colonialism to be job *seekers* instead of job *creators*. Claud Anderson in PowerNomics says, "in America 1 out of every 10 Asians is in business, 1 out of 35 Whites is in business, 1 out of every 54 Hispanics is in business, and only 1 out of every 104 Blacks is in business."[10]

    On the continent of Africa, people were by nature entrepreneurs even though on a small scale. However, the colonial masters "educated" the natives and trained them to seek office jobs. One of the greatest limitations on nations that have been previously colonized in the Caribbean and Africa is that people have a job-seeker mentality. Primary, secondary, and university education is geared toward writing nice résumés and seeking a job, and like I often say, JOB may stand for: Just Over Broke.

5. Are economically challenged particularly in the Caribbean because the economy of this region depends heavily on tourism and Caribbean migrants who send money home. This in effect binds the people to the spending pattern of other people. Other than tourism, another major sustenance of the Caribbean economy is migration as people leave for other parts of the world, particularly the United States and Europe, to work and make enough money to sustain the various Islands. This in itself is very limiting and also has direct and indirect impact because it has often meant that apart from economic challenges, the whole subcontinent is exposed to other attenuating problems.

6. Are economically challenged because of their mind-sets also. Wealth or poverty has a lot to do with mind-set. In a recent documentary on the "Millionaire Mind" in the United Kingdom, the mind-set of millionaires set them apart as people who are able to make and perpetuate wealth, and where there is wealth loss, to make it again.

On the other hand, the mind-set of the poor justifies poverty, sotimes using Scriptures to do so. The mind-set of the poor lacksthe discipline required for the making and perpetuation of wealth.

However, I believe that economic challenges for the Black person are caused by the following Money Mistakes:[11]

❖ Get rich quick schemes.

❖ Ignorance of the Biblical covenant of prosperity.

❖ Belief that there is a conspiracy to keep you poor.

❖ The belief that currency is something hard to earn.

❖ Developing "fruit eater" rather than a "seed sower" mentality.

❖ Believing that a good job is a source of creating prosperity.

❖ Saving, but not saving smartly.

❖ Irresponsible use of resources.

❖ Trying to get rich quick.

❖ Withholding benevolence.

❖ Cheating.

❖ Refusing to try again because of previous failure.

❖ Downward investment instead of upward investment.

❖ Latent belief that only greedy people can be blessed.

❖ Blaming poverty on the lack of capital for starting off.

❖ Mythical statements that we hold onto.

❖ Refusing to take risks and investing.

❖ The belief that big brother, i.e., "The Government" owes you.

❖ Living a life that is money-centered.

❖ Over-commitment to career.

❖ Investment hang-ups.

Indebtedness is often rooted in a person's compulsion to buy, and today's easy availability of credit facilitates making purchases on credit, easily clearing the path to poverty. Going into debt indirectly trains your children to follow the same path.

The rich ruleth over the poor, and the borrower is servant to the lender (Proverbs 22:7).

Train up a child in the way he should go: and when he is old, he will not depart from it (Proverbs 22:6).

So your child observes you and sees your actions. Borrowing is the father of bankruptcy. When borrowing is not controlled, bankruptcy will look you in the face. Indebtedness is an evil spirit that has your destruction as its ultimate goal. Those who provide credit facilities prefer you to borrow because it helps the economy and helps their own income. The car you were supposed to buy for $25,000, could end up costing you $31,000 at the end of four or five years.

Debtors presume that they will have a job tomorrow. In today's volatile world, that is a tall order. Debt makes Christians forget that they are promise keepers, and so when they are unable to fulfill their promise, excuses are given, and sometimes lies are told to cover their tracks.

A great percentage of those who draw the equity on their house often use it to pay off debts, whereas those who create wealth will take the equity to start a new business or buy more real estate.

You cannot really overcome indebtedness unless you are realistic about your income and how much of it is available to you. Imagine a man who earns $12,000 and pays 25 percent in tax, 7 percent in insurance, 17.5 percent value added tax on all purchases except for the children's clothing, and the few necessities we buy. In a nutshell, out of 12 months' income, only 8 months' income really stays with you. So if you earn $12,000, what is really available to you is $8,000.

Remember also that out of the $8,000, $1,200 belongs to the Lord in tithe. This leaves the believer with $6,800. Ignorance of these facts will make indebtedness spread faster than any disease; it will make such a person groan every time he wants to give to God because he calculates what 10 percent, the tithe, now means to them, forgetting that the government did not ask permission before it withdrew its own 32 percent in income tax, plus your insurance contributions.

Indebtedness makes some well-meaning couples struggle in spite of the level of wages they earn. Having bought most of the things in their house on credit, unpaid bills now stay on their mind like a bad dream. They walk on carpets that are "buy now pay later," they drive a car that is on a similar arrangement, their home is mortgaged, the television they watch is bought on credit, and they patronize catalogs and brochures of shopping companies that allow you to buy and spread the payment over years. The result—family tension and constant arguments.

Indebtedness also drains the joy out of payday. It has meant that some people have eaten the tithe and money that belongs to God. Lies and deception are easier for debtors than those who are debt free. Confidence is eroded when you are a debtor, particularly when you see the people you owe. Indebtedness enslaves you to the system of the world.

The Word says, "Borrowers are servants of lenders." The major reason for work then becomes paying all your lenders, ensuring that you keep them happy so they do not come and use the law to take everything you have. Most Western nations have empowered lenders to recover their money by using the full arm of the law, even if it means throwing you out of your accommodation and repossessing everything you have worked for to pay off the money you owe.

Indebtedness may cause the courts to determine what you spend your money on; in other words, a counselor may have to be hired to budget your own income for you, and such a counselor may decide that you have no right to bring the tithe. The "buy now pay later" marketing strategy of this world enslaves you and your children.

Of course there is time to use debt, but only as leverage for a business so that you are using other people's money to perpetuate and produce more money. Otherwise, your children are being raised in the atmosphere of debt, and when you bring up your children as debtors, you have disobeyed the Lord.

Train up a child in the way he should go: and when he is old, he will not depart from it (Proverbs 22:6).

Children catch behaviors, and children also go forth and perpetuate what they have seen. Borrowing is the guaranteed passport to financial slavery.

Unless there is a change, generation upon generation will be held in financial bondage. So while the righteous man leaves an inheritance for his children's children, the debtor leaves challenges, battles, and heartache for their spouse and relations.

A good man leaveth an inheritance to his children's children: and the wealth of the sinner is laid up for the just (Proverbs 13:22).

Now there cried a certain woman of the wives of the sons of the prophets unto Elisha, saying, Thy servant my husband is dead; and thou knowest that thy servant did fear the Lord: and the creditor is come to take unto him my two sons to be bondmen (2 Kings 4:1).

The indebtedness of the prophet, which he left for his wife and sons, added burdens, multiplied their worries, subtracted their peace, and divided their minds. He now left his wife worried because indebtedness was the only thing he left in the world for her; her sons were about to be taken by the people who provided the credit facilities.

Indebtedness produces sleepless nights and makes people question your integrity. It makes you feel the grind of borrowing on the inside. Indebtedness embarrasses you particularly when you are behind in your payments. It can lead to family acrimony. Indebtedness makes you not look forward to the postman bringing your mail because another reminder might be on the way.

Indebtedness invites the spirit of fear into your home so that you are no longer at peace but perpetually afraid of what might happen to you and your family. For the man, indebtedness takes away confidence and makes him feel inadequate as a provider for his family. Indebtedness leaves your family stressed because any little wastage by your children makes you overreact.

Debt between friends is another great challenge that causes the separation of friends. Imagine borrowing the car of your friend, and just as you are coming back from your trip, someone dents it. Having no money to repair it, you have to take it and explain. The reaction of the friend immediately changes because what is important to them has been tampered with. The spirit of debt is a bad master; it rules and it ruins.

Indebtedness can frustrate the vision of a church. People have been tempted to steal, therefore losing their job or even facing the possibility of a jail sentence because of indebtedness. Technically, the lender determines the movement of a borrower. They determine where you may go, what you may do, and how you may spend. When a debtor is led by the Holy Spirit to give a certain amount, the first thing he remembers is his line of credit which must not be jeopardized, and so he faces the temptation of disobeying the Holy Spirit, thus being rendered useless in the promotion of the Kingdom of God with his income.

Indebtedness really does frustrate one's destiny because the calling on the believer is to go out and make money in order to use it to promote the Kingdom of God. However, the rich who rule over the poor are now taking it from him.

People who get into indebtedness presume or forecast the future. They presume that the current value of their house is a certain amount and is likely to increase. They fail to realize that things could happen and that there could be calamities or disasters in the area where they live.

In summary, debt is a thief that robs one of his time and life. It is like being enslaved again to serve certain people you owe. It is the transfer of the wealth of the poor to the wealthy. Somebody somewhere is spending your money because you have chosen to walk in indebtedness. So if you cannot imagine Jesus in debt, then it is not the lifestyle you should follow.

Being economically challenged cannot stand in isolation from other conformations, other things which limit Blacks. They all are intrinsic and intertwined. However, until there is an understanding that God's plan is to bless and prosper the individual, the battle will continue, and Blacks will continue to be economically challenged. They will be economically challenged if they do not have a culture of wealth perpetuation. Every culture, nation, and geographical location presents its own opportunities.

The man of color must primarily work on the limitations which the lack of group economics put on him. The economic challenge of the Black person extends to the nations. Black nations have a habit of mortgaging their natural resources, in some instances selling the right to mine, export, and sell years ahead. This in spite of the fact that Africa is the wealthiest continent on earth. African governments are in the habit of always seeking foreign investment.

However, they are not good managers of their own economy. In the words of Daniel Etounga-Manguelle in *Cultural Matters* he writes, "African governments are not, it is evident, any better at economic management than are African individuals as our frequent economic crisis confirm."[12]

It is not enough to have a challenge. How you view the solution or the way out determines if you break free from it. Sixty-seven percent of Blacks in the United States believe that the government, rather than private businesses or individuals, have the greatest responsibility for creating jobs. Again, this is a job-seeker mentality. Poor and middle class Blacks hold this belief, and research shows that they are the ones who tend to gather liabilities.[13]

There certainly is a challenge with the Black community on the global level. In the United States where Blacks have run their own businesses and enterprises, their businesses are so fragile that a good number of them depend on government contracts by being preferred in order to perpetuate business in their community. Eighty percent of Black businesses are family-run enterprises employing no outside workers. Only 4 percent of African-American spending goes into Black-owned businesses.[14]

The most marginalized and economically challenged group of Black people outside of the continent of Africa would be European Blacks. Statistical data is almost non-existent for reference. The little information available paints a pathetic picture.

In October 2003, a television documentary was shown of White police cadets in training to become policemen—it was to show racism in the United Kingdom police force. The statements from most of the cadets showed their pathological hatred for people of other colors. When it came to the Asian, they said they hated him most because he is in the United Kingdom to take everything. They did not even reckon with the Blacks because they felt they have not much of an impact on the British economy.

ENDNOTES

1. The United Nations Development Program, Human Development Report of 2003.

2. The United Nations Development Program Report, July 8, 2003.

3. "The Buying Power of Black America," Target Market New Inc., TMN.

4. Stacey Gilliam, "Black Buying Power Up, Savings Still Lag," BET.com, posted August 21, 2003.

5. Ibid.

6. Daniel Etouaga-Manguella, "Does Africa Need..." Harrison & Huntington, *Culture Matters*, (New York: Basic Books, 2000).

7. "The Buying Power of Black America," TMN.

8. Ibid.

9. Claud Anderson, *PowerNomics* (Bethesda, Maryland: Power-Nomics Corp. of America Inc., 2001).

10. Ibid.

11. Matthew Ashimolowo, *10Ms of Money* (Mattyson Media, 2003), 215-235.

12. Daniel Etounga-Manguelle in *Culture Matters*.

13. Gerald F. Seid and Jo Davidson, "Whites, Blacks agree on problems; the issue is how to solve them," NBC News, *Wall Street Journal* Survey, September 1994.

14. National Urban League article, "The State of Black America 1993," Washington DC, p. 94, 101.

CHAPTER 14

Racism

The *Shorter Oxford English Dictionary*, volume 2, defines *race* as:

a. The offspring or posterity of a person,

b. A set of children or descendants,

c. A limited group of persons descended from a common ancestor,

d. A house, a family or kindred.

With this in mind, what then is racism?

Racism really is an ideology, a belief that one race is superior to another race. It is not only a belief; it is an action, a practice and discrimination on the basis of such belief. It is behaving toward another group of people with a perceived thought that one is superior and the other is inferior.

For example, the Funk & Wagnalls Encyclopedia 1952 edition defines a negro person thus, "The negro and Negroid people are sometimes said to represent a stage which is lower in evolutionary development than that of the white man and to be closely related to the anthropoid apes because they often have very long arms, protruding jaw, and a flat nose. These claims have no scientific justification."[1]

Martin Luther King Jr. defined racism as "A doctrine of the congenital inferiority and worthlessness of a people."[2]

Webster's Dictionary defines racism as "A doctrine or teaching which claims to find racial differences in character and intelligence; That asserts the superiority of one race over another; That seeks to maintain the supposed purity of a race." It also adds that racism is, "Any program or practice of racial discrimination or segregation based on such beliefs."[3]

Originally inspired by the various voyages of Europeans to far places like Africa and the new world, racism began when European travelers who saw, for example, Africans living in basic subsistent cultures and civilizations immediately assumed their own culture, to be superior and the people to be inferior.

This notion was then carried on by voyagers, missionaries, explorers, into literature, later to be propounded and expanded by leading philosophers. This, in effect, tainted the psyche or thought of the average European against the Black race in particular.

From then on, in addition to the dictionary definition of the word *black*, anyone of that color was considered dirty, black, inferior, etc.

Attempts were made to look for the basis for racism in biological difference. As early as the 16th century, certain biologists tried to make the Jews, for example, seem less than human or at least not to be tolerated within the Christian society.

And in recent times, psychologists like M.A. Jansen and Hans Eysenck have argued that lower IQ scores of Black children compared to White children is a reflection of their genetic deficiency. This, of course, is an attempt to not take into account whatever struggles such people face.

WHAT ACCOUNTS FOR RACISM AND WHY IS IT SO PREVALENT?

In the article "The End of Racism," Frank Furedi quotes Sir William McPherson commenting on racism and a racial incident as, "One that is perceived to be racist by the victim or by any other person."[4]

In other words, a racial act has taken place once the other person feels that an action carried out toward him is because of his race. In his book, *Beyond the Rivers of Ethiopia*, Mensa Otabil gives us insight. He writes, "The spirit of racism thrives on mis-information and stereotyping. Instead of portraying people in the likeness of God, it seeks to devalue the worth of people that are different from us or as not being as good as we are."[5]

This difference in looks, likes, and dislikes has long been used, therefore, as the reason why the Negroids may be considered inferior to the White race. Mensa buttresses his argument by saying, "Because somebody does not talk the way you talk, dress the way you dress and look the way you look does not in any way imply that they are inferior or superior to you."

Western views, having been shaped by missionaries, slave traders, and explorers, became easier for those who traded in slaves and who owned slaves to argue that the man of color was lesser in intelligence and ability. This helped justify ownership of other humans against their will and the use of their labor freely.

The situation was not helped by the fact that even great philosophers and Western thinkers like Immanuel Kant, David Hume, and Georg Hegel portrayed Blacks lesser than they should.

Immanuel Kant said, "The negros of Africa have received from nature no intelligence that rises above the foolish."[6] And as if to make his point a justification for what was to follow in the way Blacks were treated by slave traders, he said, "The difference between the two races is thus a substantial one, it appears to be just as great in respect of the faculties of the mind as in color."[7]

Kant portrayed Blacks as being less intelligent and their color as inferior.

As if that was not enough, David Hume, who lived about the same time as Kant, said, "I am apt to suspect the negros and in general all the other species of men to be naturally inferior to the white. There never was any civilised nation of any other complexion than white or even any individual eminent in action of speculation."[8]

David Hume must have deliberately ignored 4,000 years of human development and history. He must have overlooked the contribution of

Blacks in building the first civilization or other races in the subsequent developments of man. He goes on to say, "No indigenous manufactures among them, no arts, no sciences."

How wrong! He did not notice that the discovery of the wheel, iron, architecture, shipping, and astronomy preceded the evolution of the European civilizations.

Once the people purported to be the great thinkers shape the views of any generation, it is hard to undo the damage.

Hume further argued that, "The constant difference could not happen, in so many countries and ages, if nature had not made an original distinction between these breeds of men."

In this book, it has been established that there were three forms of slavery out of Africa—intertribal slavery, Arabian slavery, and Western slavery. Western slavery was driven purely by economics, and to justify it, the man of color had to be made to look inferior to everyone; and therefore, slavery to seem like a way of rescuing him from his shambolic existence. Slavery exploited and merchandized Black Africa.[9,10]

It is hard to say that the prejudice of America made her turn to slavery, rather it was the reverse; once the trade in humans had begun and those humans were looked down upon in that way, America and the West became racist.

In his book *Capitalism and Slavery*, Eric Williams stated, "Slavery was not born of racism, rather, racism was the consequence of slavery."[11]

The depth of the philosophers earlier quoted immediately becomes questionable because they made *different* to mean *better*. Because a man is different in color, race, size, or grace does not mean he is better. Racism may have existed before slavery; however, the people who seem to have suffered it the most are people of color, the Black people.

Between themselves too, Africans may have held views of prejudice or a sense of inferiority to other Africans. The Yorubas of Nigeria would think it is the worst thing to have to pay homage or respect to a Hausa although this has changed since geopolitics and colonialism have placed the latter as the supposed political power masters of Nigeria.

Racial views were spread across the world and may be found in almost every culture as far as records can be found, according to Harvard palaeontologist Steven J. Gould in his book, *The Mismeasure of Man*.[12]

But for the African, what makes prejudice and racism against him so far and widespread is a result of travelers who painted the African in a way that today shapes impressions of him. Richard Johnson, who tried to make Blacks look like sexual predators, morally loose, and incontinent, said, "The enormous size of the virile member among the Negros is an infallible proof that Blacks are descended from Noah's son and cursed for seeing their father's nakedness."[13]

The ill-conceived view of Blacks' sexual virility has also informed certain racial beliefs of him that are very negative. In addition to the explorers, philosophers, and missionaries, others have traveled into Africa and have written literature based on their own assumptions. They have also shaped views in addition to the view of Western slave owners who wanted to justify their action.

Arab and Persian writers have had firsthand relationship with Africa, particularly coming into Africa through Zanzibar and Bornu in the Elkanemi Empire below Sudan. They have written views that have not helped but rather presented Blacks in a stereotypical way. The Arab's negative impressions were not limited to Blacks; they were known to have taken Europeans as slaves and they held such views of some Europeans, particularly Eastern Europeans.

Ibn Khaldun, an Arab writer, said that, "In character, Blacks were just dumb like animals and most of them dwell in caves and thickets, live in savage isolation and eat each other." He holds the same view of the Slavics of Eastern Europe.[14] It is difficult not to bring in the fact that the largest number of slaves were taken by Arabs; therefore, even Khaldun may have served the elites who brought African slaves for their sexual pleasure in Arab lands.

The difficulty with racism is that it is today perpetrated in a greater dimension by views that have shaped and been caused by language and the use of color to differentiate people.

Among the Caucasians, once you are not White, you are ethnic. That causes a major problem because only 20 percent of humanity is White. That makes 80 percent of the world to be ethnic.

A more extreme and reverse view of racism being perpetuated because of White view is held by Michael Bradley in his book, *The Iceman Inheritance* in which he writes, "All primary threats to our survival" in his opinion are "the results of peculiarly Caucasoid behavior, Caucasoid values, Caucasoid psychology."[15]

How has Racism Been Used?

Although there is no basis in biology, science, or nature for racism, it has been used to determine the destiny of millions of people, particularly from the days of slave trade to date. Whole political systems as in the apartheid of South Africa have been built on it; segregation laws of the United States of America were founded on the bedrock of racism. In South Africa, for example, the color of skin was used to categorize people and the color level they fell into determined what opportunities and challenges they faced.

At the top of the ladder was the White, and at the bottom was the Black African. And though they were in the majority, having been classified and held down by laws and the barrel of a gun, their future was shaped by racial prejudice. The same color classification or national classification was used in other places. In Rwanda, for example, the Belgium colonialists used the difference between the Hutus and the Tutsis to perpetually rule them, deliberately giving the impression that one group was better at administrative matters while the other was only good at manual labor.

Classification into a color group other than the ruling one immediately made you unequal and a person who can potentially be nullified or ignored. Such classification affected education and the labor market. In the United Kingdom, for example, it affected housing, social care, and in my opinion, the criminal justice and the judicial system.

The number of Blacks in prison is higher, probably not because they tend to or are prone to crime but once you are classified, a knock-on effect takes place. It is hard to get jobs; therefore, with such economic deficiency, people cut corners and fall foul of the judicial system.

It seems that when Black people show up in court, they are more likely to get a harder sentence than their White counterparts. For example, the 2004 October Statistics of the United Kingdom puts the number of Whites at 54,153,898, that is 92 percent of the population, while Black Caribbeans number just over 565,876, and Black Africans 485,277.[16]

These statistics make the Black Caribbean 1 percent of the population, while the Black African is 0.8 percent of the population. Yet these two groups account for about 16 percent of the prison population. And in the greater London area where Blacks constitute probably just over 4 percent of the population, 70 percent of psychiatric beds are occupied by them, and they are disproportionately represented in the prisons.

Unemployment rates for young Black African and Caribbean men range between 25-31 percent, while the same rate for White young men was 12 percent.[17]

When a people have been classified and a racial bias exists against them, everything becomes colored by it, and they are forced to play catch-up on all things including housing, education, employment, etc.

A great number of young Blacks in the United Kingdom and America leave school without qualifications. It has been said that in the United States there are more Black men of college age in prison than there are in college.

THE CONSEQUENCES

The damage racism has done to the psyche of the Black man is enormous. People of Africa have been painted as sexual people with libidinal passion that is totally uncontrollable. This picture is untrue, particularly because Africa holds a high custom in most places of sexual purity and the celebration of virginity.[18]

The *Oxford English Dictionary* defines *blackness* as, "Deeply stained with dirt, soiled, dirty, foul, malignant, deadly, baneful, disastrous, sinister, iniquitous, atrocious, horrible, and wicked."

With the dictionary definition of the word *black*, people of the continent of Africa were then seen as primitive, backward, and totally uncivilized. Cultural anthropologists would differ. They agree that people's culture is enough definition of their situation; their music is an expression of the immediate architecture and technology around them.

One might argue that the use of the word *black* within the English language to connote negativity existed before its encounter with Africa and the color of the African cannot be said to be jet black. Those who argue about the backwardness of the Black man deliberately overlook the fact that he was the first occupant of the Mesopotamian Valley in about 3500 B.C. when the wheel was discovered and writing began.

If we accept the Bible as authentic and inspired, then Nimrod the Cushite is exactly who he is said to be, the builder of the city of Babel in the old land of Mesopotamia.

If the Sumerians were said to be the black-headed people, if they were Hamitic, and, in the words of A.R. Fausset, spoke the Galla language of the ancient occupants of the land of Ethiopia, then the racist belief that the Black man never invented anything in antiquity becomes very weak.

REVERSING RACISM

Reversing the consequence of racism is certainly a tall order. The damage has been done in many places. Views have been formed, images have been created, impressions have been given, prejudices have evolved and in some parts of the world, racism doesn't only exist, it has been institutionalized.

To reverse racism we must start by providing adequate, concrete, and proven data which shows that truly the first civilizations were developed by the man of color and that all other civilizations have only built on what he started.

We must bring into thought the things known about ancient Africa and modern Africa—its beauty and the things that show that its people are well-mannered and cultured.

The world needs to read records of African historians who have been able to capture truths about its past which show that though it lost its ability to write and develop—following the idolatry, disobedience, and its consequences—yet it has stories of conquests, glamour, beauty, and good pride.

Pathologies that are evolving as a result of the various challenges of the Black man need to be confronted head-on. At the time of the industrial revolution 300 years ago, Africa was not too far behind, but it has stagnated; and when its leaders would use their energies, it was diverted to fight colonialists. After the colonialists were gone, they turned on each other and began to scar each other.

Blacks must take pride in the fact that they truly built the first civilization and in the first 3,000-4,000 years of humanity they were not the ones considered backward or barbaric. Rather, there were those who held negative views of certain Whites. The great philosopher Aristotle had his harshest cultural observation and view of the English people. He thought they were "wanting in intelligence and skill."[19]

You must realize that the ancients, for example the Greeks, thought highly of Blacks and respected them while they had a poor view of Europeans. They thought they lacked in the very basics of civilization. This is brought out more effectively by the controversial Black writer, Martin Bernal, in his book *Black Athena*.[20]

Speaking of Greeks and their high view of Blacks, Seneca thought they were full of courage, love, and freedom. Herodotus, the father of history, indicated that Pythagoras studied maths 21 years in Egypt. His comment on the physique of the Ethiopian is that of being handsome. In his book, *Blacks in Antiquity*, Frank Snowden quotes a Greek epigrammatic, Aslepiades, who observing a Black person said, "Gazing at her beauty I melt like wax before the fire. She is Black, what is that to me? So are coals, but when we burn them, they shine like rosebuds."[21, 22]

The most major way to reverse racism is probably to take responsibility for one's actions, beliefs, and thoughts. Blacks in the Western hemisphere cannot continue to blame racism for their socioeconomic status in life.

If it has to take double the effort to prove anything, it is better to do that than to take the view of constant argument and rebuff. The excuses, attitudes, and theories of certain members of the community must be called to question. Taking responsibility includes true self-examination.

There is no plausible justification for the continuous plundering of Africa, 40 years after independence with Black majority rule. The irony of it all is the fact that in spite of apartheid, South Africa and its White presence seem like Europe or an advanced economy in the middle of a plundered Africa, thus giving credence to this self-destructive tendency within the Black community.

Blacks must confront their quest for pleasure at the expense of prosperity and investment. They must deal with the poor self-esteem and self-destructive wantonness that exists in our community.

The wanton disregard for life, the level of Black on Black crime, and the number of people who die by the hand of fellow Blacks, call for self-examination. The patronage of music which denigrates women, elevates killing, and celebrates destruction is a shame on the man of color.

The view of some may be considered conservative, and they may not be thought to have truly spoken for their community; however, because of the prominence and voice they have we cannot but quote them and listen to them also.

Black Supreme Court Justice Clarence Thomas warns young Blacks. He says, "Unlike me, you must not only overcome the repressiveness of racism, you must also overcome the lure of excuses."[23]

Dinesh Desouza also quotes Colin Powell telling African-American students to "not use racism as an excuse for your own shortcomings."[24]

The Black community in the majority is made up of people of high value, high regard for God, morality, faithfulness, holiness, purity, achievement, and advancement. It is a community of people who have taught children not to call older people by their first name; and even when people are not related, they are taught to call them "auntie" or "uncle" out of respect.

Such values should be brought back and taught to the next generations. To this again, Colin Powell reminds Black audiences that, "The worst kind of poverty is not economic poverty but rather the poverty of values."[25]

The United States has 30 million Blacks, and only 1 in 104 owns a business. Some of these businesses are appallingly small.

Business for the Black person in Europe is a new evolution that rates very low in statistics. Unemployment for Blacks in the United Kingdom is a high 18-25 percent.

Therefore Blacks must destroy this pathology of racism by their pursuit of excellence, patriotism in the nation in which they belong, entrepreneurship, and the development of a producer, not a consumer mentality.

If anything has helped racism gain ground, it is the inability of the community itself to speak or stand and build. Blacks are more likely to not invest value or respect for one another until an outsider does. Blacks are more likely to not patronize one another until an outsider does.

In the opinion of Alan Keys, a one-time Black presidential candidate of the United States of America, "The most successful economic boycott in history—is against ourselves."[26]

ENDNOTES

1. *The New Funk & Wagnalls Encyclopedia*, (New York: Unicorn Publishing, 1952).

2. Martin Luther King Jr., *Where Do We Go from Here: Chaos or Community?* (Boston: Beacon Press, 1968), 48.

3. Webster's New World Dictionary (New York: Prentice Hall, 1994), 1106.

4. Frank Furedi, "The End of Racism," *The Problem of Race in the 21st Century* (Cambridge: Harvard University Press, 2002).

5. Dr. Mensa Otabil, *Beyond the Rivers of Ethiopia* (Bakersfield, CA: Pneuma Life Publishing, 1993), 12.

6, Dinesh D'Souza, *The End of Racism* (New York: The Free Press, 1995).

7. *Observations on the Feeling of the Beautiful and Sublime*, trans. by John Goldthwait (Berkeley: University of California Press, 1960), 111-113.

8. David Hume, *Essays, Moral, Political and Literary*, eds. T.H. Grave and T. Grose (London: Longmans, Green & Co., 1875, volume 1), 252.

9. Donald Noel, *The Origins of American Slavery and Racism* (Colombus, OH: Charles E. Merill, 1972).

10. Marvin Harris, *Patterns of Race in the Americas* (West Port, CT: Greenwood Press, 1964), 70.

11. Eric Williams, *Capitalism and Slavery* (New York: Capricorn Books, 1966), 7.

12. Steven J. Gould, *The Mismeasure of Man* (New York: W.W. Norton, 1981), 31.

13. David Brion Davis, *The Problem of Slavery in Western Culture* (Oxford University Press, 1988), 452-453.

14. Ibn Khaldun, *The Muqaddimah*, trans. by Frank Rosenthal (Princeton University Press, 1967), 89, 69, 63.

15. Michael Bradley, *The Iceman Inheritance* (New York: Kayode Publications, 1978), 3.

16. National Statistics of Great Britain, www.statistics.gov.uk.

17. www.statistics.gov.uk/cci/nugget-print.asp.

18. Eugene D. Genovese, *Roll, Jordan, Roll: The World the Slaves Made* (New York: Vintage Books, 1972), 458-459.

19. Aristotle, *Politica*, quoted by Thomas Gossett, *Race: The History of an Idea in America* (Dallas: Southern Methodist Univ., 1963), 6.

20. Martin Bernal, *Black Athena: The Afroasiatic Roots of Classical Civilization* (Rutgers University Press, 1987), 28.

21. Frank Snowden, *Blacks in Antiquity: Ethiopians in the Greco-Roman Experience* (Cambridge, MA: Belknap Press of Harvard University Press, 1970).

22. Frank Snowden, "Aslepiads Didyme," *Greek, Roman and Byzantine Studies, 32 no.3* (1991), 2339.

23. Clarence Thomas, Savannah State College Commencement Address, Savannah, Georgia, June 9, 1985, as quoted in the book, *The End of Racism* by Dinesh D'Souza.

24. "Can Colin Powell save America?" *Newsweek*, October 10, 1994; "Powell on Powell: I talk to all of America," *U.S. News & World Report*, September 20, 1993.

25. Colin Powell, Fisk University Commencement address, Nashville, Tennessee, May 4, 1992.

26. "Why Asians prosper where Blacks fail," *Wall Street Journal*, May 28, 1992.

CHAPTER 15

Mis-governance

And the Egyptians will I give over into the hand of a cruel lord;
(Isaiah 19:4a).

One of the great pathologies of Blacks which has held Africa as a continent in slavery is mis-governance by its own rulers. Amnesty International, the International Monetary Fund, the World Bank, and various major organizations around the world have used different negative words to describe the mis-governance going on in Africa including: massive corruption, political instability, coups, disunity, manmade economic problems, nepotism, and human rights violations. The list goes on.

Mis-governance includes repressive governments, torture, executions, unlawful killing, and in some cases, making legitimate vigilante groups that kill or murder for the people in power. There are detentions, ill treatment, violations of the rights of prisoners of conscience, and arbitrary arrests; in some cases there is the absence of any form of freedom of speech and where it exists, it is restricted. Jungle justice, police corruption, and bribery are also present.

In some of these despotic countries, anyone who dares to speak against the government gets branded either as an agent of the colonial masters, or he might be misbranded as a representative of some United States covert organization like the CIA or the FBI, etc.

A case in point is Zimbabwe where anyone who takes an opposing view to the government in power is said to be a representative of the British government. The apparent lack of progress in such a country makes it difficult to swallow, particularly when one realizes that the government in power has held sway absolutely since 1980.

The record of the government in the apparent handling of the people of Matabelle's land in the 1980s further buttresses the argument.

PROBABLE REASONS FOR MIS-GOVERNANCE

We have established that this pathology began in the prophecy concerning the Black person in the Book of Isaiah chapter 19. The manifestation was immediate upon colonialists giving independence to the nations.

David S. Landes, in his book *The Wealth and Poverty of Nations*, ties the argument to the unpreparedness of those who agitated for independence. He said, "The postcolonial Africans had no experience of self-government, and their rulers enjoy the legitimacy branded by kingship networks and clientele loyalties."[1]

Their energies having been directed at getting the colonial masters out at all costs, they suddenly inherited a central government by geographical representation. With the massive problem of disunity on grounds of tribes, language, and cultural diversity, they were now to form alliances that were alien to their own tradition and method of government.

This sudden platter of gold, as most African governments see the opportunity to rule, was pushed upon them after they had fought the colonial masters. The masters themselves did everything but prepare the natives for the Western governmental system the people were to inherit.

The result was, in the words of David Landes, "...the legacy was ruled by a strong man, autocratic embodiment of the popular will, hence slayer of democracy. Stability depended on one man's vigour and when he weakened or died (or was helped to die), the anarchy of the short lived military coup followed."[2]

What was the result? Having come out of a lordship system, an oligarchy where a minority ruled and owned much of the land and where superstition made the people believe that whether they were poor or rich was predestined, the danger became one man taking over—as was often the case before democracy.

Such a man often demonstrated inaptitude and inability to govern and ended up pillaging the people and becoming the richest of the land. When, of course, the intelligencia of such nations clamored for democracy, a new trend began as military leaders metamorphosed into civilian clothing as politicians.

The picture hitherto painted should not give the impression that these leaders are lacking in intelligence. On the contrary, it is rather that the intelligence is utilized for personal aggrandisement. The article, "Africa's Crisis of Governance" argues that, "the popular image of African leaders as bungling buffoons is not helpful. It obscures reality. Anyone who has observed the way in which the military has dominated politics in Nigeria would see that the generals are no fools."[3]

The army generals know how to maneuver the opposition, sow confusion in their midst, and reduce the credibility they have before the public. Tunde Obadina argues further, "it would be a mistake to approach Abacha and his cronies as a bunch of idiots, ignorant of the art of politics."[4]

Donors and multilateral agencies that have come into Africa on the notion that it is the inability to govern, have initiated a lot of capacity building programs to enable African nations to put in place structures and reforms that will strengthen the rule of law, support democracy, and increase transparency and accountability.

Capacity-building programs could have been introduced at the time of the exit of the political masters. However, it is not enough of a reason; the argument still stands that some of the political leaders are savvy; there is just a misdirection of their savvyness.

Mis-governance persists because the ruling class has no commitment to see change, to reduce or eradicate poverty, or to increase the social well-being of the people of the nations. This ruling class has dominated politics from the days of independence, and even as age begins to tell on them, they have their own people in place to perpetuate the greed, misgovernance, and kleptomania they started.

THE PICTURE OF MIS-GOVERNANCE

The ruling class sees the state as a source of accumulating wealth. With that in mind, it places a high premium on the control of the state. Every economic policy, system, and action put in place are intended to make plundering and pillaging easier for them. Much of the civil war in Africa and its continuity gives credence to this fact.

The warlords benefit from the perpetuity of the war, and when the war ends they continue to benefit from the gains. In his book *The Wretched of the Earth* Frantz Fanon puts it better when he says that the ruling class is "a sort of little greedy caste, avid and voracious, with the mind of a hoxter, only too glad to accept the dividends that the former colonial powers hands out. This get-rich-quick middle class shows itself incapable of great ideas or inventiveness."[5]

The politicians of Africa do not see the government of the people for the people; governance in a sense is some form of business, and campaign money during an election is considered an investment which must bring returns.

Essentially, politics in Africa is whatever it takes the ruling class to get what they need; when they are in power, bad governance, including repression, divides and rules.

For the African politician, P is for politicking—effective politicking, not effective policies. Amnesty International reports that the following acts of mis-governance took place in several African countries:[6]

Extrajudicial executions and unlawful killings. Confirmed or possible extrajudicial executions were carried out in 17 countries: Burkina Faso, Burundi, Central Africa Republic, Democratic Republic of Congo, Congo, Cote D'Ivoire, Ethiopia, Kenya, Liberia, Madagascar, Mozambique, Namibia, Nigeria, Rwanda, Sudan, Uganda, and Zimbabwe.

Disappearances. People were "disappeared" by state agencies in five countries: Burundi, Comoros, Congo, Ethiopia, and Rwanda.

Freedom of expression restrictions. Freedom of expression came under attack in the following African countries according to Amnesty

International: Burundi, Central Africa Republic, Democratic Republic of Congo, Cote D'Ivoire, Eritrea, Ethiopia, Gambia, Guinea, Rwanda, and Sudan.

Mis-governance and human rights violations. Thousands of lives and livelihoods were destroyed in armed conflicts and civil strife. Amnesty International reports this to be common in Burundi, Central Africa Republic, Congo, Cote D'Ivoire, Democratic Republic of Congo, Liberia, Sudan, and Senegal.

Torture and ill treatment. Victims of torture and ill treatment by security forces, police, and other state authorities were reported in several African nations: Angola, Burundi, Cameroon, Central Africa Republic, Chad, Democratic Republic of Congo, Equatorial Guinea, Eritrea, Ethiopia, Kenya, Liberia, Madagascar, Mauritania, Mauritius, Mozambique, Nigeria, Rwanda, South Africa, Sudan, Togo, and Zimbabwe.

Detention without charge or trial. This is very common in Africa. However, it was reported by Amnesty International in 17 countries: Angola, Burundi, Cameroon, Central Africa Republic, Cote D'Ivoire, Eritrea, Ethiopia, Gambia, Liberia, Namibia, Niger, Rwanda, Senegal, Sierra Leone, Somalia, Sudan, and Togo.

I am amazed that certain African nations that are well known to me are missing on the list, and they have an appalling record of detaining people arbitrarily—some are rotting in jail without a trial even scheduled.

Death penalties. People are sentenced to death in several African nations, and some of the nations carry out executions. These are the nations where death sentences are passed out: Burundi, Central Africa Republic, Ethiopia, Kenya, Malawi, Mauritania, Democratic Republic of Congo, Nigeria, Rwanda, Sudan, Tanzania, Togo, Uganda, Zambia. And the executions were carried out, according to Amnesty International, in three countries: Nigeria, Sudan, and Uganda.

Human right abuses by armed opposition groups. Armed opposition groups committed serious human rights violations including deliberate and arbitrary killings of civilians, torture, and abduction, or hostage takings in 14 countries: Angola, Burundi, Cameroon, Central Africa Republic, Chad, Congo, Gambia, Liberia, Nigeria, Rwanda, Senegal, South Africa, Sudan, and Zimbabwe.

UGANDA

In Uganda for example, the judiciary and the police are considered by members of the public to be corrupt. People are jailed for the smallest offense and are expected to bribe the police for freedom. In his writing "East and East Central Africa Global Corruption Report 2001," Gatau Warigi quotes the response of one inmate, "they ask us for some money if we want our freedom, we do not have money. That is why they keep us here. Even then, our families have to come regularly to give them money. Or else they torture us and make us dig each morning before walking to court."[7] A survey of Ugandan citizens by the government's own ombudsman showed that 63 percent of responders claim that they had bribed a court official or a police officer.[8]

RWANDA

In March 2000, in Rwanda, Pascal Disumungu resigned as president for personal reasons whereas in reality it was as a result of a purge of his top officials accused of corruption and abuse of office. This also resulted in the consolidation of Tutsi elite power around post-genocide strong man, Paul Kigani.[9]

BURUNDI

In Burundi, the parliamentary commission of inquiry reported in January 2001 that within the government, theft, fraudulent management, corruption, and embezzlement was rampant.[10]

GABON AND CONGO BRAZAVILLE

Gabon and Congo Brazaville are nations that are oil rich. However, political pay-ups have been a major form of corruption. The pay was reaching as far as France where such funds have been allegedly handled by Elf Aquitaine in order to pay off officials in Gabon and Congo Brazaville.[11]

ETHIOPIA AND ERITREA

As earlier pointed out, these politicians gained from conflicts on ground. Take Ethiopia and Eritrea, for example. The conflicts between them allowed officials on both sides, particularly those who were responsible for arms procurement, to line their pockets with riches.[12]

TANZANIA

Tanzania is a case in point which shows how political powers in Africa will go for a project, not because of its efficiency and cost effectiveness, but because it helps make them rich.

The risk analysis carried out on a large power project which Tanzania was building was poorly done, thus favoring the investment from an Asian Company which therefore meant that instead of Tanzania using natural gas which it has in abundance, it will have to source foreign exchange to buy diesel.[13]

BENIN REPUBLIC

In Benin Republic, nearly every official customs officer has a "klebe"—southern Benin jargon for swindlers or bank note rippers. They are people who have either bought illegal goods from neighboring countries such as Nigeria, or act as middlemen to collect bribes from the importers on behalf of the customs men. It is reported that to clear an imported second-hand vehicle out of the Port of Cotonou, 17 separate bribes must be made, 10 of which are from the custom house alone. In some of these nations, it is hard to know when you are dealing with the government or private businesses of government officials.[14]

Gaining employment into many of these government bureaucracies is not based on merit but on who you know. It is as a matter of fact that political masters provide jobs for their henchmen, creating positions which never existed, i.e., political advisers, adviser to the political adviser, minister of transport, minister of state for transport, adviser on transport, adviser to the adviser on transport, etc.

ZIMBABWE

Corruption is pervasive in Zimbabwe. Reports carried out by the United Nations linked almost everything to the crisis of governance. Elections are thought to be unfree and unfair, yet voters are willing to wait 30 hours at the polling booths just to find their names and enough electoral ballot papers. In some places, it is alleged that 400,000 names had been added to the voter register *after* the official closure date.[15]

MOZAMBIQUE

In Mozambique, Carlos Cardoso, the journalist who decided to investigate the theft of 14 million U.S. dollars during the privatization of the Commercial Bank of Mozambique, was murdered. Antonio Siba Macuacua, the Central Bank official appointed Chairman of Austral Bank, was also murdered in August 2001 while investigating outstanding loans at the bank which led to its collapse in 2001.[16]

ZAMBIA

In Zambia, the bane of Chiluba's government was corruption. The current president, Libbi Nwanawasa, probably won the presidential ticket because of his stand and campaign to expose corruption and to demand honesty and integrity, although his comments evoked a cynical reaction in the press.[17]

SOUTH AFRICA

In South Africa, only weak provisions exist to compel political parties to disclose their financial interest, their donations, and the proceeds they have received. This allows the widest opportunities for people and businesses to influence government decision making. In March 2002, it was revealed that Taiwan gave 11 million U.S. dollars to Africa National Congress in 1994 in a bid to prevent Nelson Mandela's government from transferring the diplomatic recognition they gave to Taiwan to the People's Republic of China.[18]

NAMIBIA

In Namibia, a draft legislation to establish an independent and impartial anti-corruption commission was rejected by the upper house of Parliament and such responsibility passed on to a mere ombudsman's office whereas it is well-known that the ombudsman's office had not been able to fight corruption.[19]

NIGERIA

Nigeria is a catalog of penal legislation inspired by Islamic law. Killings, torture, and ill treatment by the police and vigilantes came to a point when state legislature established the vigilante group by law. The Anambra State government of Nigeria in 2003 established Anambra State Vigilante Service—a group officially endorsed by a law passed in 2000 by the House of Assembly. This group has its own detention centers, illegal detention centers in Ihala, Nnewi, Onitsha, Awka, and Akulubia. Political violence culminated in the death of the nation's Minister of Justice and Attorney General Bola Ige.

In addition to his death, the President of the Nigerian Bar Association for Anambra State, Barnabas Igueoa who publicly opposed the vigilante groups and openly criticised the government, was macheted to death by an armed group. Justice has not been brought for the people of Odi and Benwin who have seen violence and violation of human rights.

Peaceful protest is very difficult to carry out in many African nations. Take the case of the Delta State women in Nigeria who protested against the destruction of the environment by oil companies and ended up being beaten by the mobile police officers, Nigeria's paramilitary police.[20]

Cote D'Ivoire

In Cote D'Ivoire, more than a million people have been displaced because of the internal conflict which the bottom line most times can be traced to the selfish ends of the leaders.[21]

The spill-over of the Cote D'Ivoire crisis has been that Liberian refugees who themselves are victims of the problem in their nation are sometimes caught in the web of the conflict in Cote D'Ivoire and blamed for the violence there.

Liberia

Liberia has been ravaged because of the political differences of many war lords. The forces of former President Charles Taylor and those who opposed him resulted in Liberians being scattered all across West Africa. A former peaceful nation was torn apart with people in 11 of its 15 counties unreachable by humanitarian assistance until the war was over and gradual peace returned.[22]

KENYA

Mis-governance in East Africa gives the same picture. The government of Kenya is thought to have lost about 6 billion U.S. dollars through corruption in the six years between 1991 and 1997.[23]

Kenya is currently paying 4 U.S. dollars in debt servicing for every one U.S. dollar it receives in aid grants.[24] This has caused untold poverty for the people. Its neighbor, Uganda, lost about 500 million U.S. dollars to corruption within five years.[25]

Every attempt by those who want accountability and transparency has been met with frustration. In Kenya, a draft bill to create an anti-corruption authority published in May 2001 was widely expected to win support, but was suddenly pulled out by the government.[26]

The World Bank has repeatedly criticized Uganda for its lack of transparency, insider dealing, conflicts of interest, and corruption in some of the ways it has handled its business.[27]

Mis-governance has meant that people cannot work together because of simple cultural and language barriers, and old ethnic differences. The effect has been intertribal violence, often fermented by politicians whose interest it serves.

MAURITIUS

Corruption and mis-governance in the private and public sectors create intense unrest. In Mauritius for example, 2,000 people staged a demonstration in October 2001 following the revelation of the gravity of fraud and corruption in Air Mauritius.[28]

FAR-REACHING EFFECTS OF MIS-GOVERNANCE

The consequent effect of mis-governance has been that leaders have acted in their own selfish interests, in total disregard for the law, and without following due process. With such pillaging and devastation sweeping across the political horizon of Africa, and its subsequent effect on the people, it is not strange to hear some agitating for the return of the old political masters.

As often called for by human nature, many African nations and their nationals are now craving for the good old days. Self-doubt has set in because of the several decades of apparent failure. Independence Day celebrations in African nations only bring back memories of when electricity was in abundance and when the road network systems were working and maintained.

Today, of the 25 poorest countries in the world, 22 are in Africa. Fifty-four percent of Africa lives below the United Nations official poverty line. In David Landes's book, he indicates that Africa's debt is $313 billion; a continent where the total income is only $25 billion.[29]

Professor George B.L. Ayittey argues in his article, "The United Nations' Shameful Record in Africa," that 200 billion U.S. dollars were shipped from Africa to foreign banks in 1991 alone. This is equal to 90 percent of sub-Saharan Africa's Gross Domestic Product.[30]

In his book, *The Black Man's Burden*, Basil Davidson gives two cases. One is the now Democratic Republic of Congo, formerly known as Zaire, where Mobutu Sese Seko ruled in the capital and there were only a few other cities and localities where foreign companies worked. Prior to his ruling, when the country was under Belgium rule, the nation had 88,000 miles of usable road. But after Mobutu's takeover in 1960, by 1985 there were only 12,000 miles of usable roads and only 1,400 miles of that was paved.

The second case is the Benin Republic where, according to Mr. Davidson, after the end of each yield year, between 1960 and 1989, there was nothing to show for major investments in palm oil and peanuts. The farmers had sold it to a parallel market because they knew much of the money would go into the pocket of government officials.[31]

The populace can't find much of anything that gives them confidence in the current political elite, climate, or even the future of their nations. In his article, "Africa's Crisis of Governance," Tunde Obadina tells of the story in 1990 when a state governor in Imo State in South Eastern Nigeria explained to the public that his government was unable to solve the erosion problem the state had because it was cash-strapped. An old man in the audience stood up and said, "Since you and other Black leaders have tried your best but have not been able to improve the lives of us ordinary people, why don't we ask the whites to come back. When the white men ruled us, things were not this bad. Please ask them to come and save us."[32]

Pan-africanists will react to the old man's statements with disgust and probably offense; although another look at the current business horizon of Africa would give you the impression that there is a backdoor colonialism—the only difference this time is that the colonialism now takes and does not improve or invest.

The Way Out

For many people, the answer is to kill all kleptomaniacs and start all over. That has not worked, though, because killing the crooked leaders, particularly in the West African zone, has changed nothing. One set of corrupt people has replaced another.

Buying out corrupt leaders, warlords, and politicians as proposed by Professor George Ayitteh will not work either because it is like replacing evil with evil, especially since they know that the way to make money quickly is to be a corrupt leader and be bought out. Replacements will always be available.

At the end of this book, we will argue for transformation of the heart. Once that takes place, it is not difficult to be able to serve humanity and God, and to put wealth in its proper place.

> *Righteousness exalteth a nation: but sin is a reproach to any people* (Proverbs 14:34).

Blacks and Africans need to become politically savvy and no longer vote for people because they fit the g.o.d.—geography of their desire. Neither should people be brought back to power because of flimsy promises. Stakeholders, particularly foreign investors/stakeholders, are now demanding that anti-corruption bodies be created. That may go a long way, a body of laws being passed that would help to institute and control all forms of corruption. But the greatest change needed, is a change of heart.

It has been known in Africa that if a committee is set up to investigate a wrong, another committee might have to be set up to investigate the first.

In Kenya for example, the international financial institutions that were going to make funds available insisted that a Kenya Anti-corruption

Authority, an independent body that would by-pass the notorious corruption that hinders the investigative machinery of the Kenyan police, must be formed before they would release a loan of $220 million.[33]

Pursuant to this, the president of the World Bank, James Wolfensohn, had pressured President Moi at a meeting in July 1999 to appoint a team of technocrats who would bring reform.[34]

However, those conditions so far only deal with donations. It is very important that the politicians and leaders of the future experience the miracle of the mind. He who pays the piper dictates the tune. If Africa wants to truly be free, if the people truly want to regain their dignity, they cannot be mendicants.

In Sierra Leone, Britain's Minister of International Development at that time, Clare Short, made clear that the condition for the British government to continue to aid Sierra Leone was for the government itself to fight corruption.[35]

ENDNOTES

1. David S. Landes, *The Wealth and Poverty of Nation: Why Some are so Rich and Some so Poor* (London: W.W. Norton Company Ltd., 1998).

2. Ibid.

3. Tunde Obadina, "Africa's Crisis of Governance," www.freerepublic.com/forum/ a39b6d50d7dce.html.

4. Ibid.

5. Frantz Fanon, *The Wretched of the Earth* (New York: Grove Press, 1963).

6. www.amnesty.org/web/web.nsf/print/2af-index-eng, accessed October 2, 2003.

7. Gitau Warigi, *East and East Central Africa Global Corruption Report 2001*.

8. Uganda Inspectorate of Government, *National Integrity Survey*, 1998; Interview with inmates by Eric Ogussu Opollot.

9. United Nations' Integrated Regional Information News, July 26, 2001.

10. United Nations' Integrated Regional Information News, January 26, 2001.

11. *Agence France Presse*, January 17, 2001.

12. *News Eritrea*, March 4, 2001, and United Nations' Integrated Regional Information News, March 27, 2001.

13. *The East African Magazine*, Kenya, August 4, 2000, and *Mail & Guardian of South Africa*, April 28, 2000.

14. *Global Corruption Regional Reports for West Africa*, by Nassirou Bako Arifari, quoted in "La Corruption au Quotidien," *Politique Africaine* 83, October 2001, by G. Blondeau and J.P. Olivier Dussardon.

15. *Mail & Guardian of South Africa*, March 15, 2002; *Sunday Independent South Africa*, April 7, 2002; Commonwealth Secretariat, Commonwealth Observer Mission, Preliminary Statement, London, March 15, 2002; United Nations Economic Commission for Africa, *Economic Report on Africa, 2002*; Addis Ababa, *Planning Commission for Africa 2002*.

16. *Global Corruption Report 2003*, page 252; *South African Regional Report*.

17. *Times of Zambia*, 23 February 2002, *Financial Times of Britain,* January 8, 2002.

18. *Mail & Guardian of South Africa*, March 22, 2002.

19. *The Namibia*, February 13, 2003; Pheliat Matsheza and Constance Kunaka, "Anti-Corruption Mechanisms and Strategies in Southern Africa: (Harare – Human Rights Research and Documentation Trust of Southern Africa, 2000).

20. Amnesty International, publication 2003, www.amnestygroup.org, International Report, Amnesty International Index afr44/01/2002, Amnesty International Index afr44/023/2002.

21. www.amnesty.org/web/web.nsf/print/2af-index-eng.

22. Ibid.

23. Center for Governance and Development, policy brief, February 2001.

24. www.jubilee2000uk.org.

25. *New People's Newspaper*, Kenya, April 1, 2001.

26. *The Daily Nation*, Kenya, March 2, 2001.

27. *The East African*, Kenya, June 18, 2001.

28. *Pana Press*, October 30, 2001.

29. Landes, *The Wealth and Poverty of Nations*.

30. "The United Nations Shameful Record in Africa," *Wall Street Journal*, July 26, 1996.

31. Basil Davidson, *Black Man's Burden*.

32. Tunde Obadina, "Africa's Crisis of Governance."

33. United Nations Integrated Regional Information News, January 15, 2001.

34. *The East African* newspaper, Kenya, July 28, 1999.

35. Panafrican News Agency, *Panam*, February 28, 2002.

CHAPTER 16

Leadership Crisis

And Cush begat Nimrod: he began to be a mighty one in the earth. He was a mighty hunter before the Lord: wherefore it is said, Even as Nimrod the mighty hunter before the Lord. And the beginning of his kingdom was Babel, and Erech, and Accad, and Calneh, in the land of Shinar. Out of that land went forth Asshur, and builded Nineveh, and the city Rehoboth, and Calah, And Resen between Nineveh and Calah: the same is a great city (Genesis 10:8-12).

The princes of Zoan are become fools, the princes of Noph are deceived; they have also seduced Egypt, even they that are the stay of the tribes thereof (Isaiah 19:13).

The Bible account of Nimrod earlier quoted gives us insight on leadership as it was first made prominent in the post-diluvium era. Nimrod would go on to build Babylon, the Towers, and be the forerunner in the creation of the first greatest government that coherently and cohesively ruled the world.

While other civilizations can quote Napoleon Bonaparte, Alexander the Great, Augustus Caesar, and Julius Caesar, and modern nations quote Winston Churchill, Eisenhower, and De Gaulle, Black leadership, in general, left a vacuum.

WHO IS A LEADER?

Certainly a people would want a man before them. It can be a mentor whose life is transparent, wise, and foresighted. Leaders create a path for the coming generation to follow. Leaders put the needs of others above their own.

People need a leader they naturally desire to follow, pursue the vision he casts, and make the vision happen. True leadership, after all, is when people want to follow without coercion. A Chinese proverb says, "If you are a leader and no one wants to or is following you, you are on a long stroll by yourself."

One of the conformations which has influenced and shaped Blacks around the world is the leadership crisis within their community. From Africa to Papua New Guinea, from the Caribbean to the Aborigines of Australia and New Zealand, there is a crisis of leadership among the people of color.

In referring to the African leader in the book *Culture Matters*, Daniel Etounga-Manguelle whom we quoted earlier in another conformation said, "Take an African, give him a bit of power and he will likely become pompous, arrogant, intolerant and jealous of his prerogatives. Constantly on his guard and an enemy of competence (not a criterion for electing gods), he is ruthless until an importune decree designates his successor. He ends his career entirely devoted to the cult of mediocrity. (It is a well-known fact in our Republics that to end the career of a technocrat or a politician for good, you need only point out his excellence.)"[1]

African leaders see leadership as a dominant person, or else they must take charge or organize a coup d'état. In effect, it is hard to look into the continent and quote many African leaders who could be said to have transcended their tribal, cultural, and geo-political acceptance.

There certainly are a few and far between: the late Leopold Senghor of Senegal, Nelson Mandela of South Africa, Nnamdi Azikiwe of Nigeria,

Obafemi Awolowo of Nigeria, the late Kwame N'Krumah of Ghana, Julius Nyerere of Tanzania, and Jomo Kenyatta of Kenya.

Blacks in Diaspora face a similar challenge. While one might be able to quote Marcus Garvey and the legendary Martin Luther King, Jr. and a few others, there certainly is a lack of leadership within the Black community.

The absence of leaders causes challenges in any society.

Earl Ofari Hutchinson, in an article written for usafricaonline.com, classifies African Americans into five categories, therefore highlighting the challenges of who might be able to lead.[2]

1. Class division. There seems to be two Black Americas: one poor, the other prosperous; one desperate and angry, and the other complacent and comfortable.

2. The majority of African Americans have always voted for the Democrat candidates; however, there is a new emergence of Blacks who consider themselves Republican.

3. While most Blacks are thought to hold the same political views, which often are liberal and leaning toward the Democrat party, there is an emergence of a new breed of Black conservatives whose perspectives may not be publicly heard but certainly do not go along with the mass majority.

4. In Hutchinson's opinion the fourth challenge for a clear Black leader in the United States is the basis upon which such a person will claim his anointing. Since the death of Martin Luther King Jr., it has been very difficult to find one person who could transcend the various diversities within the community.

5. The fifth major dilemma involves the young Blacks. Mainstream Black leaders do not seem to have an answer for the new kids on the block. Their economic, social, political, and generational perspective is diverse from the older African Americans. Their musical and cultural appreciation, fashion, education, etc., is so completely diverse. Therefore a case for a central leader becomes hard and challenging to present.

Hutchinson's analysis, of course, does not rule out the fact that the search continues for role models and leaders who stand out and bring pride to their community.

In the words of the author of *No Apology Necessary, Just Respect*, "Black people seeking those who can shed light on their problems are often attracted to men who are like the flickering light of candles. Each of these modern 'wise men of Egypt' represents handles of flickering lights of hope."[3]

In the article "Black America's Leadership Vacuum" by Thomas Sowell, Sowell raises an even more critical issue. "Are the leaders presented to the African American community worth the name Leader?" The summary of his argument makes these men "free lunch" leaders.[4]

He argues that their leadership, as in the case of Jesse Jackson, is not about leading Black people but extracting all they can from White people, and above all maintaining themselves in the office or in position of visibility. To Sowell, the interest of these Black leaders is not the Black community itself, but a paranoid vision of the world where they see all economic disparities and other disparities as points of grievances and a reason to argue that Blacks need leaders to get the goodies from Whites and the government.

His argument maintains that the so-called Black leaders have made young people feel that whatever they have or do not have has been the fault of Whites, and the future lies in changing Whites, getting handouts, or being preferred when decisions are made.

Certainly from the various categories of Blacks we have seen it is difficult for this to continue to be the argument, knowing that some people are likely to refuse to go along with the opinion. Some are likely to avoid being played for suckers by a system which supports the myopic view of the said leaders.

The same argument is maintained by John H. McWhorter in an article titled, "Why Blacks Don't Need Leaders." He takes a critical look at the operation of Jesse Jackson and said, "If what Jackson does with all this ill gotten money is leadership, Black America doesn't need it. His CEF purportedly dedicates itself to the education of voters and the promotion of full participation in the electoral process." That "sounds worthy but a look at CEF finances reveal something far less noble. In 1999 out of the 10 million dollars CEF brought in for itself from various corporations almost 1.4 million dollars funded Jackson's travelling expenses while another 1.3 million bankrolled consultants. Some of the consulting reportedly included money to support the Reverend's mistress and his love child. The biggest chunk of CEF 1999 expenditures, more than 4 million, fueled the shakedown efforts themselves."[5]

As an outsider, it is very hard for me to be able to say how much Jesse Jackson has achieved for the Black community, but reading Mr. McWhorter's article seems to present a picture of a man-about-town, jack-of-all-trades, especially because Jesse Jackson appears in unusual settings that may not be the true measure of the leadership Blacks want, i.e., negotiating with Yasser Arafat to get American prisoners of war released, brokering peace in the case of the fight between two heavy weight boxers, and showing up wherever there is any race-based fracas. However, because most times success is measured by the degree of mentoring one has done in raising other leaders and the building of projects, the leadership of Jesse Jackson is not immediately obvious.

At the time of writing this book, Al Sharpton was running as a United States presidential candidate. He is the founder of the National Action Network. Much of his work has been within the Black community in New York City.

It is this kind of leadership vacuum that keeps the average African American holding on to the words of Martin Luther King, Jr., who dared to express the dream he had. It was a dream of unity, a dream of getting to the mountaintop, a dream of achievement; it was a dream of harmony, of serving God and growing in God's grace.

Martin Luther King's dream was of economic and political empowerment. He said that religion should be concerned about people and their economic conditions. The leadership who takes advantage of the people and preaches dependency has not empowered its people.

In the words of Booker T. Washington in his book *Up from Slavery*, Washington observed in the late 19th century, "among a large class of Blacks there seems to be a dependency upon the government for every conceivable thing. The members of this class had little ambition to create a position for themselves but wanted the federal officials to create one for them." No wonder he later said, "Cast down your buckets, and acquire skills and capitals, starting at the bottom instead of looking to government."[6]

The people we need are people like Reverend Eugene F. Rivers, III, who is busy training leaders and doing community projects in challenging areas of the United States.

In a letter of response to an opinion propounded by Peter Drucker, who argues that the future may not work for any people who are not ready to accept Western values and traditions, Professor Keith Orlando Hilton of the University of the Pacific in Stockton, California, presents eight characteristics of Black leadership found in one pattern or the other among them.

These patterns are:

1. Leaders who actively encourage Africans to follow, vote for, obey, endorse, etc., non-African (non Black) leaders.

2. A leadership profile which "encourages assimilation" with other groups that continue to discriminate against Africans.

3. African leadership which actively encourages Africans to accept "universal" bonds with others, with little emphasis on Africa or positive Africanisms that Africans continue to maintain.

4. A leadership profile which encourages the development of interim survival skills—interacting with those groups that continue to discriminate against Africans, but with an understanding of maintaining African values.

5. A leadership profile which focuses openly on maintaining African values culturally, scientifically, economically, linguistically, and spiritually. This is especially important within the business enterprise.

6. The longest running leadership profile, while maintaining African values, is based on communal separation from those groups that have historically and currently discriminated against Africans; and in the case of Africans outside Africa,

a "return to Africa" physically or spiritually being the ultimate goal.

7. The seventh profile focuses on Black leadership that is granted approval by non-Blacks to supervise non-Blacks.

8. African leaders assertively persuade Africans and others to accept and promote significant, positive Africanisms between all groups as a form of institution-building and as a balance to status quo ethnic/race relationships.[7]

ENDNOTES

1. Daniel Etounga-Manguelle, *Culture Matters*.

2. Earl Ofari Hutchinson, in an article, "Does Africa Need a Cultural Adjustment Program?" written for usafricaonline.com.

3. Reverend Earl Carter, *No Apology Necessary, Just Respect* (Orlando, FL, Creation House, 1997).

4. Thomas Sowell, "Black America's Leadership Vacuum," Creatus Syndicate Inc., 1998.

5. John H. McWhorter, "Why Blacks Don't Need Leaders," *City Journal*, Summer 2002; http://www.city-journal.org/html/12_3_why_blacks.html.

6. Booker T. Washington, *Up from Slavery* (New York: Dover Publications, 1995).

7. Keith Orlando Hilton, *African Leader: Patterns of Leadership* (University of the Pacific, Stockton, CA: I.C. Publications Ltd.).

CHAPTER 17

Sexploitation

At this junction, it might be necessary to define what conformation and pathologies are. The necessity stems from the fact that this particular subject in question is both a conformation and a pathology of the Black community.

Roget's New Millennium Thesaurus gives these synonyms of *conformation*: "anatomy, appearance, arrangement, articulation, cast, configuration, conformation, construction, contour, cut, design, die, embodiment, fashion, figure, formation, framework, mode, model, mold, outline, pattern, plan, profiles, scheme, silhouette, skeleton, structure, style, system."

Antonyms for *conformation* are, "non-compliant, non-conformity."

The word *embodiment* brings up "conformation" along with many other words such as "cast, embracement, form, formation, incarnation, inclusion, incorporation, integration, manifestation, matter, organization, personification,…structure, symbol, systematisation."

Again, if we look for synonyms of the word *organization*, the definition includes "arrangement," as well as "alignment, arrangement, assembly, standardization, structure, symmetry, unity, etc."

Since we have said conformation refers to what has shaped the destiny of Blacks, the meaning of the word *shape* in the same dictionary means "form" and with words synonyms such as, "appearance, architecture, aspect, build, cast, chasis, circumscription, configuration, pattern, profile, semblance, stamp, symmetry, etc."

In effect *conformation* means "anything which forms, shapes a people, a person, a thing into a fixed structure."

On the other hand, the *American Heritage Stedman's Medical Dictionary* defines *pathology* as the medical science concerned with all aspects of disease with an emphasis on the essential nature, causes and development of abnormal conditions, as well as with the structural and functional changes that result from disease processes.

Its second definition refers to the anatomical or functional manifestations of a disease.

Merriam Webster Medical Dictionary defines *pathology* as the anatomic and physiological deviation from the normal that constitute disease or characterise a particular disease.

In effect, pathology is something abnormal. *The Merriam Webster Medical Dictionary* says it is a deviation from propriety and from an assumed normal state of something nonliving or nonmaterial.

MYTHS AND GODS

The pathologies and conformations which today have evolved within the Black community, particularly in the Western Hemisphere, that is Blacks who have been displaced from Africa involuntarily, have their roots in how you were made to conform in the new world, how in effect, the pathology which followed once that conformation, shaping, and formation had taken place.

Prior to his arrival in the West as a slave, the man of color was one about whom legends and myths had preceded regarding his sexual orientations, genitalia, competence, and desires.

From ancient Mesopotamia and Egypt had gone forth theories that the darker the people, the more sexual they were. In the Museum of the

University of Pennsylvania, according to J.A. Rogers in his book *Sex and Race*, was to be found on a tablet 400 years old, which according to its translator Professor Steven H. Langdon, tells of Nimtu, the Black head Sumerian goddess who created "dark skinned creatures because of her aversion to blondes." The tablet also said, "That resulted in [a] quarrel among the gods."[1]

In ancient Egypt, sex was part of worship, sexual orgies accompanied the worship of the various gods of the land, and cohabitation was not considered wrong. If anything, J.A. Rogers in his book argues that, "The people of Egypt considered the darkest skin Egyptians to be more sexual." Egypt was to go as far as to have a god called "phallus," and the worship of the god phallus obviously included sexual orgies because the god itself was depicted with an eternally erect genital.

This phallus god was later carried to Greece and called "priapus." This desire for people of color in sex, and the looseness and promiscuity of Egypt spread all around the world, from antiquity to the days of exploration by men who traversed the whole of Africa.

J.A. Rogers argues that priapus, the same phallus god of the Greek metamorphosed into a saint in the early days of Christianity and was honorably placed in the church and invoked by sterile Christian women. He was at that point known as either Saint Foutin, Saint Rene, or Saint Guignole.[2]

These myths about Black sexuality crept into Europe and even the language of Europe. In those days, an English proverb said, "A Black man is a jewel in a fair woman's eye."[3]

Shakespeare expressed a similar point when he said, "Black men are pearls in beauteous ladies' eyes."[4]

That was to lay the foundation in the mind of Europeans that the Black sex is more virile than the White sex and therefore influenced the explorations of Europe toward the people of color, particularly in the matter of sex.

The myth spread as far as the Arabian lands so that Arabian night entertainments and stories had Black women as the very model of sexual competence.[5]

This kind of impression was passed on from one specialist to the other in Europe and formed the impression the whole of the world had about the man of color; because at this time, the seat of the dissemination of information was Europe.

Take the following for example: Sir Harry Johnston writes, "In both sexes, the development of the external sex organs is larger than in the European, white race, more considerable than among the mongoloid yellow races of Asia, America and the Pacific."[6]

Another British author, Sir Richard Button, was of the same opinion. He was quoted as having said, "I measured one man in Somali land who when quiescent, numbered nearly 6 inches. This is a characteristic of the negro race and of African animals e.g., the horse." To further buttress his case, he continues, "Whereas the pure Arab man and beast is below the average of Europe; one of the best proof by the body that the Egyptian is not an Asiatic but a negro partially white washed. Moreover these imposing parts do not increase proportionately during erection."[7]

Another author, Dr. Julian Lewis cites the content of Duckworth's book, *Morphology and Anthropology*, stating, "The relatively greater size of the penis in negroes has long been recognized…the vagina in the Black races is said to be longer than in women of white races."[8]

In *The Natural History of the Negro Race*, p.113 of 1837, J.J. Virey said, "Negresses displayed no common proficiency in the act for exciting the patients and gaining an unlimited power over individuals of the different sex. Their African blood carries them into the greatest excesses."[9]

Another author, R.W. Shufeldt in 1915, cites a doctor, William Lee Howard, said, "Nature has endowed him, the negro with several ethnic characteristics but which must be recognized as ineffaceable by man. The ethnic trades call for a large sexual area in the cortex of the negro brain which soon after puberty works night and day." This gives the impression that the Negro person thinks of nothing else.

Shufeldt himself said, "In the Negro of passions, emotions and ambitions are almost wholly subservient to the sexual instinct…negros are grossly animal and as a rule equipped far above the average man for unlawful indulgence."[10]

This kind of belief about the man of color spread all around the world, so when they were taken as slaves to Arabian lands, it was particularly to satisfy the sexual urge of the rich and famous, and although the drive for slaves to the Western world was motivated by economics, yet sexploitation played a major role and also damaged the psyche and total outlook of Blacks in the Diaspora.

The image painted by explorers of the "Lusty Moor" and used to justify the enslaving of Blacks, was carried further in dehumanizing, exploiting, and subjecting Blacks to sexual slavery. Slave owners argued that Blacks were subhumans, intellectually inferior, culturally stunted, morally underdeveloped, and having animal-like sexuality. While Whites were presented as advanced, cultured, and civilized, Blacks were barbaric in their view, and therefore deserved the sexual slavery along with the physical slavery they had suffered.

Black Slave Women

In some instances, even abolitionists like James Redpath, unbeknown to them, justified the actions of the slavers. James Redpath was quoted to have said that the slave women were, "gratified by the criminal advances of Saxons."[11]

Such opinions therefore rationalized sexual relations with the White men and the use of the women against their will by the slavers. The slavers considered the women to be property and therefore if they are of the same value as the cattle owned by the slave owner, they could not be deemed to have been raped. When the women attempted to maintain their dignity as human beings and resist the advances of their slave masters, offers of gifts and promises of reduced work in the farm or household was made in order to seduce the women into the relationship.

Thus the rape of such female slaves, "was probably the most common form of interracial sex."[12]

Frederick Douglass, an abolitionist who was also a former slave, differed from the opinion of James Redpath. In his view, he claimed that the slave women were at the mercy of the slave master, his sons, brothers, and friends. These slave women were used as sources of entertainment, concubines for anyone who visited. Remember, they were considered as property and could not be raped and had to be available for whatever the master's bid was.

While the women were used in this way, whichever of the Black men felt nature's call and slept with a White woman were castrated, hanged, or both.[13]

Beyond the master's house, the slaves were exploited in every possible way sexually. On the auction block where they were sold, they were made to be stripped or presented half naked for buyers to observe the health of their merchandise. The slaves were touched in ways that were sexually exploitative and sadistic.

Probably one of the most horrific cases of sexual slavery would be of a young Hottentot female named Sarah Baartman. Sarah was captured from Cape Town in her country of South Africa and was taken to Europe. She was displayed at various functions all over Europe, from Paris to Amsterdam, because she possessed large buttocks and deformed genitalia. The curious White people called her the "Hottentot Venus." Her body was explored because she was considered subhuman and less than her captors. At her death, she was put on display and even dissected. Sarah Baartman was reduced to a mere spectacle, something to be observed, laughed at, and to entertain the curiosity, lust, and perversion of her captors.[14]

BASTARDIZATION

With the view the West held of Blacks and the subsequent shipping of millions of them to become cheap, free farmhands of the Caribbean and Americas, they were seen as free and available to the White man. The women were not only used to work the farmlands and the slaver's house, they were also required to be as frequently pregnant as possible. This made the institution of slavery dependent on Black women to supply future slaves whom they did not have to travel across the Atlantic to capture or buy.

Slave women were encouraged to give birth as soon as possible. For every baby they had they were given gifts—a dress, a pig—and for every infant that survived, it meant that they either had their work reduced or did not have to work, probably on Saturdays. Men were also encouraged to become sexual studs. The more women they made pregnant the better.

Men were taken from one plantation to the other, particularly those who were considered to be very virile and able to easily get a woman pregnant.

The men never needed to take responsibility for the children. All they needed to do was to make a woman pregnant. This situation persisted for the whole period of slavery.

Imagine the situation where a man was taken from one plantation where he had raised a family—a wife and children—but was suddenly uprooted from his family and taken to another plantation where he was expected to have relations with another woman, and her daughter. He was moved from one plantation to another. That way, he never took responsibility for any child.

The women raised the children and so from slavery, bonding for children was only with the women. The picture is probably even worse in the United States of America. With a land that big, a man may have come home to find his wife and children had been taken to the auction block and sold. He was probably told to catch a glimpse of them on the street corner as they drove past with their new master. In a couple of weeks' time, a new wife was given him or rather, a new woman. He took no responsibility for the children of this new woman. If nature calls, he slept with her too and thus began the breaking down of the family unit among Blacks in slavery.

One must remember the point made previously that in the Western hemisphere, particularly in nations like Barbados, Jamaica, Antigua, Martinique, Surinam, Trinidad, Montserrat, as well as in the United States, there is a high rate of single-parent families among Blacks. A further observation will show us that most of these nations were once under imperial rule particularly of the United Kingdom, the Netherlands, and some other European nations.

The out-of-wedlock rate in all these nations has been very high. For example in Barbados, a 1990 census shows that only 30 percent of mothers between the ages of 15 and 49 were married. Seventy percent were not married, and of the unmarried mothers, only 3 percent were divorced. Others just had children outside of wedlock. Probably every Caribbean nation has an illegitimacy rate of between 35-72 percent.[15]

We must link all this together—here is a people who were taken against their will to a foreign land, and their sexuality had already been preconceived by their captors. Against their will, their sense of nuclear family was broken, their morality defiled, and their ethics shattered to pieces. Let us take into cognizance the fact that the Blacks of the Caribbean and the United States have a common experience of their ancestors having been taken against their will to slavery.

It would be absurd to argue that the preconception about Blacks, the devaluation of the family system among slaves, and the disrespect for the family unit by the slave owners could not have had a long-term effect on Black people. Remember again the scenario. The women took responsibility while the men were made to have no responsibility.

W.E.B. Dubois made the claim in 1908, in his book *The Negro American Family* that, "slavery weakened or destroyed family just as it impoverished and oppressed individuals."

The process of bastardization, whereby a child is denied his parent particularly the father figure, made a woman take responsibility for the home began a process of conformation thus generating a people who, for over 200 years, only knew in the majority homes a lone responsible parent, particularly the woman.

In addition to this, slavery had a damaging effect in the sense that the cruel system itself did not permit marriage and where slaves were married they could not vow and promise faithfulness to each other because they were essentially the slaver's property. They could not vote, could not sue; they could be auctioned at any moment, so could their children. If a man expressed dissatisfaction at the way the slave master spoke to his wife, he could be flogged in the presence of his family.

Distinguished historian Orlando Patterson argued that, "Slavery prevented a Black man from being either a father or a husband. He could offer to the mother and the children no security, no status, no name, no identity. That was why in effect both the children, the woman and their father took on the name of the slave master." It was bastardization at its core.

When finally some slaves overcame legal barriers, they were made to live apart from the mother and child because, in some cases, the man gained his freedom, but the woman was made to stay on the farm of the slave master to raise the children. This bastardization meant that although a man may be in love with a slave woman and took her as his wife, he could not promise a lifetime together because he might be sent to work at a distant location or sold to a new owner.

Having been used as a stud to produce more slaves, the African American man was not encouraged, told, or taught how to be a father; he was expected to be only a lover. When slavery was over, a lot of restrictions were imposed and to make ends meet he had to share crops with others who owned some small amount of land. Even that made him a marginal member of society who could barely make enough to survive. In order to claim dues from the government and make more money, most women in such circumstances claimed that they were either widows or not married at all. The man was not to live with them in order for their claim to be supported.

Take the American situation where people who came to live in the United States came of their own volition, and came with a background of a nuclear family system. The only people in this situation who did *not* come of their own volition and were not allowed to run a proper home for close to 250 years, was the African American.

A pathology had been formed as a result of being conformed or shaped by the mold created by the slave master. Children born in the same atmosphere were themselves slaves. They took on the nature, lifestyle, sociology, and culture of their parents, and obviously whatever culture they observed was the one the parents had to formulate within the confines of slavery.

It is supposed that a boy would grow up with close identification and bonding with his father, but with an absentee father and only the mother present, it made it very difficult. When a stud was supplied to sleep with the mother, his intention was not to raise anybody's child or even his, because his father never bonded or raised him to bond.

It is interesting to note that even in this 21st century, it isn't economic status that determines if a Black man in the Caribbean, Europe, or America is married. Affluent African-American men are no more likely to marry than their poorer counterparts.

So, for generations, for the Black in the Diaspora, the father has been absent. He gives the impression that fatherhood is unimportant, and when he was present, unrestricted by the slave master, infidelity and harsh punishment were the result. Boys were left with no choice but to bond with their mother.

One might think that with the number of years since slavery was abolished, things would have changed. However Janet Brown in her article titled, "Gender and Family in the Caribbean" argues that anthropological studies of the family in the Caribbean from 1940 through the 1960s has generally shown Black families to be dysfunctional compared to European and North American nuclear family models, and in effect that family life in the Caribbean is still largely consistent with what it was in the days of slavery.[16]

Another conformation which came out of bastardization was the mulatto melee. Mulattos are by-products of a sexual relationship between a White and a Black person. Many of the slave-era Blacks who were subsequently sold into prostitution were mulattos. This was because certain Whites did not want to sleep with Blacks. They therefore felt that the mulatto combined the supposed fiery passion of the Black person and the civilized culture of the White person. This in itself was a form of bastardization of the mixed race woman which meant that she was treated as an object for satisfying the sexual desire of White men.

The White men often met the Black women at what was known as "Quadroon Balls" which was really a genteel sex market. A similar thing was said to be organized even by White women who had such places where they met Black men based on the stories they had heard of Black men's passion. They subjected the Black men to an inspection of their genitalia, to see if he was the kind of size they had always heard of.

Black women were broken into categories:

- ❖ *The Mammy.* The big, fat Black woman who was seen as good enough to raise children, clean the house, and teach the children, but had to stay sexually unattractive.

- ❖ *The Mulatto.* The one who combined both natures. In the words of one writer: "The mythic woman who is always and only a mixture of Black and White."[17]

In White-authored fiction, this mulatto woman was presented as "The divided soul character who desires a white lover/husband and suffers a tragic fate as a result. Another is the happy person mulatto who denies her race and dies." They go on to say "The third is the exotic, restless and mysterious mulatto who is inherently a sexual character."[18]

Bastardization therefore meant that people became confused because they were divided on grounds of their color, they were used because of their sexuality, and they were berated because of whatever likenesses or dissimilarities they had.

THE BLACK JEZEBEL IMAGE

If any image has lasted in the minds of many Whites and today is being reinforced, whether innocently or foolishly by the MTV generation, it is the Black Jezebel image. That is the one who is considered more like the mulatto we previously referred to. This Jezebel or "tragic mulatto" is the one with thin lips, long straight hair, slender nose, thin figure, and fair complexion.[19]

Black women in the Diaspora were presented as Jezebels with insatiable sexual appetites. They were the breeders who brought forth the children that were needed for slave work, but now they are also considered as the insatiable woman. Deborah Gray White, a contemporary historian, writes, "Major periodicals carried articles detailing optimal conditions under which bonded women were known to reproduce and the merit of a particular breeder were often the topic of parlour or dinner table conversations." These slavers thought it nice to describe the women as Jezebel.

The writer continues, "The fact that something so personal and private became a matter of public discussion prompted one ex-slave to declare that, 'Women wasn't nothing but cattle.' Once reproduction became a topic of public conversation so did the slave woman's sexual activities."[20]

This portrayal of Black women as Jezebel whores continues today. In the 1950s it was common in American material culture to put the image of a Black woman on ashtrays, drinking glasses, fishing lures, postcards, sheet music, etc. These women would be naked or scantily dressed, expressing a lack of modesty or sexual restraint. This reinforced beliefs from generation to generation.

This image presented women who were Blacks either as pathetic because of their so-called sexual passions or exotic for those who desired them, giving the impression that Black women in general possess abhorrent physical, social, and cultural traits—their lips were exaggerated, their breasts were sagged, and they were waiting for a man who would take them.

An analysis of the Jezebel images used in the '50s in America reveals that Black female children were also sexually objectified. Black girls with the faces of preteenagers were drawn with adult-size buttocks, exposed or covered with skimpy blankets or towels or sometimes hiding behind a tree.

A postcard in circulation in the '50s shows a very young Black girl with the caption, "Oh I is not, it must be something I ate." This 8-year-old child was shown to have a protruding stomach to suggest pregnancy after a sexual experience.

So the image of Jezebel as a "Come-and-get-me woman" replaced the Mammy, the big, fat woman as portrayed in the film, "Gone With the Wind." Today, in small budget pornographic movies, books, and MTV-type music, the Black woman is depicted as a Jezebel. It is a perpetuation of what was begun in the days of slavery.

THE PATHOLOGY

We have defined pathology as a disease. After Black life had been shaped by the predators who took people as slaves and used them for their sexual satisfaction, the resultant effect is generations who have only known sex with almost no boundaries.

Take the United States, for example. A survey carried out by Motivational Educational Entertainment among Black teenagers shows that the views teenagers held about sex was quite alarming. The survey included responses from 2,000 teens living in households with an annual income of $25,000 or less. They saw sex simply as a necessary transaction required for social acceptance. They did not consider intimacy and informed decision making as being of any significance in their choice as to with whom and how they had sex. The same teenagers believed they had little status or value in their community, and when necessary they had used sex as a bargaining chip for acceptance, popularity, and if it becomes necessary, to stop people from teasing them or ostracizing them.[21]

In the United States, the national campaign to prevent teen pregnancy estimates that 35 percent of girls will have at least one pregnancy before they are 20 years of age, resulting in 850,000 pregnancies.[22]

In the United Kingdom for example, half of all Afro-Caribbean families are single-parent units. The sexuality of the Black man and woman in the Diaspora has thus been animalized. Their portrayal in films has only perpetually affirmed the same negative image.[23]

Black films or films which exploit Blacks have not helped dispel the Jezebel image of the Black woman. They have legitimized the belief on the street that Black females are as cheap as they come.[24]

The proliferation, 250 years on, would be difficult to argue that whatever happened to the Black family during slavery could not have influenced Black perception of marriage because after Blacks were conformed, shaped by the environment in which they found themselves, a pathology was also created. Men are not inclined to settle down at home and raise a family, young and old thinking sexual boundaries are unnecessary, and also probably believing that native Africans were sexually loose—a theory that is totally unfounded.

After all, probably 90 percent of slaves who were taken to the West were from the West coast of Africa, and most of the cultures of West Africa placed high value on sexual morality and virginity. For example, among the Yorubas of Nigeria, during courtship you could not visit a girl alone, there had to be someone afar off to observe. After a girl was established to be a virgin on the night of your wedding, you were expected to honor her family by paying a special virginity price.

In the West today, the Black family's structure is deviant from the nuclear biblical family. Sociology should not determine marriages relationships; the Bible should.

While on one hand, Blacks are known in a large sense to be committed to the Bible, the pathology of sexploitation is destroying the Black community.

The statistics in the Black community are not helping change the trend. The lack of restraint which certain people within the community have affirms impressions that are often stereotyped in White media. Imagine the "flying girl" in the Black-created and produced television show titled, "In Living Color."

Lisa Anderson notes in her book that these images reinforce stereotypes of Blacks. Anderson writes, "Black women have been associated with unrestrained sexuality, especially a destructive sexuality. The character is determined not only by action but also by attire...the Flying Girl, a regular feature on "In Living Color" on music videos becomes the Jezebel incarnate." Just as in the days of slavery, "There is no individuality or personality for she is simply a body to be exploited."[25]

This lack of sexual boundaries within the Black community, particularly in the Caribbean, is presented further by Janet Brown who argues, "The study showed that the meaning of fatherhood changes during a man's life cycle. Fatherhood frequently begins in casual relationships when a man is young. In the Caribbean, early male sexuality is even encouraged to provide testimony of virility." This again reinforces the image that has already been painted of the Black community. She continues, "Teenage pregnancy rates are high and the first child of a young mother usually remains with her in her mother's home. Even when the baby's father initially supports the young mother, most relationships do not last."[26]

Unless a people are bold enough to face the pathology in their community, the consequences could be dire.

THE CONSEQUENCE

For a nation like Jamaica, James Wilson, professor of public policy at Pepperdine University and professor emeritus at UCLA, observes that one-third of all mothers in Jamaica had no male partner at all, married or unmarried. In a nation as poor as Jamaica, he said, "This lack of a father must surely have produced grave childrearing problems."[27] He goes on to say, "Depending on where she lives, the Black West Indian girl is at risk. If she lives in the city or among itinerant cane cutters, her own mother is likely to be unmarried and so there is no father to protect her."

This stems from the fact that within the Jamaican society, there is migrant working, where people go from one island to the other and during that time, sexual relationships take place, children are born, and there is no father to connect to the child. At such places where migrant working takes place, the woman at times desires sex; West Indian boys can grant sex on their own terms, not wanting to be a father, and there is no father or brother to challenge them.

So the sexual exploitation of young girls therefore results in family disorganization and contributes to the statistics of dysfunctional homes. For example, after a girl has a child, her value in the eyes of men is reduced, and they often have little interest in raising somebody else's child. This puts the girl in a vicious circle.

The professor goes on to say that, "The economic conditions in Jamaica and probably other West Indian countries as well contribute to this pattern of casual sexual unions. Much work, such as cutting sugar cane is seasonal and some work requires migration to other islands." And so the woman is left with children again to raise, and no father in the house.

Janet Brown, a lecturer in the Caribbean Child Development Center of the University of West Indies whom we quoted earlier, said, "Apart from the minority upper classes, marriage rates throughout the Caribbean are usually low." She indicates that marriage, when it occurs, usually comes later, after children have been born.

This has resulted in the redefinition of family as indicated in a previous chapter with words like baby fatherism, baby motherism, and people unrelated being called uncles, aunties, etc.

Christien Barrow in her book *Children's Rights, Caribbean Realities*, concludes by saying, "Caribbean family life has been uniquely shaped by an African cultural and ideological heritage, by the experience of slavery and colonialism, multiracial and multi-cultural societies and by the socio-economic context of migration, unemployment and poverty."[28]

So consequentially, a man sleeps with a woman and births a child but doesn't care for the child. The relationship with the child is severed unless where in some cases there is a stepfather who immediately steps in to provide the appropriate care although in some situations, in the words of Janet Brown, "The incidence of sexual and other forms of child abuse by stepfathers, boyfriends or other male relatives and friends is high."

Please take note again that poverty really is not the most major factor in the dysfunctionality of homes. As James Wilson argues, "The Latinos who constitute a sizeable percentage of the United States of America—Mexicans, etc., are to a large extent poorer than African Americans but yet provide stronger homes and a lower divorce rate and lower out-of-wedlock births."

In the United Kingdom, the Bangladeshis would be considered to have a lower income than Blacks in the majority and yet have a stronger family unit, possibly because of their adherence to Islamic teaching and having come to Britain of their own volition unlike the majority of Caribbean Blacks who are by-products of enforced removal from Africa.

It seems inevitable to conclude with the U.S. Department of Health and Human Services whose statistics show that Black females between 13 and 19 years of age represent 66 percent of AIDS cases among young women in the United States.

Yet in spite of these dire consequences, some people still think that HIV/AIDS is a joke.

Not much has been said about Africa in this particular section because our intention is to show what impact slavery actually had in bastardizing. This does not mean there was no sexploitation in the African setting; where there are no moral boundaries, there are dire consequences.

The image of the Black stud and the female Jezebel creates phobias in the mind of other races. Joan Nagel[29] tells the story of when she was a girl in the sixth grade, her parents began to make arrangements to move to the suburbs because of the number of Black kids in her class. Their reason was simply because there were "too many Blacks." She shows in her book how decisions to retreat into ethnic ghettos and neighborhoods are often driven by the fear that proximity to Blacks would lead to interethnic or interracial sexual relationships.

Of course, certain phobias cannot be helped, but certain impressions cannot be erased. In the United Kingdom, ethnic minority children have more than a 50 percent chance of being raised in a single-parent home. That is dire because this affects everything concerning the child.

BREAKING THE CYCLE

In the West, following the end of slavery, during the era known as re-construction, the slaves combined the beautiful African heritage of the family with the exposure to Christianity and eagerly desired legitimizing their union; and this they did by holding mass marriage ceremonies and individual weddings.[30]

However today, the historical tradition of waiting for marriage, the tradition of mothers being nurturers, educators, and other rings of fire built around the home, have been belittled and forgotten. Instead it is being associated with "images of negativity and images of the big mammy."[31]

Correcting the damage of sexploitation would have to include starting young; getting teenagers and ministering the Word of God to them, letting them know what the principles of Scripture are on matters of sexual morality. In America, the Motivational Educational Entertainment Report, quoted earlier on this matter, stated that, "Teenagers need their parents and adult care givers more now than ever to pay attention to them, guide them and be clear about views and values about sex and pregnancy."

Talking of parents, in 1988-89, the University of West Indies Survey highlighted the need for increased involvement of fathers in the up-bringing of their children. According to Janet Brown, it is becoming obvious that to raise wholesome children, the absentee father situation must be reduced in homes.

In pursuance of answers to this problem, the Bible teaches that men should love their wives, wives should submit, and children should obey. When this triangle of love is broken, all kinds of issues become manifest.

Being a man and a father has strong personal meaning for a man when he takes that role seriously. It is part of what defines a man. Any male person can father a child, but it is part of maturity to be able to be there and take responsibility for children. In the natural sometimes, it seems like it slows the man down but this is why fathering a child must not be done lightly, but duly considering all the ramifications.

It is not enough to aspire to be a good father, it is important to see that it is more than an ideal and make it a reality. Absentee fatherism is the major reason for single-parent situations. In the United Kingdom for example, where half of all African Caribbean families are single-parent units, the knock-on effect is obvious. Since 1997, 77 percent of all 10 to 17 year olds accused of murder are African Caribbean youths.[32] Also, a higher proportion of African Caribbean kids are excluded from school than any other group.[33]

The report is even more grim particularly when performance of teenagers is examined in their General Certificate of Secondary Education exams (GCSE). In 2003 for example, 40 percent of 15-year-old Black girls had five or more A-C grades at GCSE, a requirement for post-secondary education. About 20 percent of Black Caribbean boys had the same kind of grades as compared to 56 percent of White girls and 46 percent of White boys.[34]

Black kids are often known to take on courses that do not have the chances for placing them in any leadership role or sitting on any board. Trevor Phillips, the Chairman of the Council for Racial Equality, said concerning Black, African Caribbean boys, who in the majority are often excluded from schools in the United Kingdom, "Black boys enter school on a par with everyone else, year by year, they fall behind. People say they don't know why but I would lay down £100 that you would find that the absence of the male role model at home is catastrophic."

Following the end of slavery and colonialism, the circumstances were not as they are today. The level of one-parent situations in homes was not as high. Janet Brown examined research recognizing that family patterns in the Caribbean had been largely consistent from the days of slavery and that they were in fact functional in terms of child and family survival under the condition of colonial and post-colonial poverty and oppression.

The story today is different because of laxity of divorce laws. On a global level, divorce is gradually being permitted for the simplest reasons, and this further weakens the sanctity of marriage. George Randall

Hekman, Michigan Family Forum's first executive officer, said, "It is easier to divorce my wife of twenty six years than to fire someone I hired one week ago. The person I hired has more legal clout...than my wife of twenty six years. That is wrong."[35]

The ones who suffer the most in a lot of cases of divorce where children are involved are the children. There is always a selfish someone who pursues the divorce process. The newsletter of the American Academy of Matrimonial Lawyers of Summer 1997 states, "Only acts of war and events of natural disasters are more harmful to a child's psyche than the divorce process." It goes on again to say, "No two people become divorced at the same time."

Sexploitation persists as we regenerate it in our community, having raised a generation of young men who see women as sexual objects. These young men, in turn, in the majority are by-products of homes where there is no father figure. Studies have shown that where fathers are present in Black families, regardless of the family's income, education, and neighborhood, the young boys' self-esteem rises. It may not necessarily be so for girls according to the report.

The experts say that what this means for boys is that the presence of a father helps to keep them away from participating in gangs, since a role model is available. Living in a fatherless family damages a boy's self-esteem while living with a father translates to the boy becoming a stronger child.[36]

In conclusion, the sanctity of marriage and the place of sex in the home cannot be underestimated. From a biblical point of view, the Scriptures do not only frown at any form of deviant sex, they encourage the expression of sexual relationship within a duly constituted marriage between a man and a woman who have vowed to share their lives.

> *Let marriage be held in honor (esteemed worthy, precious, of great price, and especially dear) in all things. And thus let the marriage bed be undefiled (kept undishonored); for God will judge and punish the unchaste [all guilty of sexual vice] and adulterous (Hebrews 13:4 AMP).*

The constant parading of nakedness in our community must stop in order for us to truly get the kind of transformation the Black community deserves and needs. Where there is a failure to recognize the need for that sanctity, the results are devastating.

A study published in *Criminology* by researchers from the University of Cincinnati and Northern Kentucky University shows that when wedding bells stop ringing in northern churches, sirens often started wailing because ambulances have to rush, carrying women, particularly African American women, who have been injured by live-in lovers. These intimate assaults are a continuation of the sexploitation.

Live-in lovers abound in African-American neighborhoods. Cohabiting without investing in marriage equals a relationship more conducive to assault. The vow of marriage is more than an exchange of paper; it is a contract, a commitment to each other. It also means that the two are in it not for sexploitation.[37]

ENDNOTES

1. J.A. Rogers, *Sex and Race*, Vol. 1 (New York: 1941), 293.

2. Ibid.

3. H.J. Bohn, *Handbook of Proverbs* (New York: 1867), 282.

4. J.A. Rogers, *Sex and Race*.

5. *Arabian Nights Entertainment*, Vol. 1, "Tale of the Ensorcelled Prince," (London: 1937), 6.

6. Sir Harry Johnston, *British Central Africa* (1898), 399.

7. J.A. Rogers, *Sex and Race*.

8. Dr. Julian Herman Lewis, *Biology of the Negro* (Chicago: University of Chicago Press, 1942), 77.

9. J.J. Virey, *The Natural History of the Negro Race* (D.J. Dowling, 1837), 113.

10. R.W. Shufeldt, *America's Greatest Problem: The Negro* (Philadelphia: 1915), 99-100.

11. James Redpath, *The Roving Editor: or, Talks with Slaves in the Southern States* (New York: Burdick, 1859), 141.

12. John D'Emilio and Estelle B. Freedman, *Intimate Matters: The Sexual History of Sexuality in America* (New York: Harper & Row, 1988), 102.

13. Winthrop D. Jordan, *White Over Black: American Attitude Toward The Negro, 1550-1812* (Baltimore: Penguin Books, 1969), 157.

14. Bell Hooks, *Black Looks: Race and Representation* (Toronto: Between the Lines, 1992), 62.

15. James Q. Wilson, *The Marriage Problem* (New York: Harper Collins Publishers, 2002).

16. Janet Brown, senior lecturer, Caribbean Child Development Center, University of the West Indies, Kingston, Jamaica.

17. Elisabeth Hadley Freydberg, Sapphire, Spitfires, Sluts and Super Bitches: Aframericans and Latinas in Contemporary American Film, *Black Women in America*, Kim Marivaz, (Sage Publication, 1995), 234.

18. Ibid.

19. K. Sue Jewell, *From Mammy to Miss America and Beyond, Cultural Images and the Shaping of U.S. Social Policy* (London: Routledge, 1993), 46.

20. Deborah Gray White, *Ar'n't I A Woman? Female Slaves in the Plantation South* (New York: W.W. Norton, 1999), 31.

21. "This Is My Reality: The Price of Sex: An Inside Look at Black Urban Youth Sexuality," MEE (Motivational Educational Entertainment) Productions; http://www.meeproductions.com.

22. http://www.teenpregnancy.org/resources/data/national.asp.

23. www.keepmedia.com/register.do?olild.

24. www.ferris.edu/news/jimcrow/jezebel.

25. Lisa M. Anderson, *Mammies No More: The Changing Image of Black Women on Stage and Screen* (New York: Rowman and Littlefield, 1997), 10.

26. Janet Brown.

27. James Q. Wilson, *The Marriage Problem*.

28. Christien Barrow, *Children's Rights, Caribbean Realities*, excerpt: Public Interest, Spring, 2002.

29. Joan Nagel, *Race, Ethnicity and Sexuality: Intimate Intersections, Forbidden Frontiers* (New York: Oxford University Press, 2003), 308.

30. John D'Emilio and Estelle B. Freedman, *Intimate Matters*.

31. Lisa M. Anderson, *Mammies no More*.

32. *Daily Telegraph*, October 10, 2004.

33. DFES Report, The Minority Ethnic Exclusion and the Race Relations Amendment Act 2000, Interim Summary, 2003.

34. DFES Minority Ethnic Attachment and Participation in Education and Training, 2003.

35. Michael McManus, *Detroit News*.

36. Divorce Reform Page, Sponsored by Americans For Divorce Reform, www.divorcereform@usa.net.

37. John Wooldredge and Amy Thistlethwaite, "Neighborhood Structure and Race Specific Rates of Intimate Assault," *Criminology,* 41 (2003), 393-418.

CHAPTER 18

Dependency Syndrome

One of the most devastating conformations of Black Africa is its dependency syndrome—that is, looking to other nations and people for practically everything to sustain and keep its society going.

Aid dependency in sub-Saharan Africa is very high. In 1980, it was 5 percent of the Gross Domestic Product (GDP) of 17 countries; in 1985, 10 percent, and 1994, 20 percent.[1]

This acute dependency on other continents can be read against a background of United Nations estimates. The population of Africa in 1984 was 537 million, more than twice what it was in 1960 when it was 257 million. The annual growth rate of Africa is 3 percent against 2 percent by the developing world. It was projected that by the year 2000, Africa would have become 877 million; life expectancy was put at a likely 47 years for males and 50 for females. For every active hundred persons in Africa, there were 92 non-active dependents.[2]

In 2003, at a meeting in Maputu, Mozambique, the Secretary-General of the United Nations, Kofi Annan, warned that the continent of Africa was increasingly getting too dependent on international aid. He said further that Africa would never know peace and prosperity if they do not take responsibility for solving their own problems.

What could have led Africa to this precarious position of having to be a beggar continent? It could be the fact that Africa's economy is, to a large extent, dependent on Europe—that is, having been a colonial dumping ground, the colonial masters prepared Africa only to plant, grow, or run industries that serve the wishes of their colonial masters.

Some over the years have advanced the dependency theory claiming that the economic development of the Western world rested on the expropriation of an economic surplus from Africa and other third world countries, and that these countries are perpetually dependent on the international community as the result of their reliance on export-orientated primary products.

Take the West African belt where the majority of land available for farming is dedicated primarily to cocoa. This is at the expense of growing enough food or developing other industries.

Some might also argue that Africa's excessive dependency on international aid is a combined exploitation of the Western world on one hand and the heads of these African states on the other. Colonialism and an attachment to the desires and dictates of the colonial master has meant that only things that are of favorable conditions to the colonial masters were planted and eventually exported.

The colonial masters pulled out; however, these societies were forced to specialize in the production of raw materials such as cocoa, cotton, rubber, and tea, which has been used to maintain the Western world. The prices are fixed in the West, the commodities exchange are in the West, and the farmers who grow the products have to make do with whatever price the Commodities Exchange in Europe and America affix.

In addition, multinational corporations dominate international trade and control the price of basic raw materials.

Farmers in Africa who venture into other products for export have also found that the West subsidizes its farmers to the detriment of African peasants; thus, the African continent is unable to compete on almost any ground with the West.

This has kept the economy of most African nations in a comatose state.

A United Nations study indicates that the progress of economic development in sub-Saharan Africa is "so slow that goals set in 2000 to have the number of extreme poor living on less than $2 a day by 2015 will take more than an additional 130 years to achieve."[3]

This precarious state has led to two things: Africa's pursuit of foreign aid, and Africa's pursuit of foreign loans. Sub-Saharan Africa, as of the year 2000, owed $230 billion. In addition, 33 of the region's 44 countries are designated HIPC (Heavily Indebted Poor Countries) by the World Bank. Most of the remaining nearly qualify for this ranking. These external debts have increased by 400 percent since 1980, excluding South Africa where the capita for the region is $365 while the Gross National Product (GNP) per capita is just $308. With an external debt of $203 billion in 1996, excluding South Africa, such monies represented 313 percent of the annual value of the total exports of Africa. Also, 20 percent of the income of sub-Saharan Africa is spent on debt servicing.

Sub-Saharan Africa spends more money on debt servicing than it does on health care services.[4, 5]

WHY DID AFRICA TURN TO FOREIGN AID?

Following its fight for independence from colonial masters, Africa suddenly like an orphan, found itself unprepared for the colossal heritage of a new system of government, democracy, etc.

With the promise of aid, it turned to the World Bank, the International Monetary Fund (IMF), and many other foreign aid organizations—Africa in general now has close to a 40-year history with the World Bank and IMF. One report claims that 63 out of 69 clients of the IMF and World Bank have become worse off economically rather than better off. Is it the same with Africa?

In order to fully appreciate what happened to Africa, we may have to take a view as to why these major funding organizations, the World Bank and IMF, exist.

A significant intergovernmental conference at the end of the Second World War took place in New Hampshire in the United States, which led to the formation of the IMF and the World Bank with the primary goal of rescuing European nations that were devastated by the war.

When these nations mostly recovered, the IMF and the World Bank had to be reengineered to suit other purposes. In its charter, the IMF was established, "To promote international monetary corporations" by maintaining fixed exchange rates among the currencies of different nations.[6]

To make this happen, the IMF was to make short-term loans to nations which had temporary balance of payment deficits—that is, the net import of the country exceeded its net exports. Each country had its own quota once it became a member of the IMF. The quota consisted of the capital each country had paid in which was usually 25 percent in gold and the rest in the member nation's currency. With its quota, a member nation could exchange a portion of its quota to buy another nation's currency, i.e., Nigeria could buy German Dutchmarks or Japanese Yen in order to get its economic house in order.

Though all nations' currencies were recognized, it was the currency of the Western nations that became the lion's share since it was considered "hard currency." In the majority the Western nations and the stronger economies never used their quota, therefore it was rolled over while the debtor governments drew and became indebted to the fund. A nation could draw beyond its regular quota by a stand-by agreement.

You might say it was a back door way for hard currency countries to loan soft currency countries funds. The loaned funds are continuously rolled over or re-loaned and not repaid to the donor country.[7]

In order to accommodate poorer countries, special facilities have been created by the IMF so that it can lend countries who could not pay for the shorter period required so that they had longer terms to pay with larger subsidies provided.[8]

Although the IMF had among its primary purpose to help to foster fixed exchange rate systems, this was impossible particularly with these poorer countries, thus leading to the devaluation of their currencies.[9]

Furthermore, instead of the high interest the commercial lender would have had the Lesser Developed Countries (LDC) pay, which was between 11 and 13 percent, the IMF asked for 6.6 percent in 1984.[10]

Until recently, when the IMF, World Bank, and most aid granting organizations began to tidy up and demand more transparency, good governance, etc., all sub-Saharan African nations jumped on the bandwagon for major and minor projects, and drew World Bank and IMF loans which magnified the economic problems of their nations.

This of course does not eliminate the fact that some foreign aid had been very helpful to handle crises in Africa especially the drought in 1983-84. In March 1984 the *United Nations Chronicle* volume 21 published an article titled "Crisis in Africa" in which it stated, "Drought has swept through the savannahs, deserts and coastlands of all parts of Africa. Food shortages are rampant throughout at least half of all African countries, affecting millions of Africans."[11] The devastating effect of this crisis was further stated as "Hundreds of thousand of cattle have died from lack of feed and epidemics of cattle plague. Rivers and streams have vanished and wells have dried up." The crisis was far-reaching. About 150 million people faced starvation in about 24 African countries including: Angola, Benin, Botswana, Cape Verdi, Central Africa Republic, Chad, Ethiopia, Gambia, Ghana, Guinea, Guinea-Bissau, Lesotho, Mali, Mauritania, Mozambique, Saotome & Principe, Senegal, Somalia, Swaziland, Togo, United Republic of Tanzania, Upper Volta, Zambia, and Zimbabwe.

The crisis was seen firsthand by then Secretary-General of the United Nations who campaigned for more aid for Africa. On January 19, 1984, the Food and Agriculture Organization of the United Nations (FAO) warned that the food supply outlook for Africa in 1984 remained serious. Remember again what kind of crops African peasants planted. This brought limitations as to how much they could achieve and even if they could afford fertilizers or not.

WHY IS AFRICA DEPENDENT ON AID?

We may start answering the question by looking at what Africa itself cannot control.

The Ecology

Satellite photos of Africa showed in 1983 that the line of vegetation as compared to the previous years had descended by 150-200 kilometres southward over the whole of the African Saharan region.[12]

Pestilence infestation of the Cassava belt, a rain of pest epidemic in West Africa, and extensive bush fires meant that in 1983 an FAO and World Food Program task force on Africa was set up to assess the affected countries and follow development. The affected countries ranged from Cape Verde to Somalia in the east, from Ethiopia in the north, and to Lesotho in the south. The same report indicated that for Africa as a whole, per capita food production had fallen throughout the 1970s. This devastation of the '80s only complicated matters because while production was falling, the population was increasing. The average person in Africa had considerably less access to food than ten years previously and the average dietary standards were below nutritional requirements.

So, with a poor ecological situation, governments that are ineffective and inefficient, and economies that were sustained by meager exports, a number of foreign aid groups came and initiated projects in Africa. This included FAO, IFAD, WFP, WFC (World Food Council), UNDP (United Nations Development Program), WHO (World Health Organization), UNICEF (United Nations Children Fund), ILO (International Labor Organization), and UNET (United Nations Environmental Program).

Africa's dependency syndrome was further complicated by the continuous civil wars that devastated most of the countries that make up the continent. This led to the formation of the International Conference on Assistance to Refugees in Africa (ICARA). It held its second meeting in 1984 in Geneva with the theme, "Time for Solution." The objective of the conference was to find solutions to refugee problems. The largest concentration at that time was in Sudan as well as Rwanda, Uganda, Democratic Republic of Congo, Burundi, United Republic of Tanzania, and Southern Africa. The refugees at that time poured into various nations—Angola, Botswana, Burundi, Ethiopia, Kenya, Lesotho, Rwanda, Somalia, Sudan, Swaziland, Uganda, United Republic of Tanzania, Democratic Republic of Congo, and Zambia—trying to escape the civil war violence in their homeland.

The aim of the organization was to create structures that would help manage the refugee problem by providing grain storages, poultry farms, and beekeeping centers. Foreign aid continued to pour into Africa and in a lot of cases sustained the government to the extent that certain African governments could not survive without foreign aid.

THE EFFECTS OF FOREIGN AID

The flow of aid to the African nations, particularly by the World Bank, IMF, or European loans, has festered corruption. Large sums were loaned to the government but did not end up facilitating any practical help to the people; rather the funds sat in private bank accounts all over Europe.

Countries who had poor monetary systems, policies, and governance also mismanaged the funds made available to them. The World Bank report of 1998 titled "Assessing Aid" analyzed the relationship between aid and growth in countries with good monetary, fiscal, and trade policies. They found a strong positive association indicating that aid is indeed effective where economic policies are supportive of growth.

Foreign aid meant that the people took their eyes off exporting their own goods and instead depended heavily on the help they got from abroad. This is described as the "Dutch disease"—in spite of discovering large mineral deposits of good foreign exchange earners, the country in question depends more on foreign aid.

Government agencies became weak as foreign aid flowed in. The governments in Africa were turning to foreign government officials and organizations to fix their problems.

There is no doubt that IMF loans to these LDC governments made possible the massive monetary inflation which has occurred in these countries. Almost in every African country the currency has been so terribly devalued that you need thousands of almost worthless bank notes to get the equivalent of a British pound or U.S. dollar.

The IMF may have inadvertently allowed governments to expropriate the wealth of their citizens, and become extraordinarily powerful. Many African nations have taken several temporary loans back to back and plunged their nations farther and farther into decades of indebtedness.

This dependency syndrome has had a knock-on effect on practically every facet of the African person's life. The situation is complicated by the fact that the African governments who drew these loans never achieved their objectives; they did not increase the material well-being of their people, neither were the large sums of money drawn put in what can be called an investment or the perpetuation of wealth.

There is no accountability; the foreign aid that came to them may have been well intentioned, but the methodology was ill-designed. Vast sums were wasted or diverted into illegitimate channels; key things that could have immediately sustained the people and lifted their standard of living as in agriculture or industrialization received little to no capitalization.

Maybe many of these bodies should not have given aid to these corrupt governments as in the words of Peter Duigan whose article, "To Really Help Africa, Promote Trade, Not Aid" argues, "Don't give aid to governments but only limited sums to volunteer groups and private enterprise."[13]

Peter Duigan reports that the IMF, World Bank, and USAID gave billions of dollars to 36 African nations with conditions that were seldom enforced, and only Ghana and Tanzania had partial success. He cited Nigeria as an example among nations with corrupt and inefficient rulers.

Another article, "Does Foreign Aid Add Up?"[14] by William Easterly, Senior Advisor of the Development Research Group at the World Bank, cites Tanzania and how the World Bank financed its Morogoro shoe factory project costing $14 million, but it has never produced at more than 4 percent of its peak capacity; and a notorious case of Nigeria drawing $5 billion from the World Bank for its Ajaokuta steel factory which produces very little steel but has generated abundant pay-ups. According to Mr. Easterly, around $2 billion of the $5 billion was given to former Nigerian officials as kickbacks.

World Bank socio-economist Lant Pritchett cites that much of what governments officially record as investment, fails in reality to create any useful production. There has been as little as 8 percent official measured growth of machinery and equipment in Africa. The donor countries and organizations are now tired.

Eveline Herfkens, former Minister for Development Cooperation for The Netherlands, presented a paper to the Economic Commission of Africa titled, "The Challenges of Financing Development in Africa." In it she argues that, "There is increasing aid fatigue in my country and it is hard to persuade tax payers to invest in Africa while Africans seem to have no confidence in their own economies." She cited the fact that The Netherlands had aid programs in about 80 countries but was now planning to reduce it to 20 countries which will have full-fledged, longterm bilateral programs.

Aid-giving countries are beginning to be concerned about the degree of mis-governance and lack of transparency. Ms. Herfkens said that going forward, her country had acknowledged its failure of the past when it imposed counterpart and recurrent costs on the budget of the countries it was giving aid to without talking to them first to find out if it was a good idea to start such projects in hand.[15]

The Way Out

Eveline Herfkens did not mince words when she argued that if countries are to avoid dependency they have to earn foreign exchange. In order to do this, Africa should take a long-term view. If it wants to be tied to the cash crops that have taken a greater percentage of its land, it must also address the issue of capital flight. Aid givers are aware that a good number of Africans will first buy a home in Paris or London before they consider investing in their country.

Good governance and reformation of government must be a high priority of a country that will bring about change and require less aid. Sub-Saharan Africa has an example possibly in South Africa which seems to have a strong commitment to good governance, and with its resources it has built an oasis in the desert. If it has happened in South Africa, it certainly could in all of Black Africa.

Ms. Herfkens' paper also presented the fact that the new criterion for giving aid to some countries is the degree of poverty, good policies, and good governance. However, it is obvious that where there are good policies, the degree of poverty will begin to be eradicated because a good policy addresses every facet of the lives of the populace.[16]

What is a good government? It is a government which involves stakeholders, and ethical and responsible officials responsible for development, finance, and planning. A good government creates a civil society—citing the Copenhagen Social Summit, Eveline Herfkens again gives us insight on some of the ten points agreed on at the Summit. She said, "Everybody now agrees on the need for pro-poor growth, investing in people through education and health, the importance of gender, the importance of development being environmentally sustainable."

The basis of this chapter is to argue that dependency on foreign aid is a bad conformation for Africans because it shapes their destiny, values, lifestyle, vision, and sense of dignity. People who have food dropped for them and who look to another race for their sustenance will perpetually believe that they are lesser and that God is more favorable to the man whose color is different from theirs, from whom all blessings flow.

The leaders of Egypt have become truly brutish, but the time has come to break free from this cycle of defeat and dependency on other people.

Urban migration is a major African problem. It will be a step forward, a major one, if Africa seeks to combine macroeconomic reforms with microeconomic enterprise programs that involve people at the grassroots. It is also the author's opinion that Africa needs to borrow from the West, methods of establishing a decentralized government system such as the Department of Transport, for example, could be in Swansea, Wales, under the United Kingdom while the Department of Health and Social Security may have its office in Nottingham. This in effect creates jobs for people in each area and people are then able to develop their immediate environment.

Rather, in a lot of African situations, jobs have been centralized to the major cities thus creating a devaluation of other parts of the environment. Ibrahim Elbadawi, as part of his material presented to the United Nations Economic Commission for Africa, said, "Aid dependency should be reduced, not because international development community believes it will eventually happen but because such dependence on foreign aid could substantially impair Africa's export competitiveness."

Much of Africa's agrarian society is post-colonial and driven by the exact products from farms that the colonial masters wanted. Africa should now be examining what products would earn it more foreign exchange than the one which it has no control over.

In addition, every form of importation should be re-examined. Some parts of Africa export oil but have no oil-chemical plants to extract plastics which have become the major replacement for metals and rubber and are used in almost every industry.[17]

Certainly the receiving of foreign aid has been paid for dearly by the common citizen in order to forestall corruption and encourage Africa toward a better future. Donor organizations must have a checklist to ensure that the government, organization, or agency handling aid in excess of a million dollars is registered and accredited by Transparency International. They must ensure that they have signed an Integrity Pact and pledge to refrain from corruption.

The World Bank, as a major player in the continent, must acknowledge the political and organizational dynamics that make corruption control difficult and therefore put within its system safeguards which make it difficult for any nation or despotic government to misuse the funds that are meant for development in the various nations. These countries must show reform and prove that they have effective methods for investigating and prosecuting financial corruption without using it as a tool for victimization or political witch-hunts.

ADDITIONAL REFERENCES

Bauer, P. 1972. *Dissent on Development.* Cambridge, MA: Harvard University Press.

Brautigam, D. 1996. "State Capacity and Effective Governance," B. Ndulu and N. van de Walle, eds., *Agenda for Africa's Economic Renewal,* Washington DC: Overseas Development Council.

Devarajan, S., A.S. Rajkumar, and V. Swaroop. 1998. "What Does Aid to Africa Finance?" *African Economic Research Consortium and Overseas Development Council Projection Managing a Smooth Transition from Aid Dependence in Africa,* Washington DC, October.

Dollar, D., et al. 1998. *Assessing Aid.* Washington DC: World Bank.

Elbadawi, I. 1999. "External Aid: Help or Hindrance to Export Orientation in Africa," *Financing Africa's Development: Issues on Aid Effectiveness,* Background Papers, Joint Conference of Ministers, April, Addis Ababa: Economic Commission for Africa.

Global Coalition for Africa. 1997-1998. *African Social and Economic Trends. Annual Report*, Washington DC: Global Coalition for Africa.

Lancaster, C. 1999. *Managing a Smooth Transition from Aid Dependence in Africa*, Washington DC: Overseas Development Council, forthcoming.

Younger, S.D. 1991. *Aid and the Dutch Disease: Macroeconomic Management When Everybody Loves You.*

ENDNOTES

1. Global Coalition for Africa, *African Social and Economic Trends*, Annual Report, (Washington DC: 1996).

2. "The Crisis in Africa," *UN Chronicle* Vol. 21, March 1984, United Nations Publications, 2002, Game Group.

3. www.expotimes.net/backissues/august2003/august3.html.

4. "The Debts of Corruption," www.jubilee2000uk.org/features/odious.

5. "Why South Africa should say no to IMF policies," www.twnside.org.sg/south/twn/title/afri/cn.html.

6. Article 1 of the original "Articles of Agreement," cited in Margaret Garritsen De Vries in her article, "The IMF in a changing world, 1945-1985," (Washington, The International Monetary Fund 1986), 14.

7. Henry Hazlitt, *From Bretton Woods to World Inflation: A study of causes and consequences* (Chicago: Regnery Gateway, 1984).

8. Richard Goode, Economic Assistance to Developing Countries through the IMF, (Washington, The Brookings Institution, 1985), 5-10.

9. Roland Vaubel, The Moral Hazard of IMF Lending, in Alan H. Meltzer, "International Lending and the IMF: a conference in memory of Wilson Schmidt," (Washington, The Heritage Foundation, 1983), 69-70.

10. Goode, p.15-16

11. Crisis in Africa, *UN Chronicle* Vol. 21.

12. Ibid.

13. Peter Duigan, "To really help Africa, promote trade, not aid," *Insight on the News*, Vol. 10, Issue 46, (November 14, 1994).

14. William Easterly, "Does foreign aid add up?" *Foreign Policy*, July 2001, Canadian Diamond for International Peace.

15. Eveline Herfkens, ECA Joint Conference of Ministers of Finance and Planning, Addis Ababa, May 6, 1999, Netherlands Minister for Development Cooperation.

16. Ibid.

17. The external aid: Help or hindrance to export orientation in Africa," *Journal of African Economies*, Vol. 8, Issue 4, 1999, 578.

CHAPTER 19

Colonial Heritage

Donald Rothchild notes, "No single factor proved to be more significant in shaping the configuration of group interactions than in territories experienced with colonial rule."[1]

By 1935, colonialism had been fastened on Africa like a steel crate and like shackles upon a lifetime prisoner. It seemed as if it was going to be there forever. This system of government which combined the absolute powers of the colonialists with their arbitrary way of changing the rule for the governance of the regions in which they were was to forever shape the lives of most Black people in the various nations of Africa.

Virtually every nation known to be part of Africa today had a colonial master except for Liberia and Ethiopia. The latter only had a brief brush with occupation by Italy until they resisted; Liberia, on the other hand, was the playing field of American conglomerates like the Firestone Corporation. Colonialism in Africa was different from that in America or Europe.

For Africa, the colonial master redistributed land and people and determined if half a village would be under French rule while the other half was under English rule. Colonial masters, for example, drew the boundary lines between Nigeria and Benin Republic, thus dividing clans and ethnic groups purely between themselves—the French and the English. The colonial master attended to the supply of labor, most times forced labor or underpaid. The colonial masters destroyed the traditional fabric in certain places, and imposed unlegislated taxes.

Some look at Africa and say the gain of colonialism was education. However, African historian Claude Ake argues differently as to the education of the people. He writes, "Colonialists went into the business of education to ensure that workers could do the jobs they were required to perform and would remain steadfast in the performance of their own tedious and disagreeable tasks."[2]

Education was only for the sake of carrying out the duties designated by colonial masters. The roads, ports, and rail tracks were built only to convey goods from the hinterland, particularly where the colonial master has chosen as being good for certain crops that were useful for Europe.

Subsequently, the roadways created brought these goods to the port for onward exportation to Europe. Thus colonies were made to produce what Europe needed or processed for export. Individual nations were chosen for certain crops. Claude Ake gives the example of Ghana which was chosen to produce cocoa.

From 1865 Ghana had cocoa, a seed originating in Brazil, as its major export. Ghana became a mono-agricultural economy. By 1939 cocoa accounted for 80 percent of the value of Ghana's exports.

Kenya is another case. British colonial masters chose Kenya as good ground for planting coffee. Claude Ake said, "The colonialists controlled the planting of the coffee seed and forbade everyone else from planting or possessing it. In Kenya, the coffee plantation registration ordinance of 1918 forbade the growing of coffee—the country's most profitable commodity, by Africans."

He points out, "The purpose was to make Africans available for wage labor by keeping them from becoming independent producers as well as to prevent them from stealing coffee from European farms."

Kenyans were not only denied the right to possess or plant coffee beans, but a market of native produce ordinance was introduced in 1935 that restricted the wholesale of coffee to Europeans.

Kenya's White settlers made huge profits, as they used cheap labor. The highlands were declared to be British Crown Lands. Lands were handed over to British aristocrats like Lord Delamere who purchased 100,000 acres of land for a mere penny per acre. Lord Francis Scott got 350,000 acres. The East African Estates got 350,000 while the East African Syndicate got 100,000. These plantations made huge profits as they used cheap labor provided by the indigenes who were already restricted from owning their own farms.[3]

With reference to land, in 1926 the Firestone Company acquired one million acres of land from Liberia at a cost of only six cents per acre.

The colonial masters restricted and even prevented the planting of cash crops so that the labor and skill of the farmers would be available to the White settlers.

One British settler in Kenya, Colonel Grogan, said of the Kikuyu's, "We have stolen his land. Now we must steal his limbs. Compulsory labor is the corollary of our occupation of the country."

This confirms the argument of Guyanese historian Walter Rodney who said that over a period of 500 years, starting in the 15th century, the two continents went into some kind of relationship. In the end "Africa helped to develop Western Europe in the same proportion as Western Europe helped to under-develop Africa." Rodney believes that the most painful part is that "so much of Africa's wealth goes to non-Africans who reside for the most part outside of the continent."[4]

Professor Ali Mazrui said, "the labor of Africa's sons and daughters was what the West needed for its industrial take off. The slave ship helped to export millions of Africans to the Americas to help in the agrarian revolution in the Americas and in the industrial revolution in Europe simultaneously."[5]

In another setting the professor also argues that "Africa's minerals became the next major contributor not only to Western technology. Uranium from the Belgian Congo (Democratic Republic of Congo) was part of the original Manhattan project which produced the first atomic bombs." The professor argues further that other minerals like cobalt became indispensable for jet engines. There were times when Africa had 90 percent of the world's known reserve of cobalt, 80 percent of the global reserve of chrome, and a hefty share of the platinum and industrial diamonds.

Africa's impact on the West's technological history in this phase was heavily based on Africa's industrial minerals. The extractive imperative made Africa's minerals fuel for world economy. Africa's minerals enriched other economies rather than Africa's own.[6]

America's largest multinational, General Electric, carried an advertisement in *Modern Government* magazine in March/April 1962 stating "from the heart of Africa to the hearths of the world's steel mills comes ore for stronger steel, better steel—steel for buildings, machinery, and more steel rails."[7]

Professor Richard Drayton who teaches European history at Cambridge University states in *The Guardian* newspaper of the United Kingdom that, "Profits from slave trading and from sugar, coffee, cotton and tobacco are only a small part of the story."

He states further that, "what mattered was how the pull and push from these industries transformed Western Europe's economies. English banking, insurance, shipbuilding, wool and cotton manufacture, copper, and iron smelting, and the cities of Bristol, Liverpool, and Glasgow multiplied in response to the direct and indirect stimulus of the slave plantations."

Such arbitrary expressions of absolute power and control of a people shaping their topography, demography, and lifestyle to satisfy the colonial masters had a major impact on the lives and mentality of slaves—to live an indentured life of inferiority.

What is the legacy left which may have conformed or shaped these people? Tessilimi Bakary puts it clearly, "Such an externally regulated hegemony system concentrated bureaucratic military education, commercial, industrial communications and other modern sector activities within a small privileged, white-led urban core. The different rates of contact with western technology as well as administrative practices and values affected the various people and regions of a territory in distinct ways, resulting over time in cleavages between an expanding urban based core and a relatively disadvantaged periphery."[8]

So against a people's wish, others invade their land, take over, suppress them, determine their life, lifestyle, livestock, where they live, how much they earn, etc. British philosopher and economist John Stuart Mill noted that, "No single member group should have the power to override the expectation of another group. If a group has such power, it will dictate its will to all others."[9] This was what colonial masters came to do and this was the method of divide and rule they also left.

Imagine the French government official who cunningly asked African males to join the army, later to be used for forced labor. This process was called "prestation."

COLONIALISM AFFECTED BLACKS

Colonialism created a whole system of divide and rule which worked effectively and comfortably for the colonial masters but was to leave an indelible mark on the ethnic landscape of Africa and create challenges of national harmony. Donald Rothchild argues that for administrative convenience the colonialists promoted a sense of unity among a number of fluid clans and ethnic groups who were hitherto disunited by different issues.

The Karamogong of Uganda, the Sukuma of Tanzania, the Yoruba and the Igbo of Nigeria, and the Kikuyu of Kenya fall in this category. Peanut producers in Senegal, for example, were not easy to control until the Marabouts, or religious leaders, were used by the colonial masters to mediate on state and societal matters.

During the colonial era, the Africans themselves did not benefit from the resources of their continent because it was mostly exported. The roads, health care, and infrastructure were only built in the areas where the raw materials existed. This is the reason why, at the end of colonialism, there was such struggle and conflict for social emancipation and access to the kind of resources that were only available to the elite of colonialism.

The British government accumulated all contributions made by the colonies into its sterling reserve as a gift to the British Treasury. By the 1950s a tiny country like Sierra Leone had contributed £60,000,000 to the sterling reserve, while Ghana contributed £210,000,000 from its sale of cocoa and gold.

Between 1940 and 1965, Firestone Company had taken rubber worth $160,000,000 out of Liberia and only returned $8,000,000 back to the government of Liberia.

At independence, most African nations had developed the appetite for foreign exchange, the by-product of exploitation. The continent increased its dependence on imported capital and consumer goods and services. This meant that the domestic economy was not developed. Everything had to be imported, and only the crops or the services which benefited the former colonial masters were continued for a long period. In effect, the desire for social emancipation and access to resources engendered struggle. This struggle was not quelled by the state of the economy but rather increased the tension as the nations depended on imported goods without any desire themselves to be technologically and industrially emancipated.

In many of the African nations, the result was a breakdown of law and order, with internal strife and civil war resulting in armed conflicts. Sunday Dare, a Nigerian journalist, wrote the following in an article titled, "African Globalisation," "In a recent study of armed conflicts around the world, the University of Maryland's Center for International Development and Conflict Management found that thirty-three countries were at high risk from instability and of these, twenty were in Africa."

Many of the problems of Africa today can be directly traced to slavery and colonialism. Africa lost freedom and resources while countries like Britain received many benefits of colonialism. John F. Conway, lecturer in political sociology at the University of Regina, writes in an article titled, "Benefiting from Crimes against Humanity"[10] that "The industrial revolution happened first in Great Britain largely due to its colonial empire and the slave trade and the speed with which this modernisation occurred had much to do with slavery and colonialism."

Someone might want to challenge John Conway's argument, but he presses further by saying, "Colonialism provided Britain and the other European nations with not only the source of slaves and raw material but access to a protected and enforced world market for manufactured goods."

Arthur Creech-Jones and Oliver Lyttleton, major figures in British colonial policy, said that in the early 1950s Britain was living on the dollar earnings of the colonies.

The by-product for the Africans was that cultures and economies were disrupted, and groups of people were disenfranchised—their lifestyles irreparably scarred. Colonialism had slight advantage for various nations, as some of its sons and daughters were exposed to modern and Western education reversing some of the negative legacy.

The UN declared two decades dedicated to "the eradication of colonization" and claimed that colonialism in all its forms is incompatible with the UN charter and therefore causes a serious threat to international peace and security. It is almost too late for Africa, and this declaration possibly only affects the various territories, particularly small Caribbean islands and the new worlds that are still territories falling under the rulership of nations like Britain, France, the United States, the Netherlands, etc.

To bring a change, Africa herself needs to wake up to her responsibility. Abiodun Ogundipe indicates that two of Africa's strongest economies, Nigeria and South Africa, are awakening to this responsibility and challenging everyone to restructure and strengthen in various economies.[11]

EDUCATION

Africa and Africans need to rethink their educational systems. They had been set up to serve the colonial master's need; in some cases, a process and method of divide and rule, a method of educating one ethnic group against the other still exists. This has created advantages and disadvantages.

The colonial systems have been adopted into modern educational policies so that in a country like Nigeria, once the quota allocated to an ethnic group has been satisfied in regard to university admission, the student's chances are gone until another year. Entrance, therefore, into a university is not only based on merit but on which ethnic group the student belongs to.

Fay Chung of Zimbabwe has served as her country's Minister of State for National Affairs, Job Creation and Cooperatives, and as Minister of Education. She now works for UNICEF in New York and says, "More than any other continent Africa needs to rethink its education system. All too often the systems of education inherited from colonialism have been preserved in Africa more or less intact generally on the grounds of maintaining standards."

Ms. Chung elucidates by saying a very small number of elite enjoy exactly the same kind of education as they would have in Europe, while the vast majority of students are deprived of any form of modern education whatsoever. This situation still holds true in most of Africa, particularly since that is the method found in European nations.

DEVELOPMENT

Another detriment of colonialism is Africa's policy of development which is based entirely on structural adjustments as required by the IMF, World Bank, and various foreign aid contributors, not on the basis of what becomes their country's immediate need or what could enhance, develop, and help the progress of Africa.

Though colonialism may have ended, systems and structures of the past have been retained without question. Out-of-the-box thinking is very limited or non-existent. Every negative ramification of African society needs to be extensively studied and understood so that policies which do not enhance progress and lead to further damage of the man of color's psyche, will be corrected and overcome.

ENDNOTES

1. Donald Rothchild, *Managing Ethnic Conflict in Africa: Pressures and Incentives for Cooperation* (Washington, DC: The Brookings Institution Press, 1997).

2. Claude Ake, *Democracy and Development in Africa* (Washington, DC: The Brookings Institution Press, 1996).

3. Ibid.

4. *New African* magazine, October 2005.

5. Ibid.

6. http://www.alimazrui.com.

7. Kwame Nkrumah, *Neo-Colonialism: The Last Stage of Imperialism* (Atlantic Highlands, NJ: Humanities Press International, 1965).

8. Tessilimi Bakary, quoted in *The Political Economy of Ivory Coast: Elite Transformation and Political Succession*, by William Zartman and Christopher Delgado (New York: Praeger, 1984), 28.

9. John Stuart Mill, *Principles of Political Economy* (London: 1848), edited by J.M. Robson in *The Improvement of Mankind: the Social and Political Thought of John Stuart Mill* (London: 1968).

10. John F. Conway, "Benefiting from Crimes against Humanity: Do We Owe Debts for Slavery and Colonialism, my opinion" World Conference Against Racism, 2001.

11. Ibid.

CHAPTER 20

Immigration

It is estimated by the International Labour Organization that 20 million African men and women are migrant workers and that by the year 2015, one in ten Africans will be living outside the country of their original birth. This, of course, excludes second-generation immigrants—men and women who were born outside of the country of the original birth of their parents.[1]

The BBC News Agency reports that one in three skilled Africans is lost to migration and replaced at a higher cost to his nation by expatriates. Between 1985 and 1990, 60,000 middle to high-level managers were lost by Africa due to migration. Approximately 23,000 qualified professionals leave the continent every year.

Africa has interregional refugee flow and migrant flow. In 1994, 2,000 Rwandans left for the Democratic Republic of Congo and Tanzania. In the same year there was an intraflow from Liberia to Guinea and Côte d'Ivoire, from Burundi to the Democratic Republic of Congo and Tanzania, from Somalia to Ethiopia. There were major repatriations since that time of White South-Africans and Zimbabweans to Mozambique.

Much of Africa's migration is because of economic reasons. Unemployment is very high, and in many places there is underemployment and low wages. For the nations of Burundi, Rwanda, and Liberia, it is because of civil war which continues to tear the continent apart. In nations like Nigeria and Ghana, which seem to have a degree of peace, a major factor in the migration pattern is political and religious persecution.

The northern part of Nigeria remains forever volatile because of the degree of conversion to Christianity by Muslims. Churches and properties of Christians have been torched, destroyed. Repressive leaders in these regions have added to the reason for migration.

The reason for looking at migration is that it shapes and conforms the person of color:

1. Prevailing abuses of migrant workers' fundamental rights.

   It goes without saying that Blacks are not known for taking up cases of abuse against themselves, and so for every one case reported there are probably 99 unreported. The level of abuse against migrant Blacks in Western nations is very high.

2. Poor labor conditions for migrant workers.

   In the east end of London where the rag trade has been operating for almost 200 years, Blacks have been employed to work in basements that are not heated in the winter; reports abound of some who are underpaid, possibly because the employer knows the workers have fallen foul of immigration laws.

3. Poor social protection.

   Most immigrants are not aware of their fundamental human rights, and if they are, they realize that they may be accosted for other legal problems.

4. Family dislocation.

   Migrant workers who move from other nations into South African mines have been known to be away from their spouses for close to two years. Immigrants into the United Kingdom who have had to endure the lengthy process of renewing and regularizing their immigration status have sometimes been separated from their family for as long as ten years. This, of course, has resulted in all kinds of social ills such as extramarital affairs, divorce, etc.

5. Integration problems.

    To be Polish American in the 19th century and early part of the 20th century was the greatest joke in America. However, they have blended into the system because of their color, and the perpetual joke of these immigrants in the United States no longer stands.

    The man of color is unable to blend in, and therefore, he has problems integrating into society; and in the case of those who are actually first-generation immigrants, they come with assumptions, cultural mores, and biases that have been shaped by the place of their original birth.

6. Social dislocation.

    Migration dislocates immigrants socially and culturally which leads to another problem—ghettoization.

7. Ghettoization.

    The city of Los Angeles is divided along racial lines, except in areas such as Beverly Hills, where one's financial status determines which community one belongs to.

    The average visitor to Paris would think there is such a great integration until he goes to 19th Arrondissement. A visit to London gives you the impression that everyone lives harmoniously until you realize that there is "White flight" from Lambeth, Peckham, and some other areas.

    There has been an introduction of draconian immigration policies since 1985 in Europe. With the upsurge in migration by Africans, particularly sub-Saharan, most European nations have changed their immigration laws, thus making it more difficult and almost hostile.

8. Growing Xenophobia.

    The skin color of Blacks makes it impossible for them to disappear into the society, particularly in the West. When newspapers and radios, therefore, talk of foreigners, Blacks are the first to come to mind. Since 1992 when most European nations came together to create a common immigration policy, limits were placed on Black entry into many European nations. This has not, though, deterred people—particularly from the Caribbean and Africa—from immigrating into Europe.

However, fear has complicated matters, with some British politicians making statements such as, "We are in danger of being swamped." Blacks account for just about 2 million of the 60 million people in the United Kingdom.

Xenophobia has given rise to a rightist political movement in Europe, with the emergence of the National Front in the United Kingdom and Mr. Le Pen in France.

The immediate effect of Black migration is an identity crisis for the Blacks living in Europe—first for the Blacks who migrate, and then for their children. Having been culturally dislocated and now also suffering from cultural conflict because the place of his original birth and the place of his current abode are so diametrically different, he finds himself immediately being shaped and conformed by the ideals of his newfound land. This has resulted in some coming into conflict with the laws of the land to which they have migrated. Particularly because the things they might have considered as inoffensive or a light matter is not so in their new place of residence.

Apart from this, the prejudice within the immigration, police services, and other law agencies complicate matters and further push the Black person down the social strata ladder.

This section on immigration would not be complete if reference is not made to those some might call sexual immigrants—people who migrate into Europe as prostitutes for economic reasons. Those who were not original carriers of venereal disease now suffer with one; and the ones who had the disease when they entered the country, pass it on to others—many others.

So with his family fractured, his identity in crisis, highly qualified from his homeland but now underemployed in a strange land, and confronted with the impossibility of total integration, immigration has served as a major agent of Black conformation.

Chris Buclier of the Pollution Research Group at Natal University in South Africa cited World Bank estimates that 100,000 expatriates from industrial countries are employed in Africa at a cost of $4 billion per year. That particular amount is 35 percent of official development assistance directed at the same Africa. Employing expatriate workers who are often more expensive than African professionals make the process of sustaining the economy of Africa and its environment even harder.

Poverty continues to be nurtured, and the economic development in Africa is delayed.

The immigration of Blacks has fractured their image and has further conformed them. Blacks in Diaspora are caught between their previous culture and that of their new world.

For more information about Black immigration, the following sources are offered:

John Hopkins University, *Migration Theories and Trends Module 8*; http//news.bbc.co.uk/I/hi/world/africa/16052425111; and, http://www-ilo-mirror.cornell.edu/public/english/dialogue/actrav/genact/socprot/migrant/291102cl.htm.

ENDNOTE

1. http://www.ilo.org/public/english/employment/strat/stratprod.htm.

CHAPTER 21

Apartheid

Basil Davidson, the doyen of African history, describes apartheid as "colonial racism carried to an extreme." Original South Africa was colonized in the 17th century by the English and the Dutch. The English had the upper hand initially thus dominating the Dutch descendants who were known as Boers or Afrikaners. This resulted in the Dutch moving to establish a new colony within South Africa known as Orange Free State and Transvaal. However, the discovery of diamonds in large quantities in these lands resulted in the Boer War between the English and the Dutch.

South Africa gained independence from England and in the 1940s the hand of the Dutch Afrikaner National Party became stronger, and therefore they gained a majority. Following its victory at the polls, the Afrikaner National Party began to enact Apartheid Laws that institutionalized and strengthened racial discrimination.

Prior to this, the policy of consistent racial separation had already been introduced in 1910 through a group of laws that curtailed the rights of the Black majority.

For example, the Mines and Works Act of 1911 limited Black workers exclusively to menial work, and so granted the availability of cheap labor and secured the better positions for White workers. The Native Land Act of 1913 set aside 7.3 percent of South African territory as a reservation for Black people and barred them from buying land outside of these areas. The land separated for them was mostly barren and therefore useless for proper agriculture.[1]

Prior to this Blacks had been deprived the right to vote, and in the places where they worked they were deprived the right to strike.

Having been deprived of the right to vote, strike, or express themselves politically, the Black majority had no choice but to start the African National Congress (ANC), another resistance and liberation movement. The ANC and various resistance groups were initially ill-equipped, ill-planned, and ill-managed.

Their formation, though, sent fear into the heart of the White community. This led, in 1948, to all of the Whites supporting the right-wing National Party to win an overwhelming majority in the elections.

D.F. Malan, who led the National Party, stood for drastic measures against the "Black Menace." He was the one who was known to have coined the concept of Apartheid and also consistently enforced this devious policy. Those who were not Blacks were also regulated and controlled as well. With the introduction of apartheid, South Africa was divided into four colors: White, Indians, Colored, and Blacks—with the Blacks at the bottom of the pile, though in the majority.

Following the general election in 1948, a flood of laws were enacted that formally institutionalized the dominance of White people over other races in South Africa.

The principal apartheid laws:[2]

- ❖ The Prohibition of Mixed Marriages Act of 1949.
- ❖ The Amendment to the Immorality Act of 1950. This law made it a criminal offense for a White person to have any sexual relation with a person of a different race.
- ❖ The Population Registration Act of 1950. This law required all citizens to register as Black, White, or Colored.

- ❖ The Suppression of Communism Act of 1950. This law banned any opposition party the government chose to label as Communist.

- ❖ The Group Area Act 27, April 1950. This law barred people of particular races from various urban areas.

- ❖ The Reservation of Separate Amenities Act, 1953. This law prohibited people of different races from using the same public amenities such as drinking fountains, restrooms, and so on.

- ❖ The Bantu Education Act, 1953. This law brought in various measures expressly designed to reduce the level of education attainable by Black people.

- ❖ The Mines and Works Act, 1956. This law formalized racial discrimination in employment.

- ❖ The Promotion of Black Self-Government Act, 1958. This law set up nominally independent "homelands" for Black people. In practice, the South African government had a strong influence over these Bantustans. Moreover, they were lands that were barren and therefore unusable.

- ❖ Black Homeland Citizenship Act, 1970. This law changed the status of the inhabitants of the homelands so that they were no longer citizens of South Africa and therefore had none of the rights that came with citizenship. There is certainly a limit to how far a people can take suppressions. Therefore this led to various demonstrations against the oppressive laws introduced against the majority of the people in the land.

Apartheid degraded Blacks in every way possible. It enacted laws that said that:

Blacks are not entitled to the freehold title to land anywhere in South Africa, nor is it the intention of the present government ever to grant such right to the Africans, even in his Bantu area.

No sporting event may take place anywhere in South Africa in which white and non-white people compete against each other whether in individual events or as teams or as parts of teams.

There are no trade union rights for Africans because the term *worker* or *employee* does not apply to an African because an employee is any person other than an African employed by or working for an employer.

Any African religious leader who conducts regular classes for his congregation in which he teaches them to read the Bible is guilty of a criminal offense. Also, a White man who spends a few hours a week in his own home teaching his African servant to read is guilty of a criminal offense.

A White person and a Black person may not have coffee together in a café anywhere in South Africa unless they have obtained a special permit to do so.

Unless a special permit has been granted, an African professor delivering a lecture at a White club, which has invited him to do so, commits a criminal offense.

A Colored person attending a public cinema in a town (even though he occupies specially separated seating) is guilty of a criminal offense, unless a special permit has been issued.

For example, on March 21, 1970, 20,000 people congregated in Sharpeville to demonstrate against the requirement to carry identity cards. The police opened fire on the demonstrators, killing 69 and injuring 180. Colonel J. Pienaar, the White senior police officer in charge on the day gave his reason as, "Hoards of natives surrounded the police station. Like I was struck with a stone. If they do these things they must learn their lesson the hard way." The reaction of the South African government was to ban the ANC and the Panafrican Africanist Congress (PAC).

The United Nations General Assembly on November 4, 1962, condemned South Africa's racist apartheid policies and called for all United Nations members to cease military and economic relationship with South Africa. In 1964, the leader of the ANC, the legendary Nelson Mandela, was sentenced to life imprisonment. The Afrikaans government did not relent. Rather, in 1974, they issued the Afrikaans' Medium Decree, which forced all schools to use the Afrikaans language to teach mathematics, social sciences, geography, and history at secondary school level. This made it compulsory for Black South Africans to learn a language that was not native to their own and also made them unable to probably work internationally.[3]

The Deputy Minister of Education, Mr. Pant Johnson, said, "I have not consulted the African people on the language issue, and I am not going to. An African knows that 'the big boss' only spoke Afrikaans or only spoke English. It would be to his advantage to know both languages."

The reaction of the United Nations General Assembly in 1973 to South Africa's apartheid was to provide a legal framework within which member states could apply sanctions to press the South African government to change the policies.

Article 11 of the International Convention for the Suppression and Punishment of the crime of Apartheid issued by the General Assembly of the United Nations reads, "For the purpose of the present convention, the term, "The Crime of Apartheid," we shall include similar policies and practices of racial segregation and discrimination as practised in Southern Africa shall apply to the following inhuman acts committed for the purpose of establishing and maintaining domination by one racial group of persons over any other racial group of persons and systematically oppressing them."

It goes on to state, "Acts of such suppression or oppression carried out through murders, mental harm, infringement of people's freedom and dignity, subjecting people to torture, cruelty, human degradation, arbitrary arrest, illegal punishments."[4] Apartheid was certainly a policy which destroyed people morally, physically, psychologically, generationally, and geographically.

Considering the fact that the population of Blacks was 19 million while Whites were 4.5 million, land allocation to Blacks was 13 percent and Whites kept 87 percent for themselves.

Large tracts of land were handed out to White commercial farmers while various oppressive laws killed every attempt Blacks made to run a viable business. The result was the availability of cheap, Black labor for exploitation and profit. The Black farmers lacked capital and access to fertile land.

The share of National Income for Blacks was 20 percent for 19 million people when 4.5 million people kept 75 percent. The ratio of average earnings was 1 for Blacks; 14 for Whites. The radio of doctors per population was one doctor for every 44,000 for Blacks; but one doctor for every 400 Whites. Infant mortality was 20 percent in the urban areas for Blacks, 40 percent in the rural area; while infant mortality for Whites was 2.7 percent. Annual expenditure on education per pupil for Blacks was $45, while for Whites it was $696.[5]

It was impossible to live in this kind of condition and not find your mind, spirit, and person shaped to convince you that you were of lesser value. Afrikaaner politics were based on racist and segregationist beliefs claiming, "The preservation of the pure race tradition of the Boerevolk must be protected at all costs, in all possible ways as a holy pledge entrusted to us by our ancestors as part of God's plan with our people. Any movement, school, or individual who sins against this must be dealt with as a racial criminal" (1941).

Having been separated from Great Britain in 1961, the National Party was now in control. It based its apartheid teaching on four key ideas:

1. The population of South Africa comprised four racial groups: White, Colored, Indian, and African—each with its own inherent culture.

2. Whites are the civilized race and are entitled to have absolute control over the state.

3. White interests should prevail over Black interests. The state is not obliged to provide equal facilities for the subordinate races.

4. The White racial group formed a single nation with Afrikaans and English-speaking components, while Africans belonged to several—ten distinct nations or potential nations, a formula that made the White nation the largest in the country.

Apartheid became a torturous instrument for shaping people from the horn of Africa, taking away their dignity so that even today there is an ongoing struggle for racial equality in South Africa, in spite of the removal of the apparatus legally. There is a low level but intense social struggle, which underscores the deep social and economic divisions that characterize South Africa.

The social economic reform has been painfully too slow. There-fore, nothing much has changed. There is an unequal economic situa-tion that has excluded the majority from the economy as key players, but only as day laborers and low-level workers. The majority of the land is still in the hands of the people who have always controlled it, and Black South Africans still serve as the laborers who earn £1.60 a day on these lands.

The use of the Afrikaans language, the lack of exposure, as well as the open border to neighboring nations, have resulted in migrating laborers with very few job skills who are largely illiterate.

South Africans have been systematically and deliberately murdered over the years—killed physically, murdered morally, destroyed mentally and psychologically so that deep damage has been done to the people's confidence.

The expression of Blacks today is an explosive mix of hopelessness be-cause of their lack of economic power, pervasive illiteracy, and treatment as third class citizens in the country of their original birth.

Complications set in to the matter with the high level of HIV/AIDS, which continues to disproportionately ravage the Black community in South Africa, thus making South Africa one of the highest rate HIV na-tions with 45 percent national infection. In today's South Africa, child labor is still a major cause for concern as people and local governments look the other way as if it is not in existence.

South Africans have been exposed to a system that has conformed them to an unequal, unjust economic disparity in the distribution of lands. And although South Africa has been specifically highlighted here, a different strand of Black subjugation, which may have not been called apartheid but is in practice, has also operated in Namibia, Swaziland, Zimbabwe, and all the sub-Kalahari nations.[6]

ENDNOTES

1. Leonard Thompson, *A History of South Africa* (Yale University Press, 2001).

2. http:/www.csstudents.stanford.edu/~cale/cs201/apartheid. hist.html.

3. http:/www.africansuntimes.com/articles/2003_0916_ SOUTH%20 AFRICA%20-%20%20Lingering%20 Apartheid.htm.

4. Thompson, *History of South Africa*: [Landing at the Cape] [Expansion of the Cape Settlers] [Great Trek] [The Xhosa People] [The Zulu Kingdom] [Battle of Blood River] [Colony of Natal] [Anglo-Boer War] [Apartheid Era] [The New South Africa].

5. Copyright of www.suedafrika.net *Online Travel Guide.* (33 Andrews Street, Hout Bay 7800, South Africa).

6. Michael Roberts, "South Africa: Lingering Apartheid, African Analysis," *African Sun Times*, Sept. 11-17, 2003.

CHAPTER 22

Faulted Educational Systems

In any society, education should be for the enhancement of the people, for the development of the individual until they become a source of help and blessing to humanity.

Education should prepare a man to be able to serve his community and humanity, bringing to the table his own quota in meeting the economic, social, intellectual, and spiritual needs of his nation and of the world.

When a nation's leaders set educational policies, it should be with the intention to achieve this purpose, to develop the individual and the talents he has and to help all persons become wholesome human beings.

Education should challenge the individual person to venture, create, and step into the unknown. After all, it was education that led to the discovery of the various principles in science and physics that helped man to walk on the moon and conquer the elements.

A nation should therefore produce citizens who will be able to achieve this, bring pride to their nation, encourage the coming generations, etc.

In almost every country, the central education system is run by the government. That is probably the reason why Thomas Jefferson, in a letter to George Washington in 1786, said, "It is an axiom of my mind that our liberty can never be safe but in the hands of the people themselves, and that too of the people with a certain degree of instruction."[1]

This great idea has not been the experience of Black students in school in Africa, Europe, or the United States of America. We will look at this conformation to show how a distorted educational system in the African context is perpetually holding back Africa in its effort to join the developed world and to practice a robust democracy.

You will also see how a system of institutionalized racism is affecting education in Europe.

Our last stop will be the United States of America and how Blacks have fared in the face of prejudice from the system as well as the behavior of the recipients which is probably turning against them.

African education was essentially a colonial legacy. Far from it being a medium for the enhancement of the total man, colonial masters only trained those they needed to help them with their administrative work as they managed their lands of conquest.

Their only drive for educating the masses was in order to prepare people who would help them with administrative responsibilities as David Court who did a study of Tanzania and Kenya reports. He writes, "At independence…the immediate perceived need was that of producing the technologists and administrators to replace the departing expatriates. Given this perception, it is likely that the new elite would take over not only existing positions but also their underpinning normative structure, defining relationships between education, wages and occupations as well as their associated rewards and lifestyle. Equally inevitable was the consequence that the access to these rewards would become the measure of popular aspiration in defiance of economic realities."[2]

First it was the colonial masters who did not have democracy, development, discovery, or Black's contribution to humanity as the basis for establishing education in Africa. Then it was the individual himself who eventually saw education as an escape route from poverty and possibly the maintenance of the lifestyle he had seen from previous colonial masters.

Mike Omolewa points out, as in the case of Nigeria that, "Many Nigerians from poor homes began to study for the London University examination to provide for themselves an opportunity to advance in political and social stature and material wealth."[3]

It was Ernest N. Emenyonu who argued about the consequence of such attitude to education. He said, "When an educational process is misconceived, the consequences are social-economic chaos, political instability, culture indecorum and moral indiscipline and laxity."

Once education fails to develop people to participate in democracy, in the words of Dr. M.I. Okpara, a one time premier in the Eastern part of Nigeria, "Education…unless it is right and purposeful, the people either crawl or limp along."[4]

In the United Kingdom, OFSTED, the educational watchdog of Britain, has found that the system is failing Black boys and girls, particularly Black boys who are more than four times as likely to be excluded from a classroom as other students.

The United Kingdom attempted to introduce a method of selection of certain students to prepare them to do degree courses. Emenyonu's argument was that this selection would work against Black young people and not bring any net improvement overall to them.

In the General Certificate of Secondary Education (GCSE) exams where there is a higher tier and a foundation tier, he observed that in certain subjects like mathematics a good number of Black children were excluded from this method. Where also gifted pupils were identified, it resulted in Black children again being excluded.

Although the context is different in the United States of America, the faulted systems inherent in American education has also held down and held back Black young people. According to John McWhorter, though, there is a rise of a new Black middle class which is giving African Americans hope of entering the economic mainstream.

However, almost 40 years after the Civil Rights Act, African American students on average record the poorest grades, and the poorest performance. They represent the ethnic group with the worst performance regardless of class level.

McWhorter indicates that in 1997 for example, 70,000 students applied for admission to American law schools. Among them were only 16 Black students who scored 64 or higher on the law school admission test.[5]

In another statistic about the Scholastic Achievement Test (SAT) exam, McWhorter indicates that in 1995 only 184 Black students in the United States got 700 on the verbal portion of the SAT. And 616 Black students scored over 700 on the math portion. And the top score in each case was 800. These two were .2 percent and .6 percent respectively of the Black test takers. The average score for all those taking the SAT is 1540.

So the society who produced the likes of Reginald F. Lewis, Ida B. Wells, H. Naylor Fitzhugh, and Mary McCleod-Bethune, etc. is also plagued with the challenge of underperformance by young people from the Black community in the United States.

Some may want to blame the restrictions put on Black people in the days of slavery when they were prohibited from education in many of the states. However, even in the face of such adverse laws and difficulties of the period of slavery, Black education made a lot of progress—unlike in modern times.

BLACK EDUCATIONAL CHALLENGES:
AFRICA, AMERICA, EUROPE

In a latent way, education in Africa entered the continent with intention by the colonial masters to make Africans accept the supposed superiority of Whites and inferiority of Blacks, and to also raise from among the people those who would help the process or the exploitation of the continent.

In pursuance of this, a crop of people were educated to help the colonial masters achieve their vision. These people were described by Paulo Freire and Donaldo Macedo as, "petit bourgeois class of functionaries who had internalised the belief that they had become white or black with white sauce and were therefore superior to African peasants."

The creation of an elite class made Western education become the heart of the internal challenge in Africa—politically and economically—resulting in the divide between those who have and those who don't.

Schools were not evenly spread throughout, so the tribes who received education first had an advantage.

As David Abernethy observed, "The uneven spread of mission schools by creating objective differences between various ethnic groups stimulated rivalry between them."[6] That way the missionaries, without consciously intending it, created an unevenness and therefore ethnic rivalry in Africa.

Today, that imbalance has still not been corrected and has therefore made Western education to be one of the reasons for conflicts, civil wars, and ethnic fighting.

The distortion in education in Africa reaches every strand of society. People read about agriculture—not in order to practice it. Thus Africa has an abundance of land but still has to depend on foreign aid and major units of the United Nations like the FAO or the WFP. Most farmers in Africa are uneducated. Were they to be, it would be a different scenario.

As observed by A.R. Thompson, "When an educated farmer settles down to farming, when he develops some commitment and abandons the off-farm preoccupations...he is likely to be a more aggressively innovative farmer. There is evidence that such a farmer is somewhat more likely to seek out useful knowledge more aggressively from other agencies and situations where it is available. There is also evidence that he is likely to use modern farming inputs more intensively and in general be more commercially oriented."[7]

In addition to a curriculum that is not immediately transmissible into the economy, there seems to be an atmosphere of domination in schools in Africa—students who are regulated and confined and made to receive a teaching that is more like indoctrination. This was the observation of Seth Kreisberg in his book.[8] He writes, "Students are confined to places where they are told and too often accept that someone else knows what is good for them, where someone else controls their lives and daily choices, where their voices are patronized or ignored."

This makes education in that setting authoritarian and promotes the hierarchical system that seems to cut across Africa. It is a system in which the teachers are the ones who teach and the students have to absorb and receive whatever he said. Paulo Freire describes this method as "banking education" and describes it as, "Teacher teaches and the students are taught: a teacher knows everything and the student knows nothing. The teacher thinks and the students are thought about: the teacher talks and the students listen meekly."[9]

Africa continues to complain about the fact that it has been four to five decades since independence. Yet it is held up in its inability to transfer its educational knowledge to practical management of the nation in the areas of government, technology, administration, etc.

What Paulo Freire calls "banking education," Jean Paul Sartres describes in his work "Philosophie Alimentaire" as the mass education which Africa has adopted as being very weak and unproductive.[10]

This problem about man's education was captured by Laurence Resnick who writes, "Mass education was from its inception concerned with inculcating routine abilities: simple computation, reading predictable texts, reciting religious or civic codes. It did not take as goals for its students the ability to interpret unfamiliar texts, create materials others would need to read, construct convincing arguments, develop original solutions to technical or social problems. The political conditions under which mass education developed encouraged instead the routinization of basic skills as well as the standardizing of teaching and education institutions."[11]

This system is devoid of dialogue and discovery and only treats students as depositories of knowledge. This is a big problem in Africa where students therefore are unable to be led along to the point through dialogue, research, self-discovery to be able to find lasting solutions for their own community.

It is no wonder that you can hardly point at discoveries—scientific, sociological, economic, electronic, electrical, etc.—that can be traced to a large number of Africans. This does not in effect negate discoveries and breakthroughs by many, but Africa has a high illiteracy level with a poor record in the field of scientific advancement and breakthroughs.

Black education in the United Kingdom is in trouble. Black Caribbean pupils, both boys and girls, appear to be in trouble more often than their peers. Reports from schools show that they are not doing very well academically.

David Gillborn, of the Institute of Education at the University of London, indicates that the overwhelming weight of existing research suggests that Black young people will be more likely to be condemned in almost every class with every system applied than their White classmates. Britain introduced a selection system which allows brilliant children and those who have displayed unusual ability to be set aside and taught differently. This was thought to bring improvement in overall achievement. However, the result was adverse for Black students. Black kids whatever their gender, social class, or background, too often find themselves working against teacher expectations. Such teacher assumption presumes criminality, a lack of motivation, and an inherent lack of ability to perform.

In the United States, the education of the man of color has had the most challenges than anywhere else in the world. Laws were passed to deliberately keep the Black man ignorant. From the time of slavery until the 20th century, various legislative acts passed by state governments and educational boards did not encourage but actually frustrated education for Blacks. In 1740 for example, South Carolina adopted the first compulsory ignorance law in America:

> "And whereas the having of slaves taught to write or suffering them to be employed in writing, may be attended with great inconveniences: be it enacted, that all and every person or persons whatsoever, who shall hereafter teach, or shall use or employ any slave as a scribe in any manner of writing whatsoever, hereafter taught to write, every such person or persons shall, for each offense, forfeit the sum of 100 pounds current money."

Shocking as it may this law was enforced; and in the words of Frederick Douglass, the great Black orator, writer, and abolitionist, many had to be taught in secret schools endangering their lives because of their quest to be educated.

The courts upheld these laws. It occasionally happened that the will of a slave owner was directed to a certain Black and indicated that he should be educated, but such provisions were not allowed, or legal.

Into the middle of the 20th century, Black children still attended seg-regated schools and were forced to learn the fundamentals in run-down school houses with outdated, worn-out books.

To date, Blacks in America are still playing catch-up with education because in the words of William H. Gray, III, President of the United Negro College Fund, "Despite our gains, education has not been suffi-cient to overcome racial barriers. Opportunities have improved certainly for African Americans but the number of those who have a Ph.D. com-pared to white counterparts clearly shows that Blacks are still to a major disadvantage."

Today, Black young children go to schools in inner cities where the school system in the majority has failed, yet nothing is more damaging to the education of the Black man in the United States than a new spirit of victimology—that behavior makes the man of color blame every chal-lenge he faces on his circumstance, and therefore he does nothing about changing or improving his circumstance.

Victimologists argue that White teachers tend to grade and discipline Black students harshly. This does not sit properly with the research car-ried out by Laurence Steinberg who surveyed 20,000 teenagers and their families and found not only that complaints of racist bias among teachers were rare but that Latinos and Asian Americans registered the same level of complaints yet they are managing to turn out more excellent school performances than African Americans.[12]

REASONS FOR THE BLACK EDUCATIONAL CRISIS

Nigeria has featured highly in our analysis of Africa set on a poor footing by the colonial masters. Education in Nigeria meant that the south had a greater advantage over the Muslim north—first because it was the entry point of the colonialist, and second because missionaries founded schools without much resistance in the south.

Eventually, as independence approached, from all indications the Yorubas, Edos, Efiks, and Ibos were certainly going to dominate. Riots broke out in northern Nigeria in the months of September and October 1966, which resulted in the Ibos being killed in the north and other tribes fleeing the north because of the economic reaction of the northerners as they observed the southerners dominate. In the words of Victor Diejo-maoh, "These southerners were able to entrench themselves in a domina-tive position in the north, largely by dent of their relatively higher levels of educational attainment."[13]

The imbalance had been created and the people were more or less vic-tims of this distorted education which did not carry such a young nation along—young in the sense that Nigeria was amalgamated, the north and the south, as a nation in 1914.

There was imbalance in income, lifestyle, education, worldview, and even today it still adversely affects the country. Diejomaoh stated cate-gorically that, "An examination of partial economic indices, such as per capita levels of human resource development, government expenditures and revenues, provision of health and transport facilities, and export lev-els, show quite clearly the differential in per capita income levels be-tween the north and the south.

"While per capita income differentials are traceable to a large number of factors, differentials in the level of modern educational attainments between the north and south are largely responsible for the differentials in per capita incomes of northern and southern Nigeria."[14]

Like most intertribal challenges in Africa, the reaction of the north was immediately apparent. The politicians and leaders of the north spoke against the administrative power and monopoly of the southerners because of their long-standing educational lead.

A Sultan of Sokoto reacted to the situation recalling, "As things were at that time, (the early 1950s), if the gates to the departments were to be opened the southern regions had a huge pool from which they could find suitable people, while we had hardly anyone. In the resulting scramble we were convinced the inevitable that the southern applicants would get al-most all the posts available. Once you get a government post you are hard indeed to shift...this was a matter of life and death to us...if the British administration had failed to give us the even development that we de-served and for which we craved so much, and they were on the whole a very fair administration—what had we to hope from an African adminis-tration, probably in the hands of a hostile party. The answer to our mind was, quite simply, just nothing, beyond a little window dressing."[15]

A northern newspaper in the country of Nigeria in an editorial reacted to the same problem: "Southerners will take the places of the Europeans in the north. What is there to stop them? They look and see it as theirs at the present time. There are Europeans but undoubtedly it is the southerner who has the power in the north. They have control of the railway stations, the post offices, government hospitals, the canteens, the majority employed in the Kaduna Secretariat and the public works department are all southerners. In all the different departments of government, it is the southerner who has the power."[16]

This sentiment goes against what others had expressed as a view of what education could do for a nation, but the Sultan of Sokoto was right in his view. Unfortunately, the nations in question, whether south or north, were all victims of another person's decision.

In the United Kingdom, Mylena Buyum, last chairwoman of the National Assembly Against Racism, is among the Black leaders who maintain that institutional racism is the real problem. White teachers do not understand the culture of Black young people. The reader must take into account that Black settlement in the United Kingdom is really no more than 55 years of age. While Blacks have been associated with the United Kingdom for upward of 300 years, there has not been an actual settlement in a large proportion until 1948 when the United Kingdom campaigned in the Caribbean for blue collar workers to come and fill the employment gap.

The commission for racial equality also warned that along with institutional racism there was peer pressure—young Blacks who pressure fellow Blacks not to pursue educational achievement.[17]

Apart from Black people's exposure to reading in antiquity, which was later lost as they found themselves in the forests of Africa, the people most exposed to education would be Blacks who were taken as slaves to the United States of America.

When finally Blacks were opportuned to read, the generation who knew slavery made efforts to see that the next generations were educated. In the last couple of decades, though, there has been an evolution of a new generation who, although they have reaped the progress and achievement that the civil rights movement made, has negated advances by their apparent anti-intellectual stands.

What accounts for a low achievement of Blacks in education? McWhorter argues that the chief cause is not racism, as seen claimed by several specialists and those whom he calls victimologists, neither is it inadequate school funding, class status, or parental educational level which in a sense is buttressed by the fact that in a place like Africa where there is a strong desire to educate in order to escape the poverty trap, parents never use their class or poverty as an excuse *not* to educate but rather as a reason *to* educate their children so the next generation will be better off than the previous.

His argument rests on one major point—anti-intellectualism—a plague which he feels is tearing and pulling down the Black community. Anti-intellectualism in the opinion of McWhorter began as a legacy of the sixties when in order for the civil rights movements and most who were in that stream, to make sense of life seemed to come up with an attitude of making all things illegitimate which have an appearance of whiteness.

The second argument he makes is that Black parents demand less of their children in school than white and Asian Americans do. Many Asian students do well, possibly in his opinion because the parents may have to run two or three shops to get the money.

McWhorter feels that the devaluation of education is local to Black American culture. His observation is drawn from the fact that Black Africans and Caribbean immigrants who come into the United States do well. So it is not the system, it is the persons who have chosen to devalue education.[18]

Joel Schwartz, drawing from the works of John Ogbu, a Nigerian-born anthropologist, working at the University of California at Berkeley, also seems to buttress the points made by McWhorter, although from a slightly different perspective.[19]

Ogbu had argued that African-American students do poorly in school in part because they don't apply themselves, and this lack of effort, in his argument, is the result of the student's lack of adaptation to the limited opportunity to benefit from their education. Ogbu also observed that a lot of the students considered academic learning as "acting White," thus making academic success a prerogative of Whites. There is the conventional explanation for Black underperformance which he also observed: Black poverty, White racism, and a Eurocentric pedagogy thought to be inadequate for Black students—a system of teaching that does not carry onboard the culture of the student. Ogbu did not deny the need for the shaping of the school system, particularly the one in which the Black student finds himself confronted by racism and the past.

However, another phenomenon is the fact that Black parents teach their children to hoard American mainstream ideals and yet on another hand, they teach them to be cynical and sceptical and guard against other races because of the hurt of the past. These same parents often do not contribute by way of working with their children when it comes to homework or attending parent/teacher association meetings.

Such parents feel, having worked long hours and paid high taxes, that they have contributed enough and it is the responsibility of the educational system to balance up with what their children need. Parents do not, in Ogbu's opinion, monitor their children enough; therefore, there is no desire to excel.

THE CONSEQUENCES

The consequences of these distorted views on education is farreaching. In Africa, education was and is distorted—that it is the quickest way to wealth, not a way to contribute to humanity, make discoveries, and help democracy work. Therefore the average educated person in Africa has one overwhelming desire—to be employed, preferably at the top of some position in an office. Commerce, industry, and private enterprise have no attraction for the educated African.

Everything that surrounds the modern man is a product of education which results in creation, investing, inventing, or venturing into the unknown.

For the African, his distorted view has given him the impression to, "get all the education you can so you can be at the top." He models himself after the White colonialists and the first set of people who were educated, whose only function was to run government machineries and bureaucracies.

One consequence in the United Kingdom is a generation who finish school and cannot even speak English fluently or spell properly. There has been a generation of Black young people who leave school without adequate qualification. The proportion of African Caribbean teenagers who scored at least five A to C grades on the GCSE dropped to 36 percent in 2002—worse than in any previous year. The fall in Black teenage achievement made them the worst performing ethnic group for the first time since the study first reported complete ethnic data in 1992.[20]

Lee Jasper, who advises the mayor of London on race issues, talking about the problem of Black teenagers and their attitude to education said, "The government's single biggest failure in its response to the McPherson report (into the murder of the Black teenager Steven Lawrence) has been its failure to tackle institutional racism. In schools, Black young kids were not expected to do well. The consequence for the Black community and the nation as a whole is far-reaching."

A Black member of parliament, Diane Abbott, observed that Black pupils in British schools are, "A silent catastrophe." The mayor of London himself admitted that these young people "contribute a rising tide of street crime and shootings in London."

So in Africa, the ethnic cleansings, genocides, and intertribal wars have been purely because of the imbalance in the education of the various tribes. It worked for the colonial masters, but it is working against national unity, peace, harmony, progress, and against a wholesome Africa.

The consequence of a poor performance in education or a distorted educational view in the United States is probably more far-reaching than anyone has taken the time to observe. Mr. Ogbu, who studied middle class Black students, observed their ambivalence about academic success, particularly because "once the success is achieved, where is the job to go with it?"

Students could not make a connection between academic performance and their future in the labor market. Consequently, these young men and women are no longer admiring those who made academic contributions to the Black community or who achieved giant strides in that field.

Their heroes today are the rappers, particularly the ones whose lyrics speak against the ills of the White community. Scotty Ballard, in an article

titled, "Why Black women more than Black men are getting an education?", indicated that 65 percent of Bachelor's degree recipients are Black
women, nearly double the number of their male counterparts according to
the U.S. Department of Education. And the education gap between the
two sexes is widening.[21]

Why?

Dr. Anthony Young, vice president of the National Association of Black
Psychologists, points out that Black women, more than men, are getting an
education because of the anti-intellectual, non-parent involvement that creates a low self-esteem especially among Black men where there is a lack of
Black on Black encouragement; rather there is Black on Black crime.

An ultimate lie Black men buy into is the fallacy that they can't afford
or compete in a higher education environment. Inadvertently, many
Black men have believed that they cannot achieve and have subsequently
been discouraged from making any effort. The U.S. Department of Education 2000 Census indicates that women age 30 and below make up
48.7 percent of the United States population, and they graduate and are
enrolled in college and high school at a higher rate than men. As a matter of fact, they made up 58 percent of college graduates in 1999.

THE WAY OUT

Blacks stand at a disadvantage if the distortion on education continues—whether it is in Africa or on the streets of New York or London,
wherever Blacks live.

Turning it around in Africa will require the vision of eastern Nigeria as
described by A.E. Afigbo in the book, *The Missions, the State and Education in South-eastern Nigeria – 1956 to 1971*, which was included in Edward Fashole Luke's work, *Christianity in Independent Africa*.[22]

Mr. Afigbo records that eastern Nigeria adopted a policy indicating,
"The colonial type of education…did not adequately meet the needs of
the country…the result is that manual, agricultural and technical education have come to be associated with inferior status and to be accorded
low instead of high regard in the scheme of things."

For Africa to make progress, the argument of Victor Uchendu who
said, "Education in Africa is more than an instrument of national

development. In postcolonial Africa, it is the simple most important national institution that allocates present and future societal privileges because of its critical role in the social structure."

He also examines the problem of the disparity between the education available in the city areas, the urban centers, and the rural areas, indicating that once an area is disadvantaged, it affects the whole politics of the nation.[23]

African governments and nations must not be dependent on foreign aid, individuals, or even missionaries to educate their people. They must formulate an educational system that will change their society and build a nation of the future, giving everyone, whether in the city or the hamlet, a future full of hope.

It is this kind of opinion which motivates the argument of the Director of UNESCO, who said, "Development can only come from within, it must be endogenous, thought out by people for themselves, springing from the soil on which they live and tuned to their aspirations, the conditions of their natural environment, the resources at their disposal and the particular genius of their culture…Education should accordingly contribute to the promotion of such indigenous development."[24]

So Africa must re-conceptualize its own education to shake off its colonial inheritance and in so doing it must not allow some of the things that metamorphosed in recent times in certain African nations where education is now what might be referred to as "ethnoeducation," that is education by an ethnic quota system—people getting university placements, placements in polytechnics, etc., purely because of the ethnic group they come from and not merit. After the quota allocated for their ethnic group is completed, they are refused admission in that particular year; as a result, there are people who have educational aspirations in Africa but are unable to fulfill them because ethnoeducation reigns in their nation.

Education in the future of Africa must be for the emancipation of the mind, the development of the nation, and the contribution of the individual to the building of the nation. It should be the type of pedagogy that challenges oppression, exposes corruption, and eradicates the sheer exploitation of the masses by the privileged few.

Henry Giroux talks of this kind of education when he said, "It should defend schools as democratic public faces responsible for providing indispensable public service to the nation, a language in this case that is capable of awakening the moral, economic, political and civic responsibilities of our youth."[25]

Ernest N. Emenyonu, quoted previously, supports this argument. He also would put forth the truth that, "If education at the top is purposeless, so will the learner, at the end of the educational process become a nuisance to the society and a liability even to himself. An educational system must be purposeful so that its products can be functional members of society."[26]

The education Africa needs is the one which informs the citizen and helps them in the process of making intelligent decisions about everyday life. It is education which helps the average student or citizen become a critical thinker; and a critical thinker is by definition a person who can adjust to different questions and domains of thought. The critical thinker is one who is able to explore and appreciate the adequacy of other people's position.

It is this absence of critical thinkers that limits Africans to an ethnic and cultural worldview, unable to accommodate those who are different.

In the United Kingdom, it is obvious that the system may need to adjust to help Blacks catch up and make progress academically. David Gilbert cites a consultation document of 2002 titled, "Extending Opportunities, Raising Standards" that indicates, "Young people should be able to develop at a pace consistent with their abilities, whether faster or slower. Those being faster might skip some examinations or take them early and use the time gained to study some subjects in great depths or to start new ones. Those progressing more slowly might take GCSEs or equivalent later than age sixteen."

The most important thing is aiding such students to finally achieve and contribute to the community. Blacks are in Britain to stay. It becomes beneficial both ways, to the government and Blacks, that the government should consult on a strategy to improve the training of school staff to reduce exclusion of certain ethnic groups, and to create a support system for them. The people's views should be sought about the best way to raise educational achievements so that there will be a greater number doing well.

In any culture or community, parental involvement helps the achievement of children. If African-Caribbean parents would get involved, there would be a higher academic performance level for the children.

To turn the educational situation around in the United States of America, everyone will have to cooperate. African-American children and students need to see and become familiar with adults, particularly Black entrepreneurs, professionals, and achievers, who are making a positive difference in their communities and country. These successful people need to make themselves more visible and available to help the coming generations.

In another conformation it was shown that there is a lack of wholesome, successful African Americans on television and therefore children form the opinion that the people of their community are not as important and are not achievers.

Children being underexposed to career options tend to go for what is suggested to them by a teacher who has a likely prejudiced opinion of what they can achieve.

In the United Kingdom it would be smart for parents to keep their children away from street culture which is defining education as being unimportant. Schools need to help by creating a learning environment that is calm, purposeful, and business-like.

The language used in challenging these young people is a significant feature if they are to be achievers. They must be spoken to, not in the style of "banking education" as we earlier noted. Not in a way that suggests that they come from an inferior culture.

Endemic views that have already been communicated to these teachers must be challenged. For example, the popular notion in the United Kingdom is that a restless young child is only being that way because of his culture, and that Blacks by nature are restless.

Schools that do well are known to have an atmosphere of praise, a reward system for achievers. Trusting relationships between teachers and pupils from ethnic groups are usually very high. This can be emulated by other schools where there is a strong ethnic presence.

The ethos of the school must be based on the fact that all students are created equal, and all can achieve when the atmosphere is conducive. If anger is expressed, teachers should help such children learn how to manage a behavior that may bring unnecessary negative views of them across.

Black children in Europe have learned the street language word *respect* in the sense of being treated either as equal or regarded. Where students are given such treatment that suggests regard and respect, achievement levels are likely to rise.

In America, in the opinion of Mr. John U. Ogbu, educational success is contingent upon broader social improvements. Success is dependent on minorities learning to respond to schooling properly and stop thinking that academic orientation is "acting White."

Alfred Edmond Jr. in his article, "How to Raise a Successful Black Child" argues that to facilitate a situation where children are committed to education, programs should include recruiting at least one college student for an internship at your company. Black businesses should learn to let a young person shadow them as they go through their business or workday. Sponsor student membership at your professional association, organise tours of colleges for children in your neighbourhood, organise a mentorship program for a school in your neighbourhood." [27]

Let us remember the illiterate slaves who risked their lives to get an education. People travel the world to come to America to gain an education. It is no longer enough to blame the system. If it is going to be, it is up to the community.

A distorted educational view has become a conformation of the Black person and is thus limiting his scope. It is time for a change.

ENDNOTES

1. Henry J. Perkinson, *The Imperfect Panacea: American Faith in Education, 1865-1965* (New York: McGraw-Hill Inc., 1991), 8.

2. David Court, "Education as Social Control: the Response to Inequality in Kenya and Tanzania," reported in Victor C. Uchendu, *Education and Politics in Tropical Africa* (New York: Conch Magazine Ltd. Publishers, 1979), 27.

3. Michael Omolewa, "London Universities Earliest Examinations in Nigeria, 1887-1931," *West African Journal of Education*, 20, no.2, (1976), 352.

4. Ernest Emenyonu, "Education and the Contemporary Malice in Nigeria," quoted by Charles E. Nnolim, *The Role of Education in Contemporary Africa* (New York: Professors World Peace Academy, 1988), 34.

5. John H. McWhorter, *Losing the Race: Self-Sabotage in Black America* (New York: Harper, 2001).

6. David B. Abernethy, *The political dilemma of popular education: an African case* (Stanford CA: Stanford University Press, 1969), 104.

7. A.R. Thompson, *Education and Development in Africa* (London: McMillan Press, 1983), p.56.

8. Seth Kreisberg, *Transforming Power, Domination Empowerment at Education* (Albany: State University of New York Press, 1992), 6.

9. Paulo Freire, *The Pedagogy of the Oppressed*, 1970 reprint (New York: Continuum Publishing Company, 1994), 54.

10. Paulo Freire, *Pedagogy of the Oppressed*, quoting Jean Paul Sartres in his Situations 1: Paris, Librairie Gallimard, 1947.

11. Lauren Resnick, *Education and Learning to Think* (Washington, DC: National Academy Press, 1987).

12. Laurence Steinberg, *Beyond the Classroom* (New York: Simon & Schuster, 1997).

13. Victor P. Diejomaoh, *The Economics of Nigerian Conflict*, in the writing of Joseph Okpaku, *Nigeria: Dilemma of Nationhood an African Analysis of the Biafran Conflict* (New York: The Third Press, 1972), 321.

14. Ibid.

15. Reference unknown.

16. James S. Coleman, *Nigeria: Background to Nationalism* (Berkeley: University of California Press, 1958), 362.

17. www.blink.org.uk/pdescription.asp.

18. John H. McWhorter, essay.

19. Joel Schwartz, joint Senior Fellow at the Hudson Institute, "Explaining Black Underachievement," and author of *Fighting Poverty with Virtue: Moral Reform and America's Urban Poor* (Indiana University Press, 2000).

20. *The Independent Newspaper*, February 21, 2003.

21. Scotty Ballard, "Why Black women more than Black men are getting an education," *Jet*, September 16, 2002; http://www.ebonyjet.com.

22. Edward Fashole Luke, *Christianity in Independent Africa*, (University of Ibandan Press, 1978), 178.

23. Victor C. Uchendu, *Education and Politics in Tropical Africa* (New York: Conch Magazine Ltd Publishers, 1979), 1.

24. A.R. Thompson, *Education and Development in Africa* (London: McMillan Press, 1983), 201.

25. Henry A. Giroux, *Living Dangerously: Multiculturalism and the Politics of Difference* (New York: Peter Lang, 1993), 20.

26. Ernest N. Emenyonu, *Education and the Contemporary Malice in Nigeria*; cited in Charles E. Nnolim, *The Role of Education in Contemporary Africa* (New York: Professors World Peace Academy, 1988), 34.

27. Alfred A. Edmond, Jr., "How to Raise a Successful Black Child," *Black Enterprise*, September 16, 2002.

CHAPTER 23

Segregation

Martin Luther King Jr., wrote, "I guess it is easy for those who have never felt the stinging darts of segregation to say, 'Wait.' When you have seen vicious mobs lynch your mothers and fathers at will and drown your sisters and brothers at whim, when you have seen hate-filled policemen curse, kick, brutalize and even kill your Black brothers and sisters with impunity, when you see the vast majority of your twenty million Negro brothers smothering in an air-tight cage of poverty in the midst of an affluent society; when you suddenly find your tongue twisted and your speech stammering as you seek to explain to your six-year-old daughter why she can't go to the public amusement park that has just been advertised on television, and see tears welling up in her little eyes when she is told that Funtown is closed to colored children, and see the depressing clouds of inferiority begin to form in her little mental sky, and see her begin to distort her little personality by unconsciously developing a bitterness toward white people; when you have to concoct an answer for a five-year-old son asking in agonizing pathos, 'Daddy, why do white people treat colored people so mean?'; when you take a cross-country drive and find it necessary to sleep night after night in the uncomfortable corners of your automobile because no motel will accept you; when you are humiliated day in and day out by nagging signs reading "white" and "colored"; when your first name becomes "nigger" and your middle name becomes "boy" (no matter how old you are) and your last name becomes "John," and when your wife and mother are never given the respected title "Mrs."; when you are harried by day and haunted by night by the fact that you are a Negro, living constantly at a tip-toe stance, never quite knowing what to expect next, and plagued with inner fears and outer resentments; when you are forever fighting a degenerating sense of "nobodiness"; then you will understand why we find it difficult to wait."[1]

This letter from the Birmingham prison where Martin Luther King Jr. was incarcerated expresses the heart of segregation by the time it took its toll in the 1960s. Following the abolition of slavery, radical racists who supported segregation made their voices known, passing various statutes and laws, ensuring that they were applied until Blacks were treated like beasts wandering about without owners.

Some of these racists lobbied that Blacks should even be deported. People like Hinton Helper lobbied to have them sent back to Africa saying, "After all, they have outlived their usefulness."[2]

Such radical deportation following emancipation was impossible, so another set of seven paternalists began to advocate for a segregation so that free Blacks did not share the same amenities, etc., with Whites.

In *The Crucible of Race: Black White Relations in the American South Since Emancipation*, Joel Williamson writes, "Segregation as executed by the conservatives was for a purpose quite different from that of the radicals. Conservatives sought segregation in public accommodations to protect Black people and their dignity. The conservatives' segregation meant giving the Black person a very special place in which he would be protected. Far from putting down the self-esteem of Black people, conservative segregation was designed to preserve and encourage it."[3]

The objective of the Conservatives may have been lofty, but it was the desire of the racists of the society which became accepted by the public. By 1910, with the support of several companies, judges, and state leaders an elaborate legal segregation system had taken over in the whole of southern America. Separate railway cars, steam ships, separate places for

Blacks and Whites in post offices, prisons, restaurants, theatres, swimming pools, churches, zoos, bowling, and rallies; even mental hospitals observed segregation so that people were assigned to different floors according to their race. So were retirement homes and institutions for the poor. Blacks and Whites did not use the same public amenities like toilets, drinking fountains, parks, and beaches. And in the words of Martin Luther King, Jr., it became very difficult for parents to explain why their children could not enjoy the amenities advertised on television.

It is interesting that today, although the amenities are available, segregation by way of prejudice with reference to what job a Black person can get or not get also keeps most families at bay from the ideal life they see advertised. Segregation wasn't only for the living. In death, funeral homes were also separate, as were cemeteries.

Private companies found that employing Black people required creating separate places of work and amenities, so the cost of running the company became very high; thus Blacks were refused employment in certain places. Every wind of economic adversity which blew in the United States only increased the plight of the person of color, so that by the late 1960s things had reached a matured proportion. There was acute unrest in urban ghettos where Blacks lived.

A Kerner Commission concluded that America was "moving towards two societies: one Black, one White, separate and unequal."

The U.S. National Advisory Commission on Civil Disorders (1888) taps on the extent of segregation. Segregation was applied under all aspects of American lifestyle. Premised upon what was known as the "One Drop Rule," anyone who had any trace of Black blood or Black relationship was considered a Black person. This meant that those previously classified as mulattos now had a worse experience under segregation.[4]

Thomas Dixon, Jr., in his book *The Leopard's Spots* writes "The blood of the Black person kinks the hair, flattens the nose, thickens the lip, puts out the light of intellect and lights the fires of brutal passions."[5]

Segregation was taken so far out that by 1920 mulattos were no longer counted separately, rather they and other races other than White were categorized as Black. So America was divided into Black versus White.

The economic sector reacted by trying to make the absurdity of such laws clear since it meant that companies could not cope with separate cars or rail, trams and ferries. However, politicians who favored this racist principle argued to the businesses that they were putting their profit above racist principles.[6,7]

With laws prohibiting Blacks from working in different categories and places of employment, prohibiting them from education, and many other benefits available to other citizens, there was an evolution of Black neighborhoods. Discrimination and prejudice against them increased the level of poverty in their midst.

In an article by the Society for the Advancement of Education written in 1997, with the subheading "Prejudice: still a big factor in housing," research shows that racial household segregation is largely caused by discrimination against minorities. The society argued that among minority groups, Blacks suffer the greatest amount of discrimination and prejudice. Meanwhile, obscurity and institutional discrimination against Black homebuyers were some of the contributing factors to segregation, indicates Camille Zubrinsky, assistant professor of sociology at Ohio State University, Columbus, and co-author of the study.

Zubrinsky maintains that when Whites were interviewed about living next door to Latinos, Blacks, or other races, the number of those who wanted to live beside Blacks fell drastically. This, according to her, shows, "That there is a rank order among minority groups—the Blacks at the bottom. The Blacks are seen as the least desirable neighbors and this is probably an important reason for the lack of integration in Los Angeles."[8]

THE CONSEQUENCES

The May 1954 landmark decision was given by the Supreme Court of the United States of America questioning the "Separate but Equal" clause on the grounds that separate educational facilities are inherently unequal.[9]

This decision was based on the challenge brought by the NAACP represented by attorney Thurgood Marshall. Marshall invited psychologists Kenneth and Mamie Clark who showed that the segregation of children based on skin color gave Black children, "A feeling of inferiority...that may affect their hearts and minds in a way unlikely ever to be undone."[10]

Western societies are run essentially on the basis of the quality of education you have. This goes on to determine the quality of life, residence, association, friendship, mobility, etc., of a person.

Indicating how it affects the residency of Blacks, Camille Zubrinsky charts in her research titled "The Dynamics of Racial Residential Segregation," that segregation was a major barrier to equality. She also quoted Taeuber and Taeuber, 1965, who wrote of segregation that, "It inhibits the development of informal neighborly relations" and "ensures the segregation of a variety of public and private facilities." Taeuber and Taeuber argued that segregation and its prejudice was to be "Freely vented on negros without hurting whites."[11]

Segregation spilled therefore mainly into the areas where people lived. Residential segregation, according to Douglas Massey and Nancy Denton, "Undermined the social and economic well-being."[12]

A landmark victory was won in the Supreme Court case of Brown versus the Board of Education. However, with legal barriers to educational, occupational, and residential opportunities removed, when Blacks could finally achieve full fledge integration, the color line had already been drawn—physically, socially, and in the minds of people nationwide.

Where we live affects our prospects for jobs, education, relationships, etc. Therefore, whether voluntarily or involuntarily, where people live has consequences on their current and future situation. Segregation may have ended officially but that conformation birthed most of the sociological pathologies in present-day inner-city United States of America.

In the book, *The Truly Disadvantaged*, the author argues that, "Geographically concentrated poverty and the subsequent development of a ghetto under class resulted from structural changes in the economy combined with the exodus of middle and working class Black families from many inner city ghetto neighborhoods."

America actually changed. It shifted from a manufacturing society to a service producing economy. Much of Black education prior to this was working class, preparing people for education. Therefore being unable to adapt to ghettoization resulted.

Massey and Denton also argue that "Without residential segregation these structural changes would not have produced the disastrous social and economic outcomes observed in inner cities."[13]

In an article titled, "Defect to segregation" by Nat Hentoff, a columnist for the *Washington Times*, claims to have had some degree of relationship with Kenneth Clark, the psychologist who was involved in the case before the Supreme Court, *Brown v. Board of Education*. Mr. Clark was the expert in the case and had argued that the segregation of children was making them feel inferior.

Many years down the road, the psychologist Mr. Clark concludes that he has lost hope that the *Brown v. Board of Education* case or any law of the land would have actually ended any segregation in schools. This is because schools are still segregated—if not on legal grounds, at least on grounds of unequal access and based on where people live.

People's residential pattern in parts of the United States has created boundary lines for the various races. In the majority Blacks and ethnic minorities still get the low income jobs and therefore send their children to schools that are essentially run down. The argument remains that America is still segregated.

We might borrow the words of Thurgood Marshall, quoted by Mr. Hentoff, when Mr. Marshall stood before the Supreme Court and said, "Children who do not learn together do not know how to live together."

Advantages to Segregation?

Some think so. The most resourceful of Blacks at that time suddenly were confronted with a niche market. Segregation created the opportunity for barbers and other professions that are specific and could serve the Black community. In the words of Thomas Sowell, "The reluctance of whites to minister to the hair, the bodies or the souls of Blacks created a class of Black barbers, physicians, undertakers and religious ministers."[14]

This also led to the evolution of Black masons, jewelers, tailors, and repairmen. Some even created cooperatives and fellowships with Black people. In that way they established their own real estate businesses and insurance businesses in the core areas where there were large Black communities.[15, 16]

With the acute segregation, Blacks had to become resilient and work their way around the system. The kind of life imposed upon them by segregation was hard, but they had to find freedom and joy in the midst of social oppression.[17]

Oppressed people often find that in the midst of oppression a new creativity flows. During the segregation, Blacks evolved their own kind of music, nightclubs, restaurants, etc.

TACKLING SEGREGATION

Since slavery ended, many schools of thought have evolved on how the Black person should handle segregation, prejudice, and racial discrimination. For the sake of argument, I present two schools—the first represented by Booker T. Washington and the second by W.E.B. DuBois.

Booker T. Washington more or less argues that handling segregation prejudice should be by dint of hard work—going out to achieve until those who condemn you can condemn you no more. It was his opinion that the only way to change the minds of those who are prejudiced against you is not by abusing them but by working hard—taking into account the fact that he overcame a lot of obstacles to become one of America's Black leading artists, educationists, and builders of institutions. He took an attitude of not reacting to White prejudice with bitterness but succeeding against all odds as the best answers.[18]

Booker T. Washington did not see political pressure as a waste of time. However, he considered it an artificial passing of hands to recognize the Black man's plight. It was his opinion that many arguments can be raised against you but no one can argue against success. He said, "The wisest among my race understand that the agitation of questions of social equality is the extremist folly, and that progress and the enjoyment of all the privileges that will come to us must be the result of severe and constant struggle rather than of artificial fussing."[19]

He solicited political activity, political strategy, and worked hard to convince others, but he felt that the greatest thing that could help Blacks is personal discipline, industrial education, and a dint of achievement.

He said that, "We have a right to enter our complaints but we shall make a futile error if we yield to the temptation of believing that mere opposition to our wrongs will take the place of progressive constructive action."

One of the most remarkable things Booker T. Washington was quoted to have said in the article "The Awakening of the Negro," in *Atlantic Monthly*, September 1896, was "Whether he will or not, a white man respects a Negro who owns a two-story brick house."

On the other side of the argument is W.E.B. DuBois. He held an almost opposing view to Booker T. Washington because DuBois was a man of French Dutch and American Indian ancestry. He was the first Black postgraduate degree holder from Harvard University. It was his view that political action and pressure was necessary for change. After all, if it is never the desire of the oppressor to release the oppressed, DuBois felt that if the Black man is to be released, it "is going to be saved by its exceptional men."[20]

DuBois lived at a time slightly different from Booker T. Washington and therefore held the view that complaining and whining was not enough. He thought that the Black man has inherent rights, needs legal rights, and economic opportunities, and should express the same. He said, "We have a right to answer and to answer insistently that the rights we are clamoring for are those that will enable us to do our duties."[21]

This was his response to the White who would say, "Do your duties first and then clamor for rights later." But to DuBois, what is duty if you have no rights? Duty is only established by the legal rights you have.

When one combines Washington's argument for Black self-help with DuBois's argument for legal rights, when one combines Washington's stand against Black promiscuity, profligacy, and crime with DuBois's argument that the Black man is already disadvantaged and it is that disadvantage that causes him to be adversarial to the system, there seems to be a picture emerging.

Consider again Washington's argument that, "A race or an individual which has no fixed habits, no fixed place of abode, no time for going to bed or getting up in the morning, for going to work, no arrangement, order or system in all the ordinary business of life. Such a race or such individuals are lacking in self-control, lacking in some of the fundamentals of civilization."[22]

DuBois does not totally agree with Booker T. Washington. Washington does not fail to recognize the deficiency in the Black community, however he still insists that, "a little less complaint and whining and a little more dogged work will do us more credit than a thousand civil right bills."[23, 24]

Generations of Blacks in America today still suffer the consequence of the years of segregation which followed slavery. This conformation in my opinion had a great impact on the self-image of the African American, and thus became the womb in which teenage pregnancy, crime, single-parent challenges, and other pathologies of the African American Black community were born.

ENDNOTES

1. Martin Luther King Jr., *Why We Can't Wait* (New York: Harper & Row, 1964).

2. Hinton Rowan Helper, *Nojoque* (New York, 1867), 251.

3. Joel Williamson, *The Crucible of Race: Black/White Relations in the American South since Emancipation* (New York: Oxford University Press, 1984), 254.

4. Marvin Harris, *Patterns of Race in the Americas* (West Port, CT: Greenwood Press, 1964), 56.

5. Cited in Joel Williamson, *The Crucible*.

6. Jennifer Roback, "The Political Economy of Segregation: The Case of Segregated Street Cars," *Journal of Economic History*, (1988), 46.

7. Edward L. Ayers, *The Promise of the New South: Life after Reconstruction* (New York: Oxford University Press, 1992), 143.

8. www.soc.upenn.edu/CVs%20and%20PDF%20Files/ camillecharles_05_06.pdf.

9. Brown v. Board of Education of Topeka, 347 U.S.483, (1954).

10. http://c250.columbia.edu/c250_celebrates/remarkable_ columbians/kenneth_mamie_clark.html.

11. http://www.questia.com/googleScholar.qst;jsessionid= GgjZZq2hKxgQ3Fy3stQTmyJ5bPKDx0hwv5DbhQvvcyn 8QrQ5119d!-1899162586?docId=5002052001

12. Douglas Massey and Nancy Denton, *American Apartheid: Segregation and the Making of the Underclass* (Cambridge: Harvard University Press, 1993).

13. Massey and Denton.

14. Thomas Sowell, *Markets and Minorities* (New York: Basic Books, 1981), 61.

15. John S. Butler, *Entrepreneurship and Self-Help Among Black Americans: A Reconsideration of Race and Economics* (Albany: State University of New York Press, 1991).

16. Abram Harris, *The Negro as Capitalist* (New York: Arno Press, 1936).

17. Albert Murray, *The Omni Americans: Black Experience and American Culture* (New York: Outer Bridge & Diensfrey, 1970).

18. Judge W. Jacobs, *The Negro in the South* (New York, 1907), 10.

19. Booker T. Washington, *Up from Slavery* (New York: Penguin Books, 1986), 201.

20. W.E.B. DuBois, "The Talented Tenth," *The Negro Problem* (New York: Arno Press, 1969), 33.

21. W.E.B. DuBois, *W.E.B. Du Bois Speaks* (New York: Pathfinder Press, 1978).

22. Emmett J. Scott & Lyman Beecher Stowe, *Booker T. Washington: Builder of a Civilization* (New York: Double Day, 1917), 231.

23. W.E.B. DuBois, *The Negro American Family* (Cambridge: MIT Press, 1970), 37.

24. W.E.B. DuBois, *The Philadelphia Negro* (Philadelphia: University of Pennsylvania Press, 1899), 389-390.

CHAPTER 24

Self-Image Problem

"Do you really think a nigger's a human being?"

That was the question Clay Hopper, the disgusted manager of the Brooklyn Dodgers, asked the general manager who ordered him to train Jackie Robinson, the first Black major league baseball player, in 1946.

The fishers also shall mourn, and all they that cast angle into the brooks shall lament, and they that spread nets upon the waters shall languish (Isaiah 19:8).

Isaiah's prophecy about the experience of the Egyptian (analyzed previously) further indicates that the person of color was likely to lose the knowledge of his ancestry or have it concealed from him.

How true. The majority of Blacks do not know their origin, and when people have stumbled onto great truths about Blacks, there has been a great effort to conceal the truth.

Moreover they that work in fine flax, and they that weave networks, shall be confounded (Isaiah 19:9).

Blacks as a people of class and culture, a people of elegance and beauty would end up becoming "confounded"—low, crude, and considered uncultured.

Isaiah 19 may be a prophecy. The subsequent experience of Blacks, the subjugation of slavery, rejection, and treatment as people inferior would continue to shape the self-image of Blacks.

In an article titled, "I am Somebody" by Christopher Shea posted on www.salon.com on June 2, 2000, the writer states, "Race and self-esteem are inextricably bound in the popular imagination. Thanks to racism and discrimination, the theory goes, a core of self-doubt lurks in the heart of every Black child and young adult."[1]

Christopher Shea's argument probably takes a different turn from this chapter. However, in that brief statement he mirrors what this pathology of the Black person is.

Jesus was keenly aware of who He was and what His mission on earth was. It was clear and obvious from His ability to accept who He was and interact with people that Jesus was comfortable with His identity. It is from this that He taught all people to have a healthy self-esteem and after that, to love their neighbors as they love themselves.

This is My commandment, that you love one another as I have loved you (John 15:12 NKJV).

In Matthew 22:39 Jesus said that the second greatest commandment is to love your neighbor as you love yourself. Paradoxically, it would be very hard to give your neighbor what you cannot give yourself. So loving yourself is at the core of a healthy self-image.

And the second is like it: 'You shall love your neighbor as yourself' (Matthew 22:39 NKJV).

In order to fully appreciate how the self-image of the Black person or the self-esteem of the people of color has affected their progress in life we may need to define what it fully means.

In the book, *Honoring the Self: Self-esteem and Personal Transformation*, the author, Dr. Nathanal Branden answers the question: "Does self-esteem mean feeling good about yourself?"

Branden says that self-esteem is an experience which involves your emotion, your intellect, and your will. Part of self-esteem, he explains, is your ability to be able to cope with the challenges of life and handle it in a way that it does not diminish your joy or your person.

A healthy self-esteem, he says, makes you know that being successful, blessed, and progressive is not unnatural or bad, but rather a healthy thing to expect. If you have difficulty handling these things, you have a problem with your self-esteem.

A healthy self-esteem is not a by-product of a drug, and it is not enhanced by drugs. It is essentially who you are on the inside without external forces having any influence. A healthy self-image or self-esteem is not narcissistic, yet it is the ability to accept yourself and have a good time just by yourself, or in the words of Oscar Wilde, "To love oneself is the beginning of a life-long romance."

So the long struggle of Black people with self-image and its various manifestations in their constant attempts to launch themselves in various kinds of shapes, images, and opinions of other people, may be a sign that one of the pathologies that have followed the things that have shaped Blacks is a self-image problem.

We cannot overlook this pathology because it may be where help is needed the most if the man of color is to gain his regal position in God and maximize his potential in life.

In an old issue of *Cosmopolitan* magazine (1959), P.F. James had this to say, "Understanding the psychology of the self can mean the difference between success and failure, love and hate, bitterness and happiness. The discovery of the real self can rescue a crumbling marriage, recreate a faltering career, transform victims of 'personality failure'."

It is hard to meet anyone who has not had self-image challenges in life, even people who seem to be very sure of themselves. We readily admit to having had bouts of low self-esteem, bouts of self-esteem challenges.

REASONS FOR BLACK POOR SELF-IMAGE

It is very difficult to deal with individual behavior or life patterns without looking at the collective factors. However remote a historical basis may be, it possibly could have resulted in shaping people's self-perception.

During the period of slavery in the new world for example, the slave master's fine house, beautiful landscaping, exquisite clothes, and objects were associated with power and status, while the slaves had to make do with the poor leftovers. They had no rights and felt perpetually inferior.

Slaves or ex-slaves who showed any inclinations or abilities of leadership were immediately put down, eliminated, isolated, killed, or ridiculed. In a previous chapter the leadership crisis within the Black community was examined.

There is a long history of Blacks being conditioned to reject natural and strong leadership in their midst, and today when individuals do manifest such ability it is sometimes tainted as not being very representative of the people they purport to lead.

This historical challenge of what Blacks have gone through in slavery and in the new world of colonialists in Africa has meant that the person of color often tends to see himself as being inferior to the White race.

Debra Dickerson said, "Blacks can't claim their own power because, in their heart of hearts, they believe the white man's version of them as immoral. Ugly. Dumb. In their heart of hearts, they believe in the white man's version of himself as smarter, good at math. Since no one believes in white superiority more than Blacks, when whites respect Blacks, Blacks will be able to respect themselves."[2]

The majority of prominent Blacks are in the world of athletics and entertainment, not in intellectual acuity, moral integrity, technological know-how, managerial efficiency, or the expression of vision; therefore this continues to convey the impression that Blacks are not really achievers.

With the abolition of slavery came segregation. Being made to apologize for who you are, having to settle for the inferior, and having to sit at the back of the bus or go to a poorer school, play in the worst park, etc., dampened and reduced the self-image of a person of color.

A more modern reason for a poor self-esteem is the atmosphere in which Blacks grow up, particularly in the West. There is a high level of single parenthood among Blacks in Europe, the Caribbean, and the United States.

There will certainly be exceptions to the rule.

Unfortunately with a great number of the new generation growing up without the presence of a father, the immediate image the young person grows up with is dented. Julia McNamee Neenan, reporter for Health-Scout in her article, "Having no dad affects Black boys' self-esteem: Life with father translates to stronger kids," writes that a report indicates that when fathers are not present in Black families, irrespective of the level of income and education afforded the young person, the self-esteem of the boy drops. But this does not appear to happen with young girls. This apparently is the reason why boys end up participating in gangs as they continue to look for male role models.[3]

While a girl can cope with a home where there is no father to a degree, it is imperative that there be a male person in the home to model a positive lifestyle for the young man. Carolyn Murray, associate professor at the University of California Riverside, is also quoted in the Health-Scout article that, "Just 25% of Black children were raised in homes in which only the mother was present in 1960 but that that number had climbed to 54% in 1993. In the 1950s, 78% of Black homes were led by both parents but only 34% in 1996 were led by both parents. And even in the 21st century the figure has now escalated to about 80% single parenthood in Black America."

Dr. Murray's report shows that boys from families headed by married couples scored higher on tests than boys from families headed solely by a mother; and when Dr. Murray scored the boys specifically on self-esteem matters, the picture became grimmer. Boys who have the presence of a father, who see and feel "macho," seem to score higher, meaning that they feel stronger and more competitive than boys from a home where there is no father present.

Once there is a struggle with self-esteem from childhood, the image becomes tougher to change as the person matures, and even if their circumstances change they have to fight the self-esteem battle in order to regain confidence.

From this report, it seems no one has it rougher than Black boys when it comes to growing up in the United States of America. The issues a Black boy has to deal with every day simply because his skin is different are enough to dampen self-esteem and reduce quality self-image.

The irony of it all is that while he is wrestling with all these feelings about himself, there is nowhere to go for help. Not only do the boys have challenges with their self-esteem but Black girls face self-esteem challenges too. They worry many times about their physical attractiveness. Many aspects of today's society seem to validate certain shades of skin above the others.

In the West, the Black people are still struggling with skin tone. Psychologists Derek and Darlene Hopson operate the Hopson Center for psychological and educational services in Connecticut and they have concluded that, "Our own community is still struggling with stereotypes about skin tone and hair structure."[4]

Even in the 21st century, Dr. Hopson notes, Blacks still make statements like, "She is dark skinned but she is pretty" as if to be dark was not to be beautiful. This influences how a girl perceives herself.

There are so many other things which affect Black self-esteem. Employability, the quality of job they have, the real estate they possess or do not possess, societal perception of their person, and in the case of Black Africans whether in the Diaspora or in their country of original birth, the feeling of having an accent inferior to the French, English, Portuguese, or Spanish languages of their colonial masters tend to sometimes determine their self-esteem. Language may become the basis of their national jokes.

THE DAMAGE

The miseducation of many people influences how they depict Blacks and has caused tremendous damage. Schools in the West still portray Africa with an image of savagery. Yolanda Harper-Garcia, who co-founded the University of Tulsa's African American Studies program, talked about the severity of this image when she said, "That many supposedly adult school teachers fear African American boys as early as pre-school and kindergarten." This fear often times, according to her, leads to an unfair treatment of such children.[5]

Once you have a self-esteem problem you begin to wonder what is exactly appropriate, what behavior is acceptable or not acceptable, what language, what word, and what action is acceptable or not. And in the end we can sabotage ourselves or hurt ourselves deeply by being self-expressive.

There is a consequence of a poor self-image that Judge Garrow, Executive Director of the National Organization of Concerned Black Men, identified when he said that, "Boys growing up in fatherless families seem to do well until around the 3rd grade when they begin to need focus." Lacking a father's influence, he says, "They begin to seek male role models."

It is Mr. Garrow's opinion that if the father's role is never fulfilled the boys may join gangs or unhealthy groups. From these mentors, Mr. Garrow says, "Such a young man is going to play out what he thinks is the image of a man."

A healthy or poor self-esteem, according to the California study we discussed earlier, makes little of income and much of the place of parental presence, particularly the male presence as it influences a boy. Once self-esteem is damaged, people either pull into their shell and become less expressive and unable to adequately participate in the wellbeing of society, or could put on egotism and end up, according to Dr. Nathaniel Branden, "Bragging, boasting, arrogating to oneself qualities one does not possess, throwing one's weight around, seeking to prove one's superiority to others, all evidences of insecurity and undeveloped self-esteem."[6]

If poor self-esteem is not dealt with, it begins to be expressed verbally, "Nobody likes me, I am ugly, I never do anything right, I am dumb, I am a failure and on and on and on…."

This kind of negative self-talk comes forth from a person who has low self-esteem. Even if it is not spoken, the individual still believes it. The interesting thing about people with poor self-esteem is that they tend to also look for someone who treats them that way, who makes statements like, "You will never amount to anything, nobody will ever want you, you are lucky to have me, you are stupid, ugly, brainless, worthless, a loser, good for nothing, you are an awful wife, mother, student, person, you are on your own on this, you drive me nuts, and so on…."

THE WAY OUT?

All humankind receives their true identity from God. It is only in tracing our history, identity, and origins back to God that we find our true godly positive image. When God created man He did not mean for him to divide and rule on the basis of the color of the skin as has been established in this book. In Bible times, language, family, and nationality were the basis for the separation of people, not the color of the skin. For what it is worth there must be a desire to have a strong positive self-esteem. This will come with a desire to succeed.

Setting yourself free is a process which comes along with a desire to succeed and the pursuit of that goal with every step you take. The desire to succeed becomes a driving force that keeps the individual from continuing and trying in the face of failure. In the article, "Your Personal Guide to Ending Abuse," Jan Black, who is also the author of *It's Not OK Anymore* says, "Success and self-esteem feed each other. Success increases your self-esteem and self-esteem leads you to more and more success. By taking charge of your life you step onto the upward path of general fulfillment."

Jan Black also recommends that you form habits of hearing messages that build self-esteem like, "You are gifted and capable, you are desirable, I am happy to have you in my life, you are bright and attractive, sensible, valuable and powerful, you are able to be a great wife, mother, student, person, I am here to help you, you are no bother."

We are dealing with self-esteem as it applies to a person of a particular race who feels continuously let down, put down, and trampled on.

This is what informs how self-esteem can be built from the point of view of Nathaniel Branden's writing in the article, "To succeed at anything in life you must know how and when to be assertive." He writes this advice:

❖ Recognize your right to exist.

❖ When in doubt, speak up. You might say something inappropriate but this is part of learning to be yourself.

❖ Demystify rejection. Rejection is more than a possibility. Learn to take rejection in stride.

❖ Rehearse new ways of expressing yourself.

How many people have shrunken into their shell once they are conscious that their particular way of expressing themselves will be viewed from the point of view of the one receiving what they are trying to communicate in a negative way. It is important to accept yourself for who you are and to put value on your person.

Earlier, we had referred to a lot of challenges young men and women face on matters of self-esteem. In order to build the confidence of a Black young person, it is important for parents to do a great deal to make the road to self-esteem easier for them.

This can be made possible by focusing on the practices which support and nurture self-esteem, encouraging young people to understand the power of self-acceptance, self-responsibility, and self-assertiveness within the boundaries of purposefulness and integrity.

Racial stereotypes are likely to be around for a long time; however its impact on a person's self-esteem can be handled if they are properly prepared. In order to protect Black young people from feeling damaged, dented, or belittled from racial slurs or attitudes, parents should discuss this possibility before the experience takes place, so is the opinion of Dr. Yolanda Harper Garcia, a licensed clinical psychologist and adjunct professor of psychology at the African American University of Tulsa. Parents in her opinion should be, "Realistic about societal impression. Discuss and debunk negative stereotypes. Explain how little things such as donning the gold rope, baggy jeans and floppy hat of his favourite rapper can color some people's perceptions."

Of course wearing a European suit and tie does not make that child immune from prejudice. Parents should discuss with their children how race influences behavior. Let them know it exists and that it must not determine the quality of their own life or how they perceive themselves. In whatever color they have come forth, they are just as beautiful as anyone else. Young people should be taught to know that racial name calling is a product of ignorance.

All humans are essentially the same, and skin difference is only 1/16th of an inch deep. Nobody can build the self-esteem of a child like the parent and this begins by the celebration of the child's birth and achievement, no matter how little, followed by the presence of the parent whenever there is an event: a sporting event, graduation, etc.

Dr. Garcia thinks that parents need to equip their children by teaching them anger management. After all, once in a while, challenges will come that have to do with race, and they could offend a child—his or her ability to manage anger will many times keep that child out of trouble. Black girls and boys must not be compared to someone else, but rather supported in all their development.

It is important that the Black community forms the habit of helping young people develop character and not focus only on talent. A young lady must be taught that it is not all right for her to be disrespected. No one deserves her hand to date if he does not respect her. When the body of a young girl begins to change, parents need to talk with her about womanhood and the changes she is likely to experience so that these strange changes are presented in a positive light and therefore she is helped in her self-esteem to see that what is happening to her body is natural, not a bad experience but a positive sign of development.

One may be tempted to conclude that this chapter deals more with young people; however, self-esteem is something we all have to deal with all our lives. When college is completed, then we are confronted with the challenges of career development, getting a place for our family, building a home, raising godly children, taking care of our physical body, and managing our lives in a way that keeps us healthy, wealthy, and wise.

For a person seeking to build their self-esteem, Mary Helen Copeland, in her writing, "Blueprints for Building Self-esteem"[7] lists exercises as a way to raise your self-esteem:

❖ Surround yourself with people who are positive, affirming, and loving.

❖ Wear something that makes you feel good.

❖ Look through old pictures, scrapbooks and photo albums; make a collage of your life.

❖ Spend ten minutes writing down everything good you can think of about yourself.

❖ Do something that makes you laugh.

❖ Pretend you are your own best friend.

❖ Repeat positive statements over and over again.

❖ Always recognize the fact that the true emancipation of Blacks must start with the restoring of a positive image of themselves.

The feeling of inferiority requires two people: the one who tries to make you feel inferior and your active participation in accepting that you really are. But once you know that no man should make you feel less than who God says you are, then you are on your way to winning and maintaining a positive self-image.

ENDNOTES

1. Christopher Shea, "I am Somebody," www.archive.salon.com/hell/feature/2000/06/02/Blackselfesteem.

2. Debra J. Dickerson, *The End Of Blackness* (New York: Anchor Books, Random House Inc., 2005).

3. Julia McNamee Neenan, HealthScout, September 2000, http://www.divorcereform.org/self.html.

4. Darlene and Derek Hopson, *Different and Wonderful: Raising Black Children in a Race-Conscious Society* (New York: Simon & Schuster, 1992).

5. www.familydigest.com/story/sons.cfm.

6. www.m_a_h.net/library/coping/article_misconceptions.html.

7. www.healthhorizons.com/care/search_details.html.

CHAPTER 25

Marginalization

The focus of this chapter will be mainly the experience of Black people in Europe. Contact with Africa and Blacks dates back 600 years, from the days of the early explorers from Portugal and Spain who visited the likes of Benin Kingdom in Nigeria in the 15th century. In those times Blacks were brought to Europe more as exotic beings and later in the 17th and 18th centuries began to be exported to the new world as slaves.

At such time Black presence in Europe was very limited. During the 19th century, the European country which was most welcoming to Blacks was France. This mass migration of Blacks from the colonies to France became necessary because of France's challenge with the decrease in birth rate and the need to fill job vacancies. Immigration of Blacks into France was not the only experience; there was also a large immigration of European and Latin people into France to meet the labor needs.

Some of the colonies that were under France's rule were Arab nations, i.e., Algeria, Morocco, Tunisia; these also had a large migration pattern into France. In 1975 France organized the right for migrants to bring their families with them. This created a major influx of people from the "third world" between the 1970s and 1990s.

Between the 1970s and the early 1980s, the number of migrants in France rose tremendously:

❖ 1.5 million from other European nations, particularly East Europeans.

❖ 1.4 million North Africans.

❖ 400,000 Asians.

During this period, about 800,000 Algerians had migrated to France, thus becoming probably one of the largest foreign nationalities in the country of France. Migration from northern French-speaking African countries also increased so that by the early nineties there were 4.2 million immigrants in France.

Fifty-five percent of the migrants came from various European countries, 8 percent Asian, and 34 percent from African countries. Here, we will include as African countries the Arab African countries.[1]

This long pattern of immigration dating back to the 19th century possibly accounts for the research by the French National Institute for Demographic Studies (INED) which assessed and concluded that 20 percent of the French population has at least one ascendant of a foreign origin.[2]

This makes France possibly the European country with the most important migratory flow and one of the countries on earth which must be said to be multicultural in a lot of ways.

The post-war industries of Europe created a new middle class which left a vacuum, resulting in the need for employing mostly lower class employees and people with specialized skills. This led to Britain's campaign in the 1940s for people from the Caribbean to come and work.

France is an example of the extensive migration of Black people into the whole of Europe. Particularly for France, since the 1970s in a larger way, and for the United Kingdom for example in the late 1940s and mid-1980s.

However, in spite of this large Black presence and the colonial relationship, statistics and the daily experience of Blacks appears to confirm a marginalization of people of color in Europe.

Some of the areas of their marginalization are in quality education, employment, their negative experience with the penal system, immigration, and their poor or non-effective presence in the media.

Other areas of marginalization could, of course, be added to this list but for the sake of argument in this book it is limited to these few subtopics.

In her writing, "Ethnic Minorities: Which Place and Which Image on French Television," Marie-France Malonga said, "French television rarely shows people of extra European origin: Blacks, Arabs, Asians. In fact this is not difficult to notice, the TV journalists or TV hosts of non-European origin are an exception, let alone speaking of their presence in the different programs: news, news magazines, shows, films, commercials etc."[3]

Marie-France argues that whenever people of color appear, they are stereotyped in negative situations. In an earlier chapter it was established that in the United States, for example, the people who probably give a larger concentration of time to television viewing are Blacks but then in Europe, because France mirrors what happens in most other European countries, there is a marginalization of people of color as far as the media is concerned.

It order to show the place of television in reporting the subject of immigration, for the first time in 1991 a research center organized a study on the subject. The Center for Information and Research on International Migration (CIEMI) looked at how French television reported the subject of immigration and how immigrants and ethnic minorities were presented on television. The aim of the research was to answer questions like, "Which image and which discourse does television give of immigration? Do private and public channels contribute to integrate or exclude people of extra-European origin? Does television contribute to create, reinforce, or destroy prejudices?"[4]

These questions raised by the researchers certainly mirrors what happens across Europe. Many times, when Blacks appear on European television, if it is not as an athlete or a musician, if it is not a Black who is making a fool of himself, then it would possibly be as Blacks in crisis in Ethiopia, Darfur, the Hutu/Tutsi crisis, or some warfare in parts of Africa.

As a matter of fact, there are people who live in the West who cannot imagine that there are skyscrapers in the Democratic Republic of Congo or beautiful restaurants in Addis Ababa, Ethiopia. Selective presentation means that Africa is mostly presented in a negative way.

However, our focus is on Blacks in Europe. Again it is hard to draw conclusions about what is happening in the Black community if you have to depend on regular television since Blacks are hardly featured. In the whole of the broadcasting time, there might be one or two newscasters representing the whole of the ethnic minority community.

The same researchers drew the conclusion that "Ethnic minorities are invisible in programs about news and general information. It does seem to belong to French social reality. Nevertheless their presence on television is limited to a simple visibility on screen because very few of them express themselves."

MARGINALIZATION EXPRESSED AT BLACKS

Minority journalists, hosts, and presenters represent only a small portion of television professionals. The oxymoron of Europe is that whenever it wants to show a strong Black setting or Black programming that is in any way positive, it airs American sitcoms such as *Different Strokes, The Cosby Show, The Prince of Bel Air, Miami Vice*, etc.

In some of the European countries, if it were not for these American imports which they superimpose their language on, there would be almost no Black actors ever on their television.

The other interesting thing about the marginalization of Blacks in the media in Europe is the fact that whenever television portrays Blacks it isn't for their worth or achievements, it has to be within a certain stereotype which the media has conjured up about Blacks: happy, athletic, sensual, noisy, passionate, etc.

This is more like a continuation of an image that dates back to the days of slavery when Blacks were never understood, and it seems there is no attempt to understand them still.

Essentially the media in Europe has not helped in multicultural cohesion. If it continues to present Blacks as being intellectually and physically lazy, socially incompetent, and sexually uncontrollable, then prejudice will continue for a long time and Blacks will continue to be marginalized.

Another area where Blacks have experienced intense marginalization is in education. A higher proportion of African and Caribbean children are excluded from schools than any other ethnic group in the United Kingdom.[5]

In 2003, for example, 40 percent of 15-year-old Black girls had five or more A to C grades at GCSE level compared to 25 percent of boys; while 56 percent of White girls had the same grade, and 46 percent of White boys had the same grade.[6]

Educational integration is vital to any society, but the disparity continues to widen the gap of society and continuously marginalizes Blacks.

Another example, Black pupils were more likely to be permanently excluded from school than any other group. Forty in every 10,000 children in the "other Black group" and 38 in every 10,000 of "Black Caribbean children" were excluded compared to 13 in every 10,000 White children and 3 in every 10,000 Indian children.[7]

The struggle for a continuous presence in education for Blacks is even worse in higher education. Black Caribbean men were least likely to have degrees and among women Pakistanis and Bangladeshis were least likely.[8]

When it comes to educational marginalization, the matter is worse when it comes to science subjects. Take the case of Ken George in an article titled, "Filling the Black Hole."[9] When people see Ken George they see an athlete, an actor, or maybe a model. When he says he is a teacher, they think he is a teacher in physical education. However Ken George is a Black teacher in the world of Science Engineering and Technology, an area most deficient of Black faces in Europe.

Earlier we talked about the absence of Black faces on television. This absence hurts aspiring Black young people because they only see others like themselves excelling in sports and entertainment, and are likely to think that these are the only areas in which they can succeed.

Sharon Witto of the Birmingham Partnership for Change, coordinating a conference on Science Engineering and Technology (SET), said, "African Caribbean children are just not aspiring to careers in SET."[10]

The fear of the likes of Sharon Witto is the fact that, for example, within the Birmingham area where she lives, within two years of her speech, 50 percent of Birmingham's school population will be from ethnic minority, and yet key areas that serve industries do not have Blacks.

The anachronism is that African Caribbean Student Population Birmingham Education Authority Statistics indicates that at the GCSE level, only 13 percent of Black students are achieving A to C grades, whereas these same kids' figures in primary school show them to be the best performers in maths in the Birmingham area.[11]

Someone often held up as a shining example in the world of Science Engineering and Technology in the Birmingham area is Liz Rasekoala, a chemical engineer and founder of the African Caribbean Network for Science & Technology, who studied originally in Nigeria and now practices in the United Kingdom.

She comments, "My personal experience and that of many other Black professionals in SET in Britain is one of isolation, invisibility and marginalization." She was part of a force known as "The Respect Campaign" to get Black children into science.[12]

There are also other reasons for Black underperformance in school. However, there is abundant evidence that teachers may possibly carry their prejudices into the classroom and do not expect much from the students.

When people have been excluded from the flow of education, certainly there will be a knock-on effect in other areas. Peter Herbert,[13] chairman of the Society of Black Lawyers and a member of the Metropolitan Police Association, notes, "The closer you go to the center of power and influence in Britain the fewer Black people you are likely to find there."

It is very interesting to see that whenever boardroom or political scenes are portrayed on television there is hardly ever a person of color featured. Peter Herbert maintains that, "If you go into a city boardroom the only Black people you are likely to see are receptionists, cleaners or security guards. When white people go out socially, they mix with Black people but in terms of who they do business with, it is generally not with us."

"Not with us" because there is a marginalization going on in Europe that describes Blacks as "the visible minority." The same applies, of course, in the economic and political heartbeat of the nations. Again Peter Herbert, "The Labour Party talks about political shortlist but nobody mentions Black and minority shortlists. If you don't want a situation where part of the population is excluded from economic and political activity you must have affirmative action."

Talking about marginalization, in the United Kingdom neither the Department for Trade and Industries, the DFEE, nor the Office for National Statistics hold any data of significance and reliability on the types of employment held by African Caribbeans in the entire country.

CRIMINAL JUSTICE SYSTEM

If "Lady Justice" is blind, she is certainly not color blind when it comes to the application of the law with Black people all across Europe.

In the United Kingdom, Blacks are three times more likely to be arrested than Whites.[14] Blacks get longer sentences than any other people—that is 54 percent get four years or more as opposed to 43 percent of whites.[15]

This has made the British prison population of Blacks soar by 54 percent. Seventy-seven percent of all young people who have been accused of murder, that is young people between the ages of 10-17 since 1997 when the Labour Party came into power, to date have been Afro-Caribbeans.[16]

In effect the whole system tends to criminalize Blacks. One must conclude that Lady Justice is not color blind because the sentence prison allocation of Blacks seems to have racial bias. For example, in 2001-2002, of 714,000 stop and searches recorded by the police, 12 percent were of Black people. Remember, they are only 1.8 percent of the total population of Britain. Black people were eight times more likely to be stopped and searched than White people.[17]

When a matter relating to a Black young person gets to court, the number of the pleas of not-guilty with Blacks is higher and eventual acquittal is also higher, 51 percent for Blacks and 41 percent for Whites. This differential is purely because many of the Black young offenders who pleaded not guilty should not have been in court in the first place.

An academic survey published in December 2002 shows that Black people are six times more likely to be sent to prison than Whites for a first sentence. This same survey shows that of the 72,406 prisoners in Britain, 15 percent are Blacks, in spite of the fact that Blacks are only slightly over 1 percent of the population.[18]

The contradictory truth about these statistics is that the only place where Blacks have a majority presence—is in the prisons.

For effective justice, how can Blacks be excluded from the police and the judicial system; it is hard to believe that they can get non-prejudicial justice when they are not represented in these career fields. People of minority ethnic backgrounds are underrepresented in all grades as employees in the police, the prison service, and in senior positions of the criminal justice agencies.

In the United Kingdom, none of the law lords or high court judges are from an ethnic minority, and out of the 610 circuit judges only 6 are of ethnic minority, which represents 1 percent.

There are 33,000 magistrates, and only 4.8 percent of that number is of the ethnic minorities. There are 1,074 Queen's counsels—senior barristers—only 7 are Black and 7 are Asians in spite of the fact that 9 percent of 13,000 barristers are from ethnic minority groups.

This magnitude of marginalization and discrimination certainly makes it very difficult to accept the British penal system as being fair to all races.

However, the most notorious use of the penal system to marginalize Blacks is when European institutions such as the judicial system, immigration agency, and police combine to control the flow of Blacks in Europe. The consequent effect has been an explosion of foreigners and immigrants in the prisons of Europe.

It has also led to "far right" political groups, like the British National Party (BNP) of Britain and Le Pen's Party in France, riding and using race as a Trojan horse to gain political popularity.

Europe is fast becoming more like the United States where in 1989 American prisons for the first time in history turned majority Black. The government of the United States says it is a result of its war on drugs, and law and order.[19, 20, 21]

Reading through the various conformations and pathologies in this book, it would not be difficult to conclude why there is such a high crime rate within the Black community in the United States of America.

A similar cause and effect situation exists in Europe where there is clear evidence of Black underemployment and ghettoization. In certain parts of Europe, Blacks are deliberately made to live in run-down, government-owned housing.

The first Blacks who were attracted to work in Europe after the Second World War, in Britain in particular, were brought to the cities where the industries were. However, European economy shifted its emphasis from goods to the service industry; and since then, it has been very difficult for the Black community to readjust.

Along with such absence of adjustment is also a new immigration of Black migrants because of the constant upheavals in the African continent. Europe now seems to be using the penal system to manage poverty and inequality by imprisoning people from the Black community who are caught in this web.

So whether it is a control mechanism, poverty, inequality, immigration, etc., the population of prisoners in the European Union has witnessed a significant increase. Between 1983 and 1995 the number of prisoners rose in England from 43,000 to 55,000. In France, from 39,000 to 53,000; Italy, 41,000 to 50,000; Spain, 14,000 to 40,000; and Holland, from 4,000 to nearly 10,000.[22, 23]

The marginalization becomes apparent when one considers the fact that Blacks, who in the majority end up foul in the penal system, are actually second generation immigrants who are really not immigrants but Europeans who are of the visible minority extraction.

Remember that because of the struggle of their parents with employment in the goods industry and the subsequent challenge of this second generation to do well in the educational system of Europe, the tendency was for them to fall within the lower class distribution and to suffer multiple discriminations.

In the Netherlands, for example, prison population has tripled in 15 years, and 43 percent of its prison population in 1993 were foreigners. The possibility of being sanctioned with an unsuspended prison sentence has become very high for people of the Surinamese or Moroccan origin in the Netherlands.[24]

France was referenced earlier where the share of foreigners in the prison population has increased from 18 percent in 1975 to 29 percent 20 years later, even though foreigners in the whole of France make up only 6 percent of the country's total population. Demographer Pierre Tournier has shown that if you were of French citizenship, you were more likely to go free, get a suspended sentence, or receive community service. However if you were a foreigner or a person who does not possess French citizenship, you were more readily imprisoned. As a matter of fact, he argues that the chances of being sentenced to prison as a foreigner was 2.4 times higher than for a French man, even if they were arrested for the same offense or the French man had a prior record.

In the area of immigration, because of the change in the laws, foreigners implicated in illegal immigration suddenly rocketed in France from 7,000 in 1976 to 44,000 in 1993. The majority of them were sanctioned based on Article 19 relating to unlawful entry and residence. Effectively, they are thrown behind bars for this which is just 1 of 16 misdemeanors most often tried before courts.

The growing share of foreigners in the prisons of France is due extensively in the past 20 years to the violation of immigration statutes and the subsequent incarceration of those who violate them. This over-representation in French prisons sends a message of Black inferiority because on one hand it uses great severity of the penal institution against them as it tries to repress illegal immigration by means of imprisonment.[25, 26]

Belgium uses a different approach but achieves the same marginalization of foreigners in its application of immigration laws. Between 1974 and 1994, the number of foreigners who had been sent to detention centers increased nine-fold. They were sent to centers for foreigners called "En situation irrégulière." There were five so-called "closed centers" surrounded by a double row of barbed wire fencing and under constant video surveillance. This place served as a launch pad for the deportation of 15,000 foreigners each year. It was the country's way of responding to far right groups who took advantage and used immigration to increase their popularity.

In Italy, deportation quintupled in only four years. By 1994 deportation had reached 57,000. This was in spite of the fact that the majority of the foreigners whose short-term visas may have elapsed originally entered the country legally to meet the demands of the job market since some of the available jobs were not sought by nationals.[27]

How much damage does this kind of conformation do to Blacks in Europe, and what is the far reaching effect?

Loic Wacquant in an article "Suitable Enemies: Foreigners and Immigrants in the Prisons of Europe" writes, "Thus it is that throughout Europe police, judicial, and penal practice converge at least in that they are applied with special diligence and severity to persons of non-European phenotype, who are easily spotted and made to bend to the police and judicial arbitrarily, to the point that one may speak of a veritable process of criminalisation of immigrants that tends, by its destructuring and criminogenic effect, to 'produce the very phenomenon that it is supposed to combat, in accord with the well-known mechanism of the self-fulfilling prophecy'."[28, 29]

This form of marginalization reduces people's dignity, takes away comforts, violates human rights, and in the case where a parent has been imprisoned for matters as flimsy as being an over-stayer, the family is destabilized and is thrown into a one-parent situation.

Some of these laws have been enforced in the crudest of ways. In France for example, the conditions of confinement in some of its detention centers and prisons violate the most basic standards of human dignity. Jean Perrin-Martin in his work "La Retention Paris"[30] highlights the case of the infamous center of Arenq near the Marseille Harbour Station, where a dilapidated hangar built in 1917, lacking any form of comfort necessary for humans, has served as a warehouse for 1,500 foreigners deported each year to North Africa.

It seems like all paths converge when it comes to the penal system and immigration—the media and the politicians. The media amplifies the cry of the politicians for the control of immigration which creates a xenophobic wave within the community.

Certainly not every Black in Europe is being criminalized. However, marginalization, possibly because of the number of Blacks in Europe, has been clearly established. People will reinforce the image they see. If the image of ethnic minority on television is that of unemployment, delinquency, poverty, and racism, then marginalization continues to be reinforced.

There is a minority that is doing quite well and contributing its positive quota to the European community. For that number to increase, media prejudice toward ethnic minority must change and so should the educational and penal system.

ENDNOTES

1. Yvan Gastaut, Association of European Migration Institutions; http://www.aemi.dk/news.php?page=120.

2. M. Triballat, National Institute for Demographic Studies, http://www.ined.fr/en/.

3. Marie-France Malonga; www.lse.ac.uk/collections/EMTEL/Minorities/papers/franceminorepres.doc.

4. Antonio Pererote; http://www.ciemi.org/.

5. DFES Report, "The Minority Ethnic Exclusions and the Race Relations Amendment Act 2000 Interim Summary," November 2003.

6. Department for Education, DFES, "Minority Ethnic Attachment and Participation in Education and Training," 2003.

7. www.jsboard.co.uk/etac/etbb/benchbook/e.

8. Ibid.

9. www.eieagwali.com/europe/england/Black-science.

10. Ibid.

11. Ibid.

12. http://www.scienceyear.com/sciteach/index.html?page= /sciteach/liz/index.html.

13. http://www.mpa.gov.uk/about/members/04herbert.htm.

14. Statistics on Race and the Criminal Justice System, 2003, Home Office Report © 2004, 8.

15. Ibid.

16. Martin Bright, "London Youth Crime: A year on year Comparison 2002-2003," *The Observer*, March 30, 2003.

17. www.irr.org.uk/2002/november.

18. Lord Chancellor's Department, Race and the Criminal Justice System, Home Office, 2002; British Crime Survey, 2003; Statistics on Race and the Criminal Justice System, Her Majesty's Inspectorate of Prison; Thematic Inspection, Thematic Inspection Report, Ethnic Differences in Decisions and Young Offenders dealt with by the CPOS, Section 95, Findings no.1, 2000; Prison Statistics England and Wales 2000; *The Observer*, December 28, 2002.

19. Michael Tonry, *Malign Neglect: Race Crime and Punishment in America* (New York: Oxford University Press, 1995).

20. Jerome Miller, *Search and Destroy: African American Males in the Criminal Justice System* (Cambridge: Cambridge University Press, 1997).

21. Catherine Beckett, *Making Crime Pay* (Oxford: Oxford University Press, 1998).

22. Pierre Tournier, "Statistiques Pénales Annuelles du Conseil de l'Europe, Enquête 1997," Strasbourg.

23. Nils Christie, *Crime Control as Industry: Towards Goulags, Western Style* (London: Routledge, 1994).

24. Josine Jondr-Tas, "Ethnic Minorities and Criminal Justice in the Netherlands" in Michael Tonry, ed., *Ethnicity, Crime, and Immigration*, 257-310.

25. Pierre Tournier, La Délinquance des Etrangers en France: Analyze de Statistiques Pénales.

26. Salvatore Palidda, *Délit d'Immigration/ Immigrant Delinquency,* (Brussels: European Commission 1996), 158.

27. Ibid.

28. www.panelreform.org/english/article_wacquant2; Loic Wacquant, Researcher, European Sociology Center, College de France, University of Berkeley, article printed in *Punishment and Society*, the international drama of Penology, Vol. 1, no.2, (October 1999).

29. Robert K. Merton, *The Self-fulfilling Prophecy: A Social Theory on Social Structure* (New York: The Free Press, 1968, Third Expanded Edition), 475-490.

30. Jean Peirre Perrin-Martin, *La Retention* (Paris: L'Harmattan, 1996).

Transforming the Heart

*And **be not conformed** to this world: but be ye **transformed** by the renewing of your mind, that ye may prove what is that good, and acceptable, and perfect, will of God* (Romans 12:2 emphasis mine).

There is nothing wrong with being black.

In fact, God created Blacks equal to all others. As you have read throughout this book, there are circumstances that have perpetuated our existence. Should we allow the negative to sustain us—or allow the positive to move us forward toward a hopeful future?

How can you transform your life and heart toward Him?

Every question, including all of the questions asked in the beginning of the book, can be answered by reading The Book—the Bible. For every "what if..." and "why," there is an answer, a personal answer for you, your community, and your nation.

Transformation of the heart is the only permanent way to take control of your life, your eternal destiny. Becoming the person God intended is the only true way to live a fulfilled and content life.

God is waiting for every Black man, woman, and child to turn their hearts toward Him, to praise Him for life—past, present, and future—and for Jesus. We must break the chains of conformations and pathologies that hold us back and destroy the bonds that keep us from achieving our goals. He will honor those who honor Him.

In walking toward God's plan for us, we need to:

* Recognize our weaknesses and climb above them through education.

* Love ourselves as God loves us.

* Realize our need for a healthy self-image.

* Read God's Word.

* Dream, plan, create, and build.

* Encourage each other daily.

* Place our trust and faith in God.

Blacks must take pride in the fact that they truly built the first civilization, and that in the first 3,000-4,000 years of humanity they were not the ones considered backward or barbaric. Egypt was a land of advanced architecture—the world's oldest stone structures are found in ancient Egypt, the great pyramids constitute one of the Seven Wonders of the World.

Africans, the Black Egyptians, were proficient in mathematics, medicine, engineering, and agriculture. Black Arabs started algebra, conquered Spain and Portugal, and carried mathematics into Europe.

We have a proud heritage; we can rise to that height again—with a proper respect for God and each other.

And we know that all things work together for good to them that love God, to them who are the called according to His purpose (Romans 8:28).

Matthew Ashimolowo Media Ministries

UK

MAMM Bookstores

C/O/57 Waterden Road, Hackney, London E15 2EE

Telephone: 0845 13 3471

USA

Matthew Ashimolowo Media Ministries

PO Box 470470, Tulsa, OK 74147

Telephone: 1-800-717-0517

Nigeria

C/O Mattyson Media

71 Allen Avenue, Ikeja, Lagos

Telephone: 01 774 2478

OTHER PRODUCTS BY MATTHEW ASHIMOLOWO

Be The Best

The 24-Hour Miracle

The 10 M's of Money

The Coming Wealth Transfer

Black & Blessed (DVD)

Congratulations, You are Going to Have a Baby

Don't Date Devils

I Am a Man, I'm Not a Chauvinist

I Am a Woman, I'm Not Dumb

The Seven Deadly Controllers

The Seven Deadly Passions

Additional copies of this book and other
book titles from DESTINY IMAGE are
available at your local bookstore.

Call toll-free: 1-800-722-6774.

Send a request for a catalog to:

Destiny Image® Publishers, Inc.

P.O. Box 310
Shippensburg, PA 17257-0310

*"Speaking to the Purposes of God for this
Generation and for the Generations to Come."*

For a complete list of our titles,
visit us at www.destinyimage.com.